Professor
WELLSTONE
Goes to
WASHINGTON

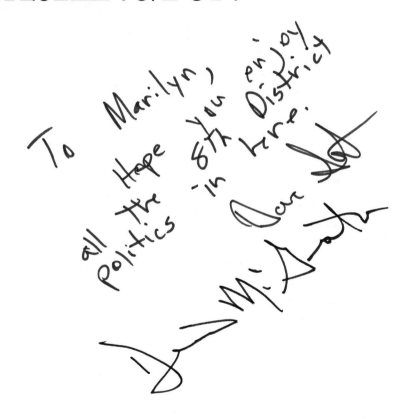

To Marilyn,
Hope you enjoy
all the 8th District
Politics in here.

Dan McGrath

Professor

WELLSTONE

Goes to

WASHINGTON

The Inside

Story of a Grassroots

U.S. Senate Campaign

Dennis J. McGrath and Dane Smith

 University of Minnesota Press
Minneapolis

Published by the University of Minnesota Press
111 Third Avenue South, Suite 290, Minneapolis, MN 55401-2520
Printed in the United States of America on acid-free paper

Library of Congress Cataloging-in-Publication Data

McGrath, Dennis J.
 Professor Wellstone goes to Washington : the inside story of a
grassroots U.S. Senate campaign / Dennis J. McGrath and Dane Smith.
   p. cm.
 Includes bibliographical references (p.   ).
 ISBN 0-8166-2662-6. — ISBN 0-8166-2663-4 (pbk.)
   1. Wellstone, Paul David. 2. Elections—Minnesota—History—20th
century. 3. Minnesota—Politics and government—1951-   4. United
States. Congress. Senate—Elections, 1990.   I. Smith, Dane.
II. Title.
 E840.8.W457M34   1995
 324.9776′053—dc20   94-41361

The University of Minnesota is an
equal-opportunity educator and employer.

To Stephanie and Mary

CONTENTS

ACKNOWLEDGMENTS

We accumulated countless debts to many people in the four years that passed between conception and delivery of this book. Here are some of them who must be thanked.

First, of course, we must thank the two main players in this book, Paul Wellstone and Rudy Boschwitz. Both were good sports and, in the best Minnesota tradition, accessible and open. Wellstone, in spite of the demands of setting up a Senate office, set aside large blocks of time for lunches, Sunday-morning breakfasts, and evening phone calls, and often submitted to repetitious questions as we plumbed his memory. Boschwitz agreed to talk at length even though it must have been painful to relive the campaign.

The candidates' campaign staffs were immensely helpful. In addition to providing us access to documents that were preserved for the next campaign, Wellstone's staff filled several boxes with the driftwood. They more than complied with our request to give us everything they otherwise would have thrown away. The boxes overflowed with duplicate letters, mailing lists, fund-raising appeals, ad scripts, and even Snickers bar wrappers and car repair bills. In the Wellstone camp, special thanks go to Pat Forciea and John Blackshaw, who agreed to the concept that eventually formed the foundation of this book: allowing one of the authors to be a full-time fly on the wall. They subjected themselves to intense scrutiny during the campaign and were just as cooperative after election day. All of the other staffers and advisers, who had no say in establishing the liberal ground rules, cooperated enthusiastically nonetheless. Those we imposed upon the most were: Liz Borg, Danny Cramer, David Graham, Scott Adams, Dick Senese, Bill Hillsman, David Lillehaug, and Jeff Blodgett. Several Boschwitz campaign staffers were enormously helpful in describing the behind-the-scenes details of that campaign; Tom Mason, Jay Novak, and Chris Georgacas were crucially important sources.

James P. McGrath, father of Dennis, was our utility player. He transcribed debates, critiqued the manuscript, and researched Wellstone's career at Carleton College. The newspaper clippings, letters, and photographs he unearthed at Carleton provided important leads and insights into Wellstone's personality and style.

We naturally are grateful to University of Minnesota Press director Lisa Freeman, who saw merit in our manuscript and oversaw publication in an extraordinarily competent and professional manner. Also at University of Minnesota Press, Todd Orjala tended to many details, scouring up photos and coordinating all aspects of the publishing. Copy editor Lynn Marasco improved our raw product tremendously, catching mistakes and inconsistencies and generally burnishing the manuscript inside and out. We know there were many many other people at the press that we never saw or met only briefly who contributed to the production of this book. Whoever you are, thank you.

We extend our gratitude to professors Hy Berman and Joseph Peschek, who gave our manuscript favorable reviews and helped us clear the last hurdle before publication.

Our colleague at the *Star Tribune* state capitol bureau, Robert Whereatt, who shares a small three-person office with us, was forced to experience every twist and turn in our torturous road to publication. We imposed on him even more by asking him to read our manuscripts, which he graciously did, devoting more time than any other colleague to reviewing our work in progress and lending us his experience and wisdom. Lori Sturdevant, who was our editor during the campaign, also provided advice on early drafts.

There are many other people at the *Star Tribune* to thank, but chief among them is Ron Meador. He instantly recognized the potential of the proposal to go inside the Wellstone campaign. When one of the authors proposed it, Ron ensured that it happened, clearing a path internally at the *Star Tribune* and negotiating ground rules with Wellstone and his campaign officials. Ron's guidance and editing of a six-page postelection newspaper article on the campaign was so masterful that many of the ideas and even turns of phrase have made their way into this book.

Joey McLeister, the photographer who teamed up with one of the authors for the newspaper project, was helpful not only in providing photos for this book, but also in being at least an equal partner in making the *Star Tribune* article such a success.

Our agents, Frances Goldin and, in particular, Sydelle Kramer, by turns inspired us, challenged us, comforted us, held our hands, and, ultimately, rejoiced with us.

Finally, our children, Kerry and Cailin McGrath and Vanessa, Daniel, and Laura Smith, spent too much of their childhoods without their dads' full attention. It's over now. We promise. And we extend our deepest thanks to our wives, Mary Smith and Stephanie McGrath. They filled the parental roles we neglected, heaping even more work on their already full schedules, so we could have time to indulge in every writer's dream. Despite their unfair workload, they supported us and encouraged us not to give up. They willingly and lovingly sacrificed time with us that we can never repay.

INTRODUCTION

Late in the afternoon on the last day of 1990, a dirty, battered bus crossed the Potomac River into Washington, D.C., and headed up Constitution Avenue. Pedestrians on the Capitol Mall stared as the bus rumbled past the stately Lincoln Memorial, past the black slab of the Vietnam Veterans Memorial, and then labored up the gentle incline of Capitol Hill. The bus turned into the Capitol parking lot, swung around 180 degrees to face the north, and stopped amid a gathering of three dozen people. They burst into cheers and pounded out a muffled applause, mittens striking mittens.

A handful of bystanders paused to see who might emerge from this rattletrap with the green and white signs—"Wellstone, U.S. Senate, DFL"—taped to grimy windows. The bus first discharged a dozen television, radio, and newspaper reporters. A few minutes after the reporters and photographers had set up, the star passenger finally appeared: U.S. Senator-elect Paul Wellstone.

The Washington media's first view of this curiosity was of a very short man with a misshapen nose and frizzy hair, wearing a formless olive-green raincoat described in one newspaper account as "unfortunate," and ragged black shoes. To some it must have looked like pure hokum, as if Wellstone was badly overplaying the role of the populist outsider misfit. It was a publicity stunt, but his fatigued appearance was hard-earned. Wellstone was haggard from three days and 1,100 miles of bone-jarring travel that began in the subzero temperatures of Minnesota, from stops in Chicago and Pittsburgh and long days and nights meeting with labor union supporters and others en route. He grinned, waded into the small crowd, and began hugging those who had waited, some for hours, to welcome him.

Slowly he made his way to the rear of the bus and climbed once more onto a platform mounted on the back. He held aloft in his hands the shredded remains of two fan belts that had snapped along the way. In the staccato cadence that had become familiar to Minnesota voters, Wellstone spoke:

> I wanted to come to Washington, D.C., in this bus I guess for a lot of different reasons. The bus was a symbol of everything that's not slick, of everything that isn't big money. The bus was our campaign, which we took to the people in Minnesota. . . . I said to the students and to the young people in Minnesota maybe more times than they ever wanted to hear it, politics is not money and power games. Politics is about the improvement of people's lives. It is about lessening human suffering and it is about—and what a time to say this—advancing the cause of justice and peace in the world. That is what politics is all about.

Three days later Wellstone would be sworn in as a U.S. senator, the only Senate candidate to beat an incumbent in the 1990 election.

Almost nobody believed that Wellstone, a forty-five-year-old political science professor, had a ghost of a chance when he opened his campaign in early 1989 to unseat Rudy Boschwitz, a popular, wealthy businessman and one of the nation's most skillful politicians and money raisers. Boschwitz, a plucky and personable entrepreneur who built up a chain of home-improvement stores, personified the Republican ideal of self-reliance and the Midwestern ideal of neighborly friendliness. After almost thirty years in the public eye—first promoting his Plywood Minnesota products on television and then twelve years as a U.S. senator—he was the most popular elected official in the state. He and Republican colleague Dave Durenberger had won five straight Senate election contests in Minnesota after taking seats in 1978 that liberal champions Hubert Humphrey and Walter Mondale once held. Wellstone just six months earlier was virtually unknown to Minnesota voters. And polls hinted that a hefty percentage of the few people who did recognize his name regarded him as a crackpot.

He was described by *Mother Jones* magazine after his election as "the first 1960s radical elected to the U.S. Senate," and nothing about him belied that image. On first hearing a Wellstone speech, many Minnesotans, famous for their emotional reserve, were literally frightened by the emotion and sheer, screaming volume, if not the content.

In both substance and style, Wellstone broke most of the rules governing mainstream Democratic politics. He was an active member of Minnesota's Democratic Party (called Democratic-Farmer-Labor, or DFL), but the party hierarchy always was nervous about him because he was too hot, too loud, too far to the left. He had never held public office and his résumé included two much-publicized arrests for civil disobedience and involvement in a string of controversial causes. To many, he was a fringe figure, a firehouse dog who rushed to protest every injustice and every flame of social controversy he could find.

But Wellstone was given his party's nomination, partly because incumbent Boschwitz scared off bigger names, but partly also because Wellstone convinced DFLers to press forward—almost in a just-for-the-hell-of-it spirit—with an uncompromising, all-encompassing, progressive-liberal-populist package. But most important, Wellstone and a committed cohort of activists wrote a new blueprint for campaigning, a grassroots, bottoms-up, low-budget crusade.

Wellstone laid out a program featuring a demand for universal health care, much heavier tax burdens on the wealthy, more spending on education and social programs, tough new environmental and energy standards, and radical reforms of the money-polluted political campaign system. And he delivered this vision to Minnesota voters with a new attitude—anger and good-humored irreverence and hope all at once—toward a system that he claimed was leaving too many people behind and shifting too much money to the upper classes. Wellstone claimed to be offering real change and not just accommodation, and he rammed this message home with a defiant new posture toward the plutocracy that, in the progressive worldview, has controlled the United States since the days of the founding fathers and Alexander Hamilton.

Wellstone understood, as did George Bush's 1988 campaign manager, the late Lee Atwater, the burgeoning power of the class issue. After the 1988 election, and before he was diagnosed as having a fatal brain tumor, Atwater told the *Boston Globe*: "The way to win a presidential race against the Republicans is to develop the class warfare issue, as Dukakis did at the end. To divide up the haves and have nots and try to reinvigorate the New Deal coalition and to attack."

That was Wellstone's essential accomplishment. He infused energy into the remnants of the "rainbow coalition" that he had helped build for Jesse Jackson in 1988. He patched together an alliance that included hard hats, gays and lesbians, inner-city poor people, middle-class suburbanites and maturing baby boomers, black and Hispanic minorities, family farmers, feminists, environmentalists, and sundry reformers.

The 1990 elections were the most entertaining and lurid in Minnesota history, and Wellstone's victory was aided by some spectacular fumbles by his opponent and a sex scandal involving the Republican gubernatorial candidate. He very well might have lost without these miscues by his opponents. And to be sure, Wellstone's traits and talents—his energy, passionate rhetorical style, telegenic friendliness, and inspired sloganeering—gave him a strong personal appeal, which is always half the game in American politics.

Minnesota Democrats, like those in many other state parties, had a history of offering up polite, bland Senate candidates who mouthed the proper, innocuous Democratic slogans, tried not to offend business interests, and were muscled out by Republicans (Independent-Republicans in Minnesota) while fighting for the philosophical middle ground. Wellstone synthesized a different model of Democratic politics with a high moral tone, indignant and at times downright discourteous. Above all, he promised economic fairness and social justice, focusing on the plight of women and children, a message that was authenticated by his two decades of firsthand experience helping people in need, and in his front-line conflict with both corporate and government establishments. His was no remote, elitist, limousine liberalism. His personal code was "Try not to separate the life you live from the words you speak."

The politics and specific policies put together by this professor of political science were a fusion of previous Democratic strains. He may have been the closest thing to a radical that a major party had seen in decades, but his radicalism had always been of the responsible and nonviolent variety, and it was grounded in an appreciation of history. The foundation was populism and progressivism, the insurgent movements of turn-of-the-century farmers, workers, and altruistic reformers who rose up together to challenge the accumulation of wealth and power by the robber barons of the late 1800s. Wellstone's politics also contained a strong element of 1930s New Deal liberalism and its expansive government programs to provide universal public goods to a nation ravaged by a speculative capitalistic boom and bust. And his politics were flavored strongly with 1960s progressivism and activism, with its emphasis on the global village, nonviolent protest, grassroots organizing and local action, and a basic impulse to challenge at every turn the abuses of both big business and big government.

He preached a provocative populist sermon out of the 1890s agrarian revolt, even employing evangelical cadences he had picked up as a college student in the South. Like the Midwestern firebrands a hundred years before, he rallied farmers and working people against the alleged abuses of the merchant class and their agents, but he exorcised all traces of the racism and nativism that has afflicted populism from William Jennings Bryan to David Duke. Wellstone, in contrast to populists then and now, was an internationalist; he never evoked resentment of foreigners or pushed for isolationism. His anger was directed strictly at the top, at a politico-economic system that he claimed divided blacks and whites and pitted the welfare poor against the working poor and middle class, all the while widening the gap between the wealthy and everyone else.

He promoted the civic activism and political reforms of turn-of-the-century progressivism but emphasized local action, "empowerment and involvement," rather than structural reforms in the democratic process and technocratic formulas. Wellstone was anything but an abstract, good-government tinkerer. He spent most of twenty years fighting exclusively local battles: for striking workers and bankrupt farmers, against nuclear power and high-voltage power lines. His progressivism incorporated a strong streak of the PIRG movement, the public interest research groups spawned by Ralph Nader, and the 1960s environmental and consumer movements.

Finally, he was a bona fide liberal, pro-choice on abortion, a civil libertarian, a feminist, an integrationist. But never in his career was he preoccupied with issues such as flag burning or gun ownership or busing or the rights of criminals, nor did he allow them to define his campaign. His was a politics of economics and social justice, first, last, and foremost.

Perhaps the most distinguishing feature of Wellstone's brand of liberalism was his emphatic rejection of the central American creed that the business of America is business and that commercial leaders ought to maintain the control that they have over American institutions. Although avowedly not a socialist, Wellstone was downright disrespectful of the free market and made no attempt to seek the support of the business class or their money. Because monied interests did not invest in his campaign and thus had no control over his message, he was able to give full-throated power to his populist progressive agenda.

Wellstone's constant refrain was that America must turn its attention to the public good, toward community and sharing wealth, and abandon yet another failed experiment in unbridled capitalism. He convinced a large sector of the middle class in Minnesota that the interests of the wealthy were not their interests. He tactfully tried to tell middle- and lower-class Minnesotans that they had been suckered by Ronald Reagan and George Bush and deprived of most of their share of seven and a half years of economic growth. Sixteen months later the *New York Times* would report that the richest 1 percent of Americans had captured 60 percent of the income from economic growth between 1977 and 1989, while the top fifth had walked away with 94 percent.

No Minnesota candidate since the Depression and very few in any state have stood so unambiguously for "the little fellers," as he incessantly said, and so clearly against "the Rockefellers." His rhetoric on this score at times bordered on demagoguery. A simpler and less provocative expression of the sentiment was this frequent line: "Some people have way too much wealth and power and say, and too many other people have way too little."

Few Democratic senators today will admit, as Wellstone has, to being at heart "not far away at all from the European social democrats." These are the dominant parties that have produced a model of capitalism that includes extensive governmental control over the direction of the economy and universal benefits in health care, education, and job security—the so-called social welfare state. France, Germany, Britain, and the Scandinavian countries typically devote 50-60 percent of their gross national product to social services and other public enterprises, through taxes or other revenues. By contrast, the "take" by governments at all levels in the United States, which has one of the lowest nondefense public service budgets in the industrialized world, is closer to 40 percent.

This difference in capitalist models has been noted and analyzed for years, and even Wellstone concedes that the United States may be too big and too diverse to fit into the European mold. He professes "a commitment to a strong private sector" and says he believes that America cannot simply copy other models. But the European model undeniably is the one that progressives want to emulate, even as the social democratic nations in recent years have veered toward the American model with privatization and freer markets. Wellstone says:

> It's part of the orthodoxy in our country, what [economist] Walter Dean Burnham calls "a politics of excluded alternatives," that if we go to more equity you lose efficiency. But a lot of these [European] countries devote a high percentage to [the] public sector, in education, health care, and economic investment, [which] go together to improve productivity. And we're

paying the price for not doing so. The bottom line is not the only line. There are certain places where commercial logic stops and social logic begins.

The progressive agenda obviously was a repudiation of political trends and was utterly unacceptable to many business owners and managers, powerful professional associations, and free-market economists—in sum, most of the most influential and powerful people in every community in the nation. To millions of others who might actually benefit from the progressive agenda, it looks impractical, inefficient, out of sync with American tradition and culture, and eventually destructive of the incentives that presumably have produced general prosperity for forty years. The American public, while searching for change, remains distrustful of the federal government and big government programs. The lack of national consensus about how to deal with severe and frightening social and economic problems may continue indefinitely, or until things get much worse.

But Wellstone's successful campaign has meaning beyond the grand philosophical conflict of our time. It contains lessons for candidates in both parties about how to change the political game, about how to take on entrenched interests, about the effectiveness of people-based politics rather than money-based and media-based politics. Wellstone decided early on that he could not and would not try to match Boschwitz dollar for dollar, image maker for image maker, TV ad for TV ad. He refused to troop along the national fund-raising circuit, which requires several stops each in the money pits of New York, Florida, and California. He ran instead what he called a "café campaign," and at times it resembled a Norman Rockwell painting.

Entering a small-town coffee shop with television cameras in tow, Wellstone would spend a few minutes with the customers and the owner, but he would also make sure to spend time behind the counter with the waitresses and in the kitchen with the dishwashers. Striding down Main Street, he would duck into a garage and shake hands with grimy mechanics. It was more than just show business, and the objects of this attention seemed to sense a genuine interest in them. In moments when there was no apparent public-relations benefit, Wellstone would seek out and ask for the support of parking lot attendants, street people, and others who by their appearance seemed clearly to be at the bottom of the economic ladder, and maybe even not likely to vote. Sometimes these folks appeared to be bewildered by the attention, but more often than not they responded with embraces and familiar banter, and the rapport grew stronger as his fame spread.

Eventually Wellstone had to buy television ads and employ sophisticated managers and handlers. But even with this concession to convention, he broke new ground. Wellstone's ads featured an irreverent, humorous style that had never been seen before and later became the toast of the political advertising world. Still, a great irony of his campaign was that it confirmed that the political game cannot be played without the infernal tube. Despite Wellstone's contempt for the sound bite, he found that even a progressive agenda must be sold to voters with simple messages and images—two minutes or less—on television.

He also discovered that the gimmicks he employed on the campaign trail were ill-suited for a U.S. senator, who is expected to act with at least a semblance of decorum. In his first year in office, under extraordinary pressure and media scrutiny, Wellstone made errors in judgment that depleted much of the goodwill he had built up.

His first days on the job were marked by grandstand plays and protests against American involvement in the impending Gulf War. His tactics embarrassed many of his new constituents and sent his approval ratings plummeting. He discovered that while a bare majority of voters might take a chance on the progressive domestic agenda, another majority rejects the essential antiwar principles of the left and views as disloyal any dissent once a war has been joined.

Amid this stress, Capitol Hill observers began to detect a self-righteousness and an egotistical nature to this allegedly selfless idealist, and Wellstone turned out to be rather thin-skinned in his dealings with the media. There were resignations from his staff and estrangements from some of his most valuable political aides.

On almost every other front, Wellstone soon discovered the great paradox of the successful antiestablishment candidate: gaining entry into a club by denouncing the behavior of its members. As an outsider, Wellstone could run against every part of the system; as a senator, he had to choose which parts and persons to defend and join. As a populist, he could press for reform everywhere; as a senator he had to set priorities and make deals. This proved to be a hard lesson, and in learning it he disappointed both ends of his constituencies—moderates who thought he might not be such a rabble-rouser after all, and progressive purists who wanted him never to waver on any cause.

But by 1994, Wellstone had recovered from his blunders and had regained his political equilibrium. He almost single-handedly forced through the Senate a bill banning gifts from lobbyists and other interested parties. His work on that issue drew lavish, almost fawning praise from the New York Times editorial page, and others in the national media applauded his persistence and skill in advocating the reform. He was considered the leading advocate in Congress of the single-payer health care plan. And with his wife, Sheila Wellstone, he had carved out a niche as an advocate for abused women and children.

This work stabilized his approval ratings in the polls back home at slightly more than 50 percent, about as high as such a controversial figure could hope for. Although his disapproval ratings remained relatively high, they were dropping, a sign that many Minnesotans were grudgingly forgiving him his opposition to the Gulf War.

Perhaps even more telling, Republicans in Minnesota launched a focused campaign aimed at trying to keep Wellstone off balance and to prevent him from solidifying a base. Through a series of attacks by press release and the *Wellstone Watch* newsletter, Republicans used him like a dog-track rabbit to get their supporters and contributors revved up. Buoyed by the Republican sweep of 1994 and the crushing defeat of liberal candidates for governor and the U.S. Senate in Minnesota, Republican Party leaders were publicly salivating over the prospect of knocking him off in 1996. Privately, some admitted he would not be an easy mark. Either way, it was evident that Republicans will never again underestimate him or forget the lessons of his extraordinary campaign.

Repeatedly, Wellstone was told by ordinary citizens that it was a pleasure to vote again because he was on the ballot. Many others told him after the victory, with no disrespect, that the astounding victory belonged to them, not him.

Wellstone drew that kind of response in part because of the grassroots nature of his campaign, especially in the formative months, but also because the campaign was not blackened by gloom and pessimism. Republicans have rightly chastised Democrats for their dour outlook, for wallowing in despair. Wellstone highlighted societal ills, but there was a Reagan-like "morning in America" message that overwhelmed the negative strains. "We can do better than this" was the overriding theme. He exuded joy and hope about what he saw as "a new world in the making" and about the potential for politics to be, as he said a thousand times, "about improving people's lives."

The authors had a unique view of this unorthodox candidate and his campaign. In 1989 and through most of 1990, as reporters for the *Star Tribune* of Minneapolis, we covered the campaign from a journalist's usual position—from the outside looking in. But beginning the day after Wellstone won the primary election, he granted one of us unrestricted access to the inner workings of his campaign.

For eight weeks, while Dane Smith continued to report on the Wellstone and Boschwitz campaigns for the daily newspaper, Dennis McGrath moved inside the campaign. He was allowed to travel everywhere with Wellstone and his staff, to attend private staff meetings, strategy sessions, debate preparations, fundraisers, and the taping of ads. He was permitted to read confidential memos, internal poll results, and financial reports. Nothing was off limits. The only restriction was that McGrath not write anything about the Wellstone organization until after the election, so as not to disclose inside information to the Boschwitz campaign.

When McGrath began the project, he expected to write a story of frustration and failure, of big money clobbering a well-intentioned but overmatched army of volunteers, of the essential rules of politics being reaffirmed.

It didn't turn out that way.

1

DREAMS AND SCHEMES

The scheme was cooked up over a campfire on an unseasonably warm night in early June 1988, on the fertile savanna of southeastern Minnesota. The state's Democrats were gathered in Rochester, a prosperous city and a medical mecca that is the home of the legendary Mayo Clinic, for their state convention. Many of the party regulars, who were closing ranks behind the presidential candidacy of Michael Dukakis, stayed in the venerable Kahler Hotel and dined almost every night at Michael's, the city's finest restaurant. A handful of insurgents who still supported the Reverend Jesse Jackson could not afford such accommodations and slept at a public campground a few miles north of town.

When the convention opened, the Jackson faction was pressing for a platform debate on the issue of a Palestinian homeland. Most of the party's leaders sought to stifle such discussion. They feared that a messy debate about Israeli occupation of the West Bank would antagonize Jewish Democrats, who were heavy contributors to the party. Although a few radicals pressed for a floor debate, the party regulars won and squelched the issue.

But that did not settle the matter. In a move that some saw as an act of revenge by the party's establishment, the convention's nominating committee refused to support one of the dissidents, Paul Wellstone, for reelection to the Democratic National Committee.

The Jackson delegates were outraged at the snub of Wellstone, an intense five-foot-five-inch firebrand of a public speaker, and a leader of the Jackson campaign. They staged a small revolt from the convention floor. In a flurry of resistance, a handful of labor organizers, community activists, and farmers' advocates worked from aisle to aisle building support for Wellstone's return to the national committee. After an impassioned speech, Wellstone won reelection rather easily, demonstrating his broad popularity within the rank and file of a party for which he had labored for more than a decade.

Later that night, as sparks from the campfire rose into the tree canopy, the Jackson group reveled in its triumph. The crew included Scott Adams, an activist in his late twenties with a perpetual five-day beard who had worked as an organizer in poor neighborhoods and on Indian reservations; Kris Blake, a community theater producer and cochair with Wellstone of Jesse Jackson's Minnesota campaign; Andy Dawkins, a recently elected state representative from a St. Paul district with a heavy concentration of minorities; and about a dozen others. After recounting the day's events, and aided by a few bottles of wine, the campers returned to a theme that had dominated each night's fireside session: dissatisfaction with the party leadership, which they believed to be a tool of the monied interests and too timid in challenging Republican presidents Ronald Reagan and George Bush. Talk shifted to the 1990 U.S. Senate race and who might take on Republican senator Rudy Boschwitz, a millionaire businessman who had spent most of his two terms vigorously advocating the Reagan agenda.

Adams recalled the dissatisfaction they shared about the state party's choice of Dukakis as the presidential candidate and of Hubert H. Humphrey III as the Senate candidate in 1988. To the Jackson delegates, Humphrey was an uninspiring and unacceptable moderate. "There were lots of comments like 'Who are they [DFL leaders] going to run after Hubert Humphrey III loses?'" Adams recounted, "and 'We're tired of . . . their hand-picked people. Let's get our own; we've got enough people to do it.'"

The underlying sentiment was that "we had brought a lot of new people into a movement and the Jackson part of it was almost over," Adams said. "We had all these people involved and we didn't want to let it die. We were having fun." Dawkins concurred: "We all felt like we had gotten Jackson to a better spot than anybody thought we could, and it was a matter of 'Where are we gonna go next? We gotta keep this group intact.' And the Senate in 1990 was the next big race."

Around 2:00 A.M. Adams mentioned that Wellstone's activism had earned him support in rural areas, in inner cities, and also with trade unions. When he suggested Wellstone as their 1990 Senate candidate, "we latched onto it, and people got real excited," Blake recalled. The next morning and over the next few weeks, a few of these Jackson delegates began testing a new form of address on the man who championed their causes. "Senator Wellstone," they called him, with teasing grins.

At forty-three, Wellstone was a politician out of time, still clinging to the principles that shaped him in the 1960s. Like so many of his generation, he was swept up in the epic battles to desegregate the South and to end the war in Vietnam. But unlike many of his peers, Wellstone never changed his 1960s view of politics as a struggle for peace, justice, and equality, the downtrodden on one side and entrenched elites on the other. And he held on to 1960s tactics as well: peaceful confrontation and civil disobedience. Wellstone explained:

I guess my indignation stayed on because I got so totally in-volved organizing with people on the very bottom, and one thing led to another. I kept seeing these people who were on the bottom, who deserved better, who were truly great people. And I have to say I was helping myself. It was self-serving in the sense that it was what I really enjoyed doing and it made me feel good.

Many Minnesotans came to view Wellstone as the state Democratic Party's loudest and most obnoxious troublemaker. Others saw him as the party's conscience and as a prophet. Over the years, welfare mothers, farmers, and workers devastated by an unforgiving economy knew they could always count on him to lead their rallies and walk their picket lines. Throughout the 1970s Wellstone's main activity outside the classroom was orga-nizing welfare recipients in the rural county just south of the Twin Cities where he taught political science at Carleton Col-lege. In the late 1970s and mid-1980s he had been swept up in two rural populist crusades, the protest against construction of a power line and the battle against the economic forces driving farmers off the land. His involvement in the farm movement re-sulted in an arrest for civil disobedience when he joined a hun-dred farmers at a sit-in at a bank office in the central Minnesota town of Paynesville.

A year later Wellstone engaged in another controversial cru-sade when he sided with militant meat plant workers on strike in southern Minnesota in a bitter labor dispute with the Hormel Company that attracted national attention. But while he was working the farmyards and factories, Wellstone also kept a strong hand in politics, rubbing elbows occasionally with lead-ers of the state's Democratic-Farmer-Labor (DFL) Party.

In 1982 Wellstone pushed his way into a race for state audi-tor, a job that involves overseeing local government expendi-tures and membership on a board that invests public pension funds. Wellstone said at the time that he ran for statewide office because he wanted to move the DFL Party toward a more populist-progressive agenda, but he had a personal agenda as well. His candidacy was the first visible sign of Wellstone's yearning for public office. "We talked about his, down the road, running for governor," said his wife, Sheila, one of his most influential advisers. "He knew he couldn't run for governor unless he had run before and people knew who he was." Wellstone bewildered his incumbent opponent, Republican Arne Carlson, by running a campaign for economic justice, railing against nuclear power plants, and marching with poor people in Washington, D.C.

At the time, Carlson complained: "We're running for the office of auditor, and Paul is running for senator or president or something." It was an eminently fair criticism. Even some of Wellstone's more germane proposals made DFL Party members nervous. For example, he suggested tapping public employee pension funds to finance low-interest loans for financially strapped farmers and small businesses, an idea that was regarded by some as a violation of fiduciary responsibility by the investment board. Wellstone also called for formation of a state bank that would be more forgiving to farmers than were private, commercial banks. That proposal, a throwback to populist schemes of many decades before, was seen as a threat to private bankers. Wellstone ran such a low-budget campaign that he often hitchhiked between stops. He lost that election by 10 percentage points, but he served notice that he was one of the party's most aggressive challengers.

In 1984, as Walter Mondale geared up for the presidential campaign, Wellstone used his own labor support in the party to win a spot on the Democratic National Committee, an ideal vantage point from which he could both speak out on the issues of the day and stay alert for opportunities to further his political ambitions. One such opportunity arose in November 1987, when he was asked to enlist in another movement. The invitation was proffered in a car traveling between Minneapolis and the little farm town of Castle Rock, Minnesota, where the Reverend Jesse Jackson had scheduled a rally. Jackson wanted Wellstone to be a leader of his embryonic presidential campaign in Minnesota, but Wellstone was reluctant. He was still angry over Jackson's 1984 reference to New York City as "Hymietown" and his links to Black Muslim leader Louis Farrakhan. But as Wellstone listened to Jackson speak at events that weekend, and as he quizzed him during the car ride, his hostility melted. Jackson told him: "We're both targets. You as a Jew and me as a black." Wellstone concluded that while Jackson had made mistakes, he believed that he was "struggling to be sensitive to Jewish history and Jewish pain, that he certainly was not anti-Semitic."

With that issue neutralized in Wellstone's mind, he found it easy to embrace Jackson's message of economic fairness and social justice. Jackson alone among the "seven dwarfs" of the 1988 campaign addressed the causes to which Wellstone had devoted his life, so he accepted Jackson's invitation and became co-chair of Jackson's Minnesota campaign. His assignment was to organize the entire state outside the Twin Cities metropolitan area—and to do it with virtually no money. Wellstone plunged into the task, criss-crossing the state, establishing telephone trees, speaking at small gatherings in people's homes as well as at larger rallies.

The state party's chair at the time, Ruth Stanoch, said that Wellstone was virtually alone among top members of the Minnesota DFL Party in supporting Jackson. But "nobody on the national committee was surprised by his support," Stanoch said. "Paul, of course, was very well known and vocal. And there were pockets of support elsewhere on the committee." The link to Jackson, with his pro-Palestinian sympathies, would cost

Wellstone dearly in the Jewish community when he ran for the Senate. Nevertheless, through his work for Jackson, Wellstone at last got a small taste of success. At Minnesota's precinct caucuses, despite being outspent by Massachusetts governor Michael Dukakis and running against a well-connected "Humphrey Democrat," Senator Paul Simon, of Illinois, Jackson captured 20 percent of the state's delegates. He tied Simon for second place behind Dukakis, who received the allegiance of about one-third of the delegates. Jackson's showing was stunning in a virtually all-white state, and it attracted national attention.

After the national Democratic convention, when Dukakis won the party's nomination and tried to make peace with Jackson, Wellstone was a key player in the smooth merger of the two camps in Minnesota. As part of that alliance, Wellstone was named a cochair of Dukakis's Minnesota campaign, and he worked almost as hard for Dukakis as he had for Jackson.

All these high points, however, were ruined on election day, which brought a humiliating rejection for liberals and the DFL Party. Although Dukakis carried Minnesota, he was crushed nationally by George Bush, who leaped past a one-time 17-point deficit in the polls, in large part by identifying Dukakis as a liberal, a "card-carrying member" of the American Civil Liberties Union. Meanwhile, the Minnesota Democrats' Senate candidate, Hubert H. Humphrey III, the son of Minnesota's most famous politician, was clobbered by incumbent senator Dave Durenberger. The fact that this magic name could lose by 15 percentage points to the somewhat tarnished Republican, accused of but not yet denounced for several ethical transgressions, was a devastating blow.

These defeats provoked much soul searching among Democrats about whether to move closer to the middle or to offer a bolder alternative to conservatism, a dilemma that has racked the party for years. One thing was clear. *Liberal* was a dirty word, and Wellstone's sassy, man-the-barricades activism put him well to the left of Dukakis's professional, technocratic liberalism.

Looking to 1990

As Bush prepared for his inauguration in 1989, Wellstone set his own sights on 1990, piecing together a team of advisers from both the Dukakis and the Jackson factions in Minnesota. While many major statewide campaigns are incubated in the Twin Cities offices of lawyers and consultants, these men and women gathered in the modest, vacant Minneapolis home of a Wellstone relative who was preparing to move in and whose furniture had not yet arrived.

Sitting cross-legged on the hardwood floor, the core group included Mel Duncan, a former community organizer who now lobbied at the statehouse on behalf of a coalition of low-income and progressive groups; Bea Underwood, a prominent voice in Minneapolis's black community and executive secretary to Minneapolis mayor Don Fraser; Kris Blake, who managed Jesse Jackson's 1988 campaign in Minnesota; the Reverend Tom Van Leer, an African Methodist Episcopal minister; party activists Mick and Dick Senese; Wellstone's closest friend, Mike Casper, a Carleton College physics professor; and a precocious political pro, Pat Forciea, a thirty-one-year-old former small-college All-American hockey goalie who had just completed his stint as director of the Dukakis campaign in Minnesota. With the possible exception of Forciea, there wasn't a true power broker in the house.

While this nucleus of supporters never gave Wellstone a clear-cut recommendation on whether he should run, they agreed on several points that helped him make up his mind. First, they rejected any efforts to bring Democrats toward the political center. Citing the lifeless Dukakis campaign, the group agreed that the party's national leadership failed to emphasize the substance of any Democratic campaign—commitment to government as a tool of social change. "A lot of us in that room shared the analysis that Michael Dukakis did not lose because he was too far to the left," recalled Mel Duncan. "He lost because he was so tepid and vacillating on so many issues."

Second, they discovered that everyone admired the Jackson campaign's ability to unite races and get people to think about the barriers of economic class. Forciea, citing his experience with the Dukakis campaign, explained that he witnessed how class issues worked from the vantage point of both the aggressor and the helpless victim. As manager of Dukakis's effort during the pivotal Democratic primary in Wisconsin, Forciea had watched his candidate spend six straight days railing against the Reagan legacy in working-class cities like Racine and Green Bay, the scene of massive layoffs in the wood products and meat packing industries. Desperately fighting against Jackson's charisma and oratory, the staid and reserved Dukakis knew he had to make class issues work for his candidacy. The tactic paid off as northern Wisconsin delivered the primary to Dukakis. But after this success, Forciea added, the Massachusetts governor dropped his focus on the politics of class, believing that it would not be helpful nationally. That move, ironically, allowed the patrician Bush to exploit class issues by casting himself as the candidate who ate pork rinds and Dukakis, the son of immigrants, as a member of the liberal Boston academic elite. In desperation, Dukakis late in the campaign tried to resurrect his working-class appeal. It helped, Forciea said, but the move was far too little and far too late:

> If that had been the message coming out of the convention, Bush never would have succeeded in portraying Dukakis the way he did. Down the homestretch, I saw how that issue, when

used effectively, not only kept Democrats in line but also brought back blue-collar, ethnic folks in places like Milwaukee, Cleveland, St. Louis—people who voted for Reagan in 1980 and 1984. But it also appealed in many instances to yuppies, for lack of a better word.

I was just very confident coming out of 1988 that we were on the very front edge of this issue.

A third area of agreement among those planning Wellstone's run for the Senate centered on the vulnerability of incumbent senator Rudy Boschwitz. Though conventional wisdom within the Democratic and Republican Parties held that the two-term senator was invincible, the group figured that the millions of dollars he raised could be used against him in a campaign based on class differences. Wellstone could deftly play a populist David and force Boschwitz into the role of an overstuffed Goliath. Forciea continued:

> I think in many ways Rudy Boschwitz came to symbolize what was wrong with politics in the 1980s, what was wrong with big money in government in the 1980s, what was wrong with the economic decisions that were made by people in charge in Washington. He laid all the seed for this campaign by himself.

Like Wellstone, Boschwitz traced his interest in politics to the 1960s, when he was a successful businessman who joined the ranks of the Republican Party. Having won statewide recognition as a result of television ads promising great bargains at his chain of retail home-improvement stores, then called Plywood Minnesota, Boschwitz mixed a folksy campaign style with his aggressive, persuasive, and shrewd marketing techniques. Within a decade of his entrance into Minnesota's GOP elite, he made himself a contender for the U.S. Senate seat in 1978. Running as a moderate Republican who stood for the environment and energy conservation, he beat the Democratic incumbent, Senator

Wendell Anderson. Two years later, he favored Tennessee senator Howard Baker, a moderate Republican, over Ronald Reagan for the GOP presidential nomination.

By his 1984 reelection campaign, however, Boschwitz had shed his middle-of-the-road Republicanism and earned the sobriquet Mr. Big Business from consumer advocate Ralph Nader. His voting record showed staunch support of the Reagan tax cuts, military buildup, and government deregulation. While the Democrats offered a bright, capable, liberal adversary, Minnesota secretary of state Joan Growe, Boschwitz romped to a win with 58 percent to Growe's 41 percent.

Immediately after that election, Boschwitz gained even more attention from the GOP leadership, who placed him on the National Republican Senatorial Committee, a key component of the party's multi-million-dollar fund-raising arm. He relished the role, proudly displaying his ability to haul in donations on behalf of lawmakers who pledged their allegiance to the Reagan administration. "Nobody in politics (except me!) likes to raise money," Boschwitz once wrote in a letter revealing his secrets to Republican colleagues, a letter discovered and reprinted by the *Wall Street Journal*. It was not the first time he boasted of his money-raising prowess.

Crashing the Party

Sitting in the empty house in Minneapolis, Wellstone and his advisers sensed that Boschwitz's swollen campaign coffers, which most observers considered one of his strongest assets, could be used to cast crucial doubts about his clean image and to overshadow years of goodwill. They could portray Boschwitz as the candidate of monied interests, Wellstone as the friend and representative of ordinary people.

"It wasn't something we had made up for the campaign,"

said Mike Casper, Wellstone's best friend. "It was what Paul had been doing forever. Paul's whole history in the state was one of association with people on the bottom, with welfare mothers, farmers, laborers, workers."

Wellstone was encouraged also by his involvement in Jackson's campaign. He said:

> Because of what I'd seen in '88, I thought there was a lot of enthusiasm in the state for a different kind of politics. Jackson's appeal was rather astounding in Minnesota. I thought it had a lot to do with the message. I could see that a populist type of campaign could maybe catch fire.

While Wellstone and his friends had no doubts about how they would distinguish Wellstone from Boschwitz, they first had to figure out how to outmaneuver the state's Democratic leadership. Wellstone recalled a chronic feeling of indignation at the treatment he was getting from party leaders:

> I remember I went out to speak to the DFL executive committee at a meeting up in Brainerd [a resort town in central Minnesota]. I gave them a good speech and they were applauding and cheering and I asked them to support me. Then that same night, after I left, they passed a unanimous endorsement urging Walter Mondale to run. I always felt I had good support among the regulars, the rank and file. But it was the leadership I had trouble with.

Initially tolerant of Wellstone and the fragmented forces behind him, the hierarchy grew increasingly annoyed at his determination to play for a share of power. Though Wellstone knew he had beaten the leadership at the 1988 state convention, he was keenly aware that winning a U.S. Senate nomination required an intensive statewide effort over many months, not just a few days of organizing in a convention auditorium. Even more problematic, to sustain this effort through November 6, probably including a primary, Forciea estimated that Wellstone would have to raise at least $1.75 million.

It was a preposterous goal for a rabble-rousing enemy of wealthy interests. Who would contribute that kind of money? The welfare recipients and working poor whom Wellstone had helped through community organizing? Bankrupt farmers? Unemployed strikers? Minnesota unions might back him, but maybe not; his activism had angered some labor leaders. Donations from wealthy contributors would not amount to much because Wellstone had spent his life working on issues affecting the poor and simply had no connections to those with fat wallets. "I couldn't even figure out how he could get to $500,000, let alone $1.75 million," Forciea said.

Wellstone also would have to overcome a party that was skeptical of his populist agenda. Though Minnesota was the home of Midwestern liberalism, the party had suffered bruising defeats throughout the 1970s and 1980s when voters pulled to the right. One faction of party strategists believed it was time to replace the old liberal guard of Humphreys and Mondales with younger candidates eager to hold the political center. Most, however, figured that Walter Mondale, the former vice president, was their only chance against Boschwitz.

As the Wellstone advisers met in January and February of 1989, Mondale was seriously considering the contest. After returning to Minnesota from Washington in 1986, he had settled into a comfortable and lucrative law practice, eagerly accepting the mantle of the party's respected elder. He enjoyed this role, as well as his job as a radio commentator on the state's largest station, and he relished frequent fishing trips. Although some of the party leaders implored him to take a run at Boschwitz, Mondale was coy. While the former vice president kept everyone guessing, Wellstone discounted the power of the old guard. If Mondale were to run, Wellstone told his advisers, "I'd gladly take him on. I think a spirited contest would be good for the party."

But some of his advisers worried about potential vulnerabilities in Wellstone's long record of protests and demonstrations. They raised fears that adversaries would dismiss the candidate with a few well-chosen epithets, such as "ivory-tower professor" or "Jesse Jackson's chairman" or "socialist."

In addition to this general vulnerability, Forciea worried about Wellstone's association with a violent 1985 strike at the George A. Hormel plant in Austin, Minnesota. Five months after fourteen hundred workers went on strike over the company's demands for givebacks, Hormel reopened the plant and vowed to hire permanent replacement workers—"scabs," in union parlance. More than a hundred defectors returned to their jobs and the plant began hiring replacements. The strikers, members of Meatpackers Local P-9, vented their anger by smashing windshields, slashing tires, and assembling into a mob on the verge of a riot. Faced with the possibility of violence, the state's Democratic governor, Rudy Perpich, called out the National Guard to maintain peace and to help keep the plant open.

Wellstone rushed to the governor's office to berate him for bringing in troops, and he pressured Perpich to use his influence to force a settlement. But Wellstone also counseled the union's militant leaders to abandon their struggle, to return to work and continue bargaining. "He wanted P-9 to fight but not to commit suicide," Paul Klauda and Dave Hage wrote in their book *No Retreat, No Surrender: Labor's War at Hormel.*

The strikers became a symbol of resistance against concessions and against attempts to break unions, and, because of this, Wellstone told the union president, he must not let the union be crushed. Some members of the defiant union heckled Wellstone when he voiced the same concerns at a membership meeting. "People are going to be destroyed," he warned them.

Wellstone vividly recalled his own terror more than a decade earlier when, as a loud, antiadministration voice on the Carleton College campus, he had been told that he was being fired from his teaching position. He said he was struck then by a sickening, empty feeling of not knowing how he would support his family. During the Hormel strike, he recognized the same fear in the face of a young striker who joined him in appealing to the union president to give up the strike. The young striker pledged not to cross the picket line if the strike continued, but he said he was worried about his two children. "What's going to happen to them?" the striker asked. "That's ultimately what it was all about," Wellstone said. "At a certain point in time, you make a decision to live and fight another day. It was so damned discouraging." The strike was broken, and six hundred to seven hundred strikers lost their jobs.

As in his earlier involvement in the farm protest, Wellstone's true role in the Hormel strike was that of a realist who worked behind the scenes to bring about a resolution. That strong streak of pragmatism and self-preservation is a dimension to Wellstone that remains unappreciated. His practical side is underestimated by those who dismiss him as a fanatic, and it has been assailed by those who question his purity.

Still, his ardent and early support for the strikers showed that there was no cause too controversial for Wellstone to touch. Although he had been seriously thinking about running for statewide office since the early 1980s, he did not choose his struggles with an eye to their political benefits and liabilities. To the contrary, the strike left a sour taste in many mouths. No politician elected to statewide office, or anyone who aspired to a statewide office, could be found anywhere near Austin—except Wellstone.

Democrats traditionally depend on the support of labor, and Minnesota Democrats are no exception. Any Democrat hoping to mount a statewide campaign must have the support of key unions. Yet the Hormel strike caused a rift in the state's organized labor camp, and Wellstone sided with the most militant faction. Wellstone prodded labor, just as he pushed the Democratic Party, to adopt a more progressive stance and was at odds with more conservative AFL-CIO and Teamsters leaders.

But most disconcerting was the fact that the P-9 battle resulted in a rout for union members, which left Wellstone depressed and shaken, doubting the efficacy of activism. He said later:

> I was really down, very, very depressed, because the two things that I had been involved in we lost. The farmers—I mean we didn't win. We didn't reverse the conditions that were destroying people's livelihoods. And the P-9ers were busted. . . . I felt not personally responsible, but I felt responsible.

Wellstone's stand in the Hormel strike, as well as in other activist arenas, represented such a minefield of liabilities that Forciea and others feared he would have to burn all his energy in a Senate campaign beating back attacks. But the professor came up with a rejoinder from his classroom. Noting that he frequently told his students to "walk your talk"—to act on the beliefs they espoused—Wellstone told his crew that he would display his liberal tilt openly and campaign aggressively on his commitment to reverse the policies that broadened the gap between the rich and everyone else. That was the essence of Wellstone's own political philosophy, and he refused to believe that voters would reject it.

2

FINDING A HOME ON THE RANGE

By mid-February 1989, less than a month after George Bush
took office, Wellstone and his advisers prepared to test his candidacy on the miners and steelworkers on Minnesota's Iron
Range, where statewide Democratic primaries usually are decided. A sprawling, rugged landscape of man-made buttes and
open pit mines located about sixty miles northwest of Duluth,
the Range had been treacherous ground for liberals like Wellstone. The population of around 100,000 is relatively small, but
voter turnout on the Range is usually high—often 75 to 80
percent—and voters have a knack for unifying behind a candidate and voting as a bloc, giving the region a disproportionate
say in picking officeholders.

Settled in the mid-1890s, when gold prospectors stumbled
upon a hundred-mile swath of uncommonly rich iron ore, the
territory consists of mines that have long since seen better days.
In the heyday of the Range, waves of European immigrants took
the dirty, back-breaking jobs, blasting billions of tons of rock
and rooting out the iron ore that helped transform the United
States into the world's dominant industrial power. Finns, Serbs,
Croatians, Lithuanians, Slovenes, Poles, Russians, Italians, and

the Irish worked every part of the operation—the explosives, the drills, the steam shovels, the rails, the depots and the docks of Duluth, where ships were filled with ore before heading east on Lake Superior and down to the Great Lakes mills of Chicago and Gary, Indiana.

Meeting in clapboard union halls across the Range, workers began to unify and demand better wages and protection from dangerous conditions, demands that led to long and sometimes bloody battles. Through generations on the Range, a strong antimanagement, anticorporation attitude runs deep. The current generation of miners grew up listening to their fathers' stories about the mine companies' relentless attempts to quash unions. Their bitterness also arises out of a century of absentee ownership and exploitation of the area's enormous mineral wealth, accomplished in large part by eastern capitalists with names like Rockefeller and Carnegie.

"We have absentee owners still to this day," said Gary Cerkvenik, a college philosophy teacher, inventor, and DFL political consultant from Britt, a small Range town. "No corporate headquarters are located here for the taconite industry. Decisions are always made in places like Pittsburgh, Cleveland, and Detroit, not in [Range towns like] Eveleth, Hibbing, and Virginia."

Despite these labor-management tensions, the American domination of the international steel market fostered boom times on the Range through much of the twentieth century. Union demands for higher wages were not easily won, but they were possible in the absence of much foreign competition. By 1980, two-thirds of the homeowners on the Range had paid off their home loans, nearly three times the statewide rate.

In 1981, however, pink slips started replacing time cards. Demand for domestic steel plummeted because the American automobile industry was faltering and cheaper, subsidized foreign steel was abundant. Layoffs, plant closings, and bankruptcies quickly upended the company-town economies of places like Mountain Iron, Hibbing, and Iron Junction. By 1986, only two thousand miners were working, a staggering decline from the fifteen thousand who were employed when Rudy Boschwitz was elected to the Senate in 1978.

U-Haul trucks fleeing south and west became a daily sight. Families moved away in search of work, many simply abandoning homes that had declined rapidly in value. Those lucky enough to hold on to jobs, or stubborn enough to stay without work, saw the demise of clothing stores, barber shops, weekly newspapers. Churches cut services. Embarrassed families lined up at food shelves for free provisions.

By the spring of 1989, when Wellstone began his political exploration of the Range, a surge in the demand for steel had brought economic recovery to the region. A decline in the value of the U.S. dollar abroad made imported steel more expensive, and President Reagan's voluntary restraint agreement with a number of foreign steel exporters had given the mine owners incentives to unlock the gates and fire up again. But few believed that the upheaval was over. While the mines had started reopening a year earlier, employment was less than half of what it had been seven years before.

Though Wellstone and his advisers figured the region still was ripe for a campaign rooted in class issues, the Range could not be assumed to be an easy mark for a liberal. In two critical primaries during the previous twelve years, the voters rose up against DFL Party-endorsed liberals and delivered stunning upsets to underdog challengers perceived as conservatives or moderates, especially on the issues of gun control, environmental protections, and abortion. The unionized men and women of the Range could be called "God and Country" Democrats, people who revere the flag, who love to fish and hunt. They resent talk about gun control and wilderness restrictions on their woods and waters.

"There are liberals who are out to, in some cases, antagonize normal folks on the Range," said Gary Cerkvenik. "They want to shove things down people's throats. People on the Range are socially and economically liberal, but they also have a strong sense of personal responsibility and rugged individualism." They also are predominantly Catholic and opposed to abortion.

When Wellstone drove to the Range in April 1989, his first meeting took place in the kitchen of a farmhouse owned by Becky and Bill Noyes, near the small town of Tower. In front of a small group of local officials and party activists, Wellstone excitedly sketched the outline of a campaign based on demands for economic justice. Then he asked what they thought about his running.

"Sounds to me like you've already decided you're going to run," said Herb Lamppa, a St. Louis County commissioner. "Why don't you quit talking about it and do it?" Wellstone burst into laughter. "That was the absolute clincher. Any lingering doubt was over at that point," remembered Dick Senese, a Wellstone supporter who helped set up the meeting. "This guy had the fire in his belly and people could see it."

An hour later, in Hibbing, Wellstone walked into the home of Gabe and Mary Ann Brisbois, two of the Range's most influential activists. They had a reputation for performing loaves-and-fishes type miracles, taking meager resources and multiplying them into viable grassroots organizations. Wellstone had caught Gabe Brisbois's attention the first time Brisbois saw him, at a local party convention in 1982. As convention delegates went about the business of endorsing a congressional candidate, a troop of candidates for state offices gave speeches that were largely ignored by the delegates. "Then they introduced this guy running for state auditor," Brisbois recalled. "Nobody was listening when he started speaking. Pretty soon some people were listening, then more people. Pretty soon the whole place was thumping and jumping."

Wellstone and the Brisboises had little contact during that campaign, and even less after it was over. A couple of years later, however, Gabe was attending a track meet at Carleton College when someone tapped him on the shoulder, and he turned around to see Wellstone. "He said, 'Gabe?' My name was right at the top of his head. It was impressive," Brisbois said.

They met again by accident in 1988 in St. Paul, when Brisbois was in a brief but deep funk about his job as a high school history teacher. Over lunch in the state capitol cafeteria, Brisbois mentioned to Wellstone that he was thinking about quitting teaching. "A week later I got this letter from Paul encouraging me to stay in teaching," Brisbois said. In the note, Wellstone reassured him that there was no more important work than teaching and that he could see Brisbois cared about kids. "It was really nice of him to take the time to do it. It was an example of the character of the individual," Brisbois said.

So when the Brisboises greeted Wellstone in April 1989, they handed him the key to their home and told him to use it whenever he needed a place to sleep. They also pledged to help him carry the Range. Their support meant that Wellstone would receive the backing of dozens of other officeholders and activists who were indebted to the Brisboises or who followed their lead. "Before the snow melted in 1989, Paul was in very good shape politically on the Iron Range," said Pat Forciea.

Russian Roots

Wellstone's ability to connect with Iron Rangers can be traced in part to his own heritage of immigration and hardship, and he made frequent references to his own humble background throughout his campaign. Wellstone's father, Leon Wexelstein, came to America from Russian in 1914, at the outbreak of World War I. He arrived at the age of seventeen, having earned a scholarship to study mathematics at the University of Washington. He would never see his parents again. They insisted that their son remain abroad during the 1917 revolt, and they disappeared during a Stalinist purge.

A natural linguist, Wexelstein quickly adapted to the language and life of America, educating himself and fixing his sights on becoming a playwright. "He only wanted to be another Chekhov," Wellstone said of his father's ambition. Wexelstein never achieved this goal. Instead he drifted through a series of jobs and cities across the country, displaying an amazing variety of skills. He was an electrical engineer in Seattle, a freelance writer in New York, a newspaper editorial writer in Boston, an economist for the federal government in Washington, and finally a writer for the U.S. Information Agency under Edward R. Murrow.

The USIA job was the only one that he liked, and that was because he deeply admired Murrow. The broadcast journalist was just one of a handful of noteworthy figures with whom Wexelstein was acquainted. He was friends with American communist leader Gus Hall and with Alexander Kerensky, a leader of the moderate socialist movement that helped overthrow Russia's czarist government in 1917. He knew diplomat George Kennan and wrote for H. L. Mencken's *American Mercury* magazine. He also landed a job with the federal government with the help of Supreme Court Justice Felix Frankfurter. (It was while he was living in Washington, D.C., in the late 1930s that Wexelstein encountered "virulent anti-Semitism" and changed the family name to Wellstone, his son said.)

Wellstone's intellect clearly was molded by his father, but he believes his personality and temperament were inherited from his mother's side of the family, particularly from his grandfather, Menasha Danishevsky, also a Russian immigrant. Danishevsky was a garment factory worker and labor organizer who turned his family's apartment in a Jewish ghetto on Manhattan's Lower East Side into a shelter for the homeless. Wellstone described his grandfather:

> He was famous for having people over every night, anybody who was out in the streets. The family used to get furious at him. They lived in a tenement and they had no room, but he was always bringing people in to feed them and to house them. He was very emotional, very warm, very gregarious. He used to take my mother to hear [Socialist Party presidential nominee Eugene V.] Debs. It's pretty obvious I take after him.

As Wellstone's father settled into the federal bureaucracy in the 1950s, the family eventually acquired the symbol of the American dream—a boxy, red-brick rambler in a respectable neighborhood in Arlington, Virginia. Tucked into a wooded hill at the end of a cul-de-sac, this house represented acceptance into America and a relatively comfortable life for Leon and Minnie Wexelstein and their two boys. But it eventually became the setting for a family tragedy.

Shortly after their elder son, Stephen, went away to college he was struck with a mental illness, a form of severe depression and occasional fits of violence, from which he never fully recovered. At first, they sought treatment at a private hospital, but after a year the cost overwhelmed the family and Stephen was transferred to a state institution in Virginia.

Each Saturday morning, Paul, then eleven years old, and his mother would board a bus to visit Stephen. At the state asylum, Wellstone's social and political education began. The bright young child was haunted and frightened by scores of mentally ill people shuffling through dark, airless wards and rocking aimlessly on spartan furniture. When he recounted the visits thirty years later, the emotional wounds seemed almost fresh and he virtually spit with hatred:

> It was a snakepit. I visited him every week and I would go in the wards and I'd see the way people looked. The whole place was just a nightmare. It was a very radicalizing experience. I hated it. I just hated that institution and the way people were treated. . . . It was all these people just sitting around on benches, nobody taking care of them. It was obvious nobody was really getting any help. People were just getting warehoused. It was grim. . . . I literally have the image of it in my mind right now. It will never leave me.

More than any other event, his brother's illness and its aftershocks, which burdened him and the family for decades, shaped Wellstone's political philosophy and motivations. At home, Wellstone remembers a distraught household, constantly on edge, his parents frequently crying. "That was . . . the worst time in my life because my mother and father . . . were always crying," Wellstone said. "It was just an awful several years."

The emotional strain was multiplied by the crushing debt. "It was so clear that we could barely hold on, all because of a medical bill," added Wellstone. "I've never understood why people should just have to go under because of medical bills."

To pay off these debts, Minnie took a job in the cafeteria of the junior high school that Paul attended. With a strain of regret and guilt in his voice, Wellstone said he was embarrassed by his mother's menial work:

> It was humiliating because all the kids would make fun of these women. They all viewed them as white trash. It made me pretty damn aware of class in America, and I'm not overinterpreting it. It really did. I didn't use the word *class* then, but I sure as hell

was aware of the situation. And I knew how hard she was working, even though I was kind of ashamed.

Here are the origins of Wellstone's sharp sensitivity to class divisions and inequities, and some of the events that produced an antiestablishment reformer.

Openly resentful of his parents' preoccupation with his brother's problems and their debts, Wellstone turned into an angry child. A sixth-grade teacher described him as buoyant and "irrepressible," but for the next two or three years Wellstone came perilously close to ruining his life. He grew into a frustrated, angry juvenile delinquent who fell in with a tough crowd, got into lots of fistfights, carried a switchblade, and even stole cars for joyrides on several occasions.

At junior high school, where his grades fell to D's and C's from nearly straight A's, he spent a lot of time in the principal's office. On weekends, a night at the movies sometimes ended with an impromptu "rumble" between him and his friends and a rival group. Punches would be thrown, bloody noses would be wiped clean, and then it was time to go home.

This was a manifestation of 1950s suburban ennui inspired by James Dean, not a gang. Wellstone even strutted around in a black leather jacket and short-sleeved T-shirt with sleeves rolled up onto his shoulders. His hair was greased and swept back in the ducktail style that was fashionable among tough guys. He said of the group:

> "Rebel without a cause" was just about right to describe us. It wasn't an organized gang or hardened criminal activity. It was a bunch of guys who were very mixed up. I wasn't a mean kid, but I was a mixed-up kid. I think I'm lucky that I didn't end up in reform school [as his best friend at school did]. God knows what would've happened to me then.

Wellstone attributes his rebellion partly to family stress and partly to a combative, bantam-rooster mentality that came with being the shortest boy around. He found it difficult to accept that he was a head shorter than his peers, so he felt a need to prove himself. "I was a short kid with a chip on my shoulder," he said. His rescue came in the form of high school wrestling, which suited his personality and channeled his aggression into discipline and competition. "Athletics . . . really literally saved me," Wellstone said. "It completely changed my life. . . . I began to feel good about myself."

Almost immediately, he pulled out of his self-destructive spin. He became a star wrestler, competing in the 98- and 103-pound weight classes. He was undefeated in matches with other high schools, and he finished second in the state championship finals in his sophomore and junior years. In his senior year, slowed by a case of mononucleosis, he finished third.

Meanwhile, his grades improved, and by his senior year he had discovered a new appreciation for his father. With his long black coat and a hat pulled down to his eyes, Leon Wexelstein was a mysterious and conspicuous sight in the Virginia suburbs, and for a while Wellstone was embarrassed by him. But now, maturity edging out rebellion, Wellstone cherished their nightly talks over sponge cake and tea, served in the kitchen at ten o'clock. After Paul gave his father a review of school and wrestling, Leon launched into the big issues—history and economics, the moral failure of the Bolshevik revolution, the horror of nuclear war. Leon inculcated in his son the importance of education and urged him to be more rigorous in his analysis of ideas and world events and to be compassionate toward the less fortunate.

"He was someone who seemed to be very sad about the world," Wellstone recalled:

I remember he once wrote [in an essay Wellstone found among his father's papers] that man has this kind of tremendous capacity to do good and man has this tremendous capacity to do evil, and the question is whether, given that parallelism, the world can survive. He used to really write a lot about that. He was very, very preoccupied with the possibility of nuclear war.

Leon also talked at length and with tremendous emotion about the Soviet leaders, who had, in all likelihood, killed his parents. "My father was virulently anticommunist," Wellstone remembered. "He felt betrayed by the Bolsheviks, he felt betrayed by Lenin, and he felt betrayed by the communists."

Wellstone's own political epiphany occurred not at home but at the University of North Carolina at Chapel Hill, where he was swept up in the drama of the civil rights movement. For the first few years at college, Wellstone was preoccupied with academics, athletics, and fatherhood. He married Sheila Ison, his high school sweetheart, after their first year in college. Sheila had grown up in Kentucky in a more affluent and less distressed family than Paul's. In the middle of her junior year in high school, her family moved to Washington, D.C. She was miserable about being uprooted, but that changed during the summer after her junior year, when she met Paul through mutual friends. Sheila recalled falling for an "extremely good-looking guy . . . with this great build."

After a year of dating they parted to attend different colleges, but they could not bear to be separated and were married in the summer of 1963, both at the age of nineteen. Sheila was raised as a Southern Baptist and Paul, while he had no formal religious training and no bar mitzvah, was a Jew. They wanted to be married in a Presbyterian church, but the first minister they asked said he would perform the ceremony only if Wellstone said he believed in Jesus Christ. "There I was, and without any religious upbringing and with no hesitation, I said, 'No, I'm a Jew,' "

Wellstone remembered. They found another minister at the same church who acceded to Wellstone's request that neither Jesus Christ nor the Holy Ghost be mentioned in the ceremony.

As a married student, Wellstone set a furious pace that would establish a pattern for his life. While Sheila worked in the college library to support them, Paul won a regional wrestling title, crammed his final three years of undergraduate schooling into just two years, and graduated Phi Beta Kappa. In the midst of all this, they produced a son, David.

Political Awakening

As Wellstone studied political science at Chapel Hill, the political and social structure of the South began to explode around him. After happening upon a confrontation in the town of Chapel Hill in which whites pelted civil rights protesters with eggs, spit on them, and beat them, the Wellstones became active in the civil rights movement. But Paul shied away from civil disobedience, afraid that an arrest would slow down his rush through school and keep him from fulfilling his role as a father and provider. "I just didn't think I could go to jail for any length of time," he said. For the same reason, Wellstone, unlike many members of the "flower generation," abstained totally from drugs, even marijuana. The complete absence of any gossip about personal habits and his family life was valuable when he ran for office more than two decades later.

While Wellstone kept himself at arm's length from many of the most dramatic confrontations that shaped the 1960s, he did attend an event that was burned into his memory and forever committed him to social activism. The incident was a Ku Klux Klan rally in the countryside outside Chapel Hill in 1967. Wellstone had finished his graduate work and was teaching political science at Chapel Hill while he worked on his dissertation on race relations, titled "Black Militants in the Ghetto: Why They Believe in Violence." Several black students told him of the Klan rally, and the curious Wellstones and two others decided they would attend.

When they arrived, they saw the Klan's trademark burning cross, which threw shadows of elongated, pointed hoods. At first they were reassured to see a line of state patrol cars and a man with a holster and gun strapped to his hip, standing guard. Sheila, figuring the man was a state trooper, told him she was glad to see him. "Yes, ma'am," he said to her. "All white Anglo-Saxons are welcome here."

The crowd was mostly "poor white people who were victimized themselves," Wellstone said. "In a strange way, I felt sorry for them." The crowd listened to a venomous speech by KKK Grand Dragon Robert Sheldon. He screamed about blacks and "Christ-killing Zionist Jews," and the crowd responded with a refrain of "Niggers!" A Klansman worked the crowd for donations, and when the bucket was thrust in front of Wellstone, his anger overwhelmed his fear. "I don't give my money to you people," he said loudly. "I give my money to the black power movement." The Klansman directed Wellstone to the edge of the rally, where he snapped open a car trunk full of rifles. Wellstone's bravado vanished and he sprinted back to his car, where he joined his wife and friends. They raced home along a deserted road, bracing for an ambush.

Back on campus, Wellstone soon began a long career of provoking authorities. He was a leading supporter of a strike by cafeteria workers, and as a teaching assistant he upset department elders by not assigning the standard textbook for a freshman political science lecture class of more than five hundred students. The textbook was written by two professors at the university who received royalties from the sales.

Wellstone's activism on and off campus soon made him realize that he was not prepared for the staid life of a traditional scholar. "I didn't like graduate school," he said. "I wasn't interested in publishing in professional journals." He became disillusioned with the academic profession of political science because he felt that it lacked any connection with the real world. It was more concerned with methodology and technique and dry theory than in affecting change, he said. He even questioned his own work, particularly his study of black militancy for his dissertation. That research had been converted into two articles that were accepted by political science journals, but Wellstone pulled them before they were published:

> After I wrote them and took a look at them, I felt like the people had really been more the objects of the research rather than the subjects. And I didn't see any connection between the publishing of these articles and the betterment of the lives of the people studied. I couldn't see any connection. Therefore I thought it was dishonest.

At the same time, however, Wellstone discovered a true affinity for teaching, and he developed a plan to link a career in academia with a lifetime of social and political activism. He described his academic philosophy at the outset of the 1990 Senate race:

> I came out of that experience [in graduate school] determined to use the tools of scholarship and my understanding of political power to make a difference in the lives of people, determined not to decouple my values from my work—not to stand back as a dispassionate observer, but to step forward and stand with people struggling for justice and equality.

To Minnesota

Within months after earning his doctorate in 1969, the twenty-five-year-old Wellstone was given a chance to test his ideals. The government department at Carleton College in Northfield, Minnesota, offered to hire him as an adjunct professor, and Wellstone accepted, even though he knew it meant moving from a large public school in his native South to a small, expensive private school in the Midwest. Wellstone appreciated the irony and was determined to be an influence for progressive change in a college that catered to a privileged elite. "I got involved in every conflict," he said.

From the start, Wellstone was an incendiary figure, wearing his curly hair in a big Afro that stuck out at least eight inches. At times the curls were parted and bunched into a lopsided cone. Instead of tweed jackets, the uniform of the college professor, Wellstone wore tight muscle shirts.

Just eight months after his arrival in Minnesota, Wellstone faced his first major crisis of conscience and crossed the line for the first time into civil disobedience. He agreed to accompany students to a sit-in protesting the Vietnam War, a protest that would be staged at the Federal Building in Minneapolis, about fifty miles north of the Carleton campus. Though he promised Sheila that he would not be arrested, he changed his mind when he saw the police hauling students away:

> I didn't actually go up intending to be arrested. I went up there because they [the students] asked me. They were very nervous, and they wanted me there as a teacher. . . . But when I was with them, and I saw the police grabbing them, I couldn't just stand there. It wasn't enough to just be supportive.

Using his single phone call to reach Sheila, he told her he had been arrested. After frantically asking a neighbor for directions and to mind her children, Sheila eventually found her way to Minneapolis and the jail. She found her husband in a crowded cell, lying on the floor, using his sport coat as a pillow.

As Wellstone established himself on the Carleton campus, students began to flock to his courses—the Politics of Poverty and the Politics of Social Welfare—which focused on the unequal distribution of money and power in American society. His former students remember him as a passionate teacher who challenged them to approach a subject from more than an academic perspective. "He forced you to step [into] the equation," remembered Steve Emerson, now a news analyst with the Cable News Network. "You couldn't be one of those disinterested observers sitting outside the political circle."

Besides teaching his courses, Wellstone directed three independent study projects in which seventy students measured the problems and needs of the poor in communities around the college. Working out of a union hall in the nearby town of Faribault, students solicited the opinions of area residents, stopping them on Main Street, walking through neighborhoods, and hanging out in laundromats. In addition to gathering information, they distributed booklets on the rights of tenants and welfare recipients. Out of this effort came the Organization for a Better Rice County, which helped poor residents to assert themselves and to negotiate with state and local officials for grants and expanded social programs. The project also inspired Wellstone's first book, *How the Rural Poor Got Power.*

As part of his tutoring in the art of community organizing, Wellstone brought nationally recognized activists to Carleton. He invited Saul Alinsky, the executive director of Chicago's Industrial Areas Foundation and author of *Rules for Radicals.* George Wiley, founder of the National Welfare Rights Organization, also came to the campus.

"A lot of students would say they wanted to take a Wellstone course to have had the Wellstone experience," said fellow political science professor Steven Schier. "It was sort of like a Tilt-a-Whirl ride. It was something to experience."

Although some students practically worshipped him, Wellstone became an irritant to many of his colleagues and administrators and a pariah among them. He ignored rules and traditions of curriculum, earned a reputation as an easy grader, and struck many as a lightweight scholar. At the same time, he refused to blend into Carleton's social life. Instead of living in the neighborhood near campus where so many of the professors occupied nice old homes, he and Sheila bought a small house in the blue-collar part of town, where he could surround his family with a neighborhood full of children. "He made it clear from the beginning that he didn't want to be part of the academic club. He was from the start an outsider," said Norm Vig, a political science professor who initially was critical of Wellstone but later became a close friend and ally.

In 1971, Wellstone pushed disrespect to the limits when he attacked the college's highest official, Edson Spencer, chairman of the board of trustees. Writing in the May 12 edition of the *Noon News Bulletin*, a compendium of announcements and comments published by students, Wellstone accused Spencer, an executive vice president of Honeywell, of "immoral behavior" for managing a "criminal corporation." Honeywell, known for its thermostats and other household products, also manufactured deadly, disfiguring antipersonnel bombs for use in the Vietnam War, and its Twin Cities facilities were frequently the scene of antiwar protests.

"I firmly believe," Wellstone wrote, "that as members of this college community we should demand that Edson Spencer—vice president of Honeywell—which continues to produce weapons to carve up the Vietnamesse [*sic*] people—be removed from OUR Bd. of trustees, much less the position of being chairman." This letter summarized neatly what many faculty members felt was wrong with this rabble-rouser posing as a scholar. Not only did Wellstone rashly call the top official a war criminal, but his writing was marred by several misspellings, clumsy usage, and grammatical errors.

The letter was followed by a confrontation between Spencer and some six hundred or seven hundred students and faculty at an evening meeting on campus. There was a lengthy question-and-answer period, and Spencer recalled that Wellstone was constantly at one of the two audience microphones:

> He was badgering, driving, and intense. There were other people who asked me better questions, very deep philosophical questions. Paul was attacking head on and he was not hard to confront, in my view. He was playing to the audience rather than engaging in a debate over philosophical issues.

By January 1974, college administrators and the government department faculty decided they had had enough, and Wellstone was notified by letter that he would be fired after the 1974-75 academic year. The reasons cited were his lack of interest in "the discipline of political science" and a "narrowness of focus." His fellow political scientists rated him as being deficient in "scholarly development and activity." Judged strictly by the "publish or perish" standard used by many colleges, Wellstone surely had not distinguished himself. With the exception of an article on urban black militancy published in *Public Opinion Quarterly,* Wellstone had placed hardly any work in political science journals. The department chairman said that the decision by department faculty members was unanimous.

With the help of students he had schooled in organizing tactics, Wellstone fought back. "The fact that some people want me to leave so badly makes me want to stay all the more," he told the student newspaper. The students marshaled opposition through a series of evening meetings, petitions, and published attacks on the administration. They lobbied college administrators and the board of trustees. They even talked of boycotting classes and withholding tuition payments. Black and Hispanic students denounced the administration for firing one of the few faculty members who openly concerned himself with their problems and well-being. A number of Northfield residents submitted a letter describing how Wellstone's off-campus activities had helped their lives. Theresa VanZuillen, president of the Organization for a Better Rice County, wrote to the college:

> Dr. Wellstone treats everyone as his equal, no matter what their status in life. He has (for the first time in their lives, maybe) given incentive to old people, some who can't even read or write, to speak up clearly and express themselves to city councils, county commissioners, etc., to let their needs be known. He gave them dignity.

On the inside, Wellstone was aided in this fight by Sy Schuster, a math professor and antiwar activist who had befriended him shortly after his arrival five years earlier. Schuster, a former wrestler who had a locker adjacent to Wellstone's in the faculty locker room, made strong personal appeals to the college's top officials, warning them that their case was not strong and that proceeding could "tear the campus apart." He finally got them to agree to outside evaluation, which Schuster considered to be an extraordinary victory in itself.

The growing pressure and continued confrontations forced administrators to bring in the evaluators, who gave Wellstone glowing reviews. "Professor Wellstone is a remarkable teacher, there is no doubt about it," wrote one evaluator, Peter Bachrach, a political science professor at Temple University. "The difficulty arose because some of his colleagues and administrators didn't understand what the hell he was doing," Bachrach said later. "The usual scholar and teacher who can't understand a teacher like Wellstone sees him as a threat. After all, you can't compete with someone if you have no idea what he's about."

The administration finally reversed itself and awarded Well-stone tenure, but the fight left scars. Seven years later, when Steve Schier accepted a teaching job at Carleton and stayed at Wellstone's house while he looked for a place to live, Wellstone warned him not to tell others in the department where he was staying: some might hold Schier's association with Wellstone against him. Schier soon learned why. At the rare department meetings Wellstone attended, "the atmosphere would crackle with tension," Schier recalled.

Locking Up the Range

Fifteen years after he was granted job security at Carleton, Well-stone began building the foundation of his Senate campaign on the Iron Range, where black coffee sustained hours of conversations in modest kitchens and living rooms. In one home after another during the spring and summer of 1989, Wellstone sparked little fires. Most importantly, he persuaded the people of the Range that he was not a metropolitan liberal preoccupied with issues that meant little or nothing to them—issues like the right to burn the flag or First Amendment protection for pornography. Instead, he proved that he was just as angry as they were about plant closings, the savings and loan bailout, and the other legacies of Reagan-Bush economics. Gary Cerkvenik explained:

> What Rangers are looking for in a candidate is a tough fighter. When you are fighting mining companies or fighting in politics, you have to be tough. Wellstone was perceived as being tough, not a laid-back liberal but someone who would be on the firing line, someone who would walk the picket line with you. That was the attraction of Paul Wellstone.

Wellstone's appeal and the diversity of the coalition he built were evident in the Range steering committee that Gabe Brisbois assembled on Wellstone's behalf. One of the earliest supporters was Bill Ojala, a former state representative who made his own mark on the Range in 1970 and 1971 by campaigning for abortion rights—three years before *Roe v. Wade*—and against the Vietnam War. Ojala, a part-time bus driver, especially liked Wellstone's disregard for the party elites.

"He took his candidacy to the people," said Ojala. "He didn't direct his campaign to the party leaders to gain their support. He took it to the people." A major reason Wellstone succeeded in firing up regular folks on the Range was his sincerity, Ojala added. "We've heard lots of songs and dances from a lot of people coming up here looking for votes. But here was a guy they instinctively believed and trusted."

Another person Wellstone drew into his circle of admirers was Pamela Reynolds, a Holiday Inn bartender who used her spare time and money to organize a support group for low-income women, most of them single mothers on welfare. Wellstone and Brisbois also signed up party activist Joe Moren. Mary Anderson, a bar owner and the feisty mayor of the town of Kinney (population 257), gave Wellstone her blessing, too. Mary's Bar is a required stop for any politician passing through the Range, and Anderson liked what she saw of Wellstone. "You felt comfortable with him," said Anderson. "He was a different type of candidate."

Colleen Baker, a part-time computer operator, became another member of the steering committee. And, despite Wellstone's support for abortion rights, he drew the backing of Jayne Marsnik, a party activist who was strongly against abortion. Marsnik generally was suspicious of liberals, but she said she was swept away after hearing Wellstone speak.

In rollicking speeches at local political gatherings and in

union halls and in animated conversations in people's houses, Wellstone's message and his personal magnetism spread across the Iron Range and excited voters as no outsider had in years.

Recalled Reynolds: "He had these little coals deep inside him that kept burning."

3

SHAPING THE AGENDA

After securing a beachhead on the Iron Range, Wellstone and his advisers turned to the task of formally launching the campaign and sending its message across the state. Essential as the Range was to his emerging strategy, Wellstone also recognized that it was far from the main source of free publicity—the state's media center of Minneapolis-St. Paul. So for the convenience of the statewide television and radio stations and newspapers with headquarters in the Twin Cities, Wellstone had to declare his candidacy in the metropolitan area. Most statewide candidates go to the capitol, where the state's political reporters are based, because it increases the chances of drawing coverage. But Wellstone, an outsider who had never held public office, chose a location that better symbolized the campaign he had in mind.

The site was the Sabathani Community Center in south Minneapolis, a neighborhood hub for nutrition, job training, housing, and other programs targeted at residents of the inner-city area. Choosing Sabathani was a distinct statement about who the campaign intended to appeal to: minorities, the poor, the homeless, the disenfranchised. Kris Blake, who was to become the campaign's first manager, elaborated:

> Sabathani, despite the fact [that] it was worn around the edges, was the perfect place. It didn't look fancy, and our campaign wasn't going to be fancy. It was going to be a hard-working, different campaign and this was our chance to cement that idea in the minds of party leaders and the press—that this was going to be different.

The setting also drew attention to Wellstone's close ties to the black community, and was therefore of questionable political value in a state where 94 percent of the population is white. Through his work on Jackson's campaign, Wellstone probably was better known among blacks than among whites and would have enjoyed their support no matter where he announced his campaign.

Much of the planning for Wellstone's speech at Sabathani, like so much of the early stage of the campaign, was conducted during Wellstone's noontime runs through the woods north of the Carleton College campus with Mike Casper, a theoretical physicist, and Norm Vig, a fellow political science professor. As Wellstone's closest friend and adviser, Casper was the most influential in helping shape the early campaign strategy. Wellstone remembers when he first saw Casper at a collegewide faculty meeting held in the fall of 1969 to talk about the Vietnam War. ("This is when I still went to faculty meetings," he said.) There was heated discussion about whether to cancel regular classes so professors and students could conduct discussions about the war. The president, Howard Swearer, and other faculty endorsed a one-day cancellation of classes in October, but rejected a proposal to repeat the event in November. "This hand shoots up," Wellstone said, describing Casper perched in the front row:

> Mike says, "What's so compelling in October that's not just as compelling in November?" I fell out of my chair laughing. It's one of those questions that just pisses people off because it's

right. . . . That was the beginning of the friendship. This was a guy I wanted to meet.

Casper, a few years older than Wellstone, was his intellectual soul mate and probably the most supportive influence in the development of his politics over twenty years. They shared remarkably similar backgrounds. Both grew up in Arlington, Virginia, in Jewish households headed by fathers who worked for the federal government, Wellstone's for the U.S. Information Agency, Casper's for the Atomic Energy Commission. Casper said:

> There was something about growing up in the Washington area, where local news is always national news, and maybe being from Jewish traditions, that made us similar. Our politics was not quite the same as Midwestern populism, but still we both grew up with the idea of struggling against the rich and powerful and we both were very much ready to join in the populist tradition of the Midwest when we arrived at Carleton.

They became a team, researching, writing, and even teaching together, and once they joined students in a sit-in at the campus library to block a board of trustees meeting and to urge the trustees to sell the college's investments in South Africa. Casper and Wellstone talked together almost every day over the years. "There was a time when he wouldn't give a speech without calling and talking to me," Casper said. "We had a variety of running jokes where he claimed he thought of something and I claimed I thought of something."

In the spring of 1989, Casper wrote outlines for Wellstone's opening speech at Sabathani. In every draft of the speech, Casper pounded on the idea that Wellstone would run a different kind of campaign. He wrote in one version:

The good news is that there are many signs that the conventional politics will not be the winning politics in Minnesota in 1990, signs that Minnesotans are fed up with the superficial appeals and the negative innuendo of the 1988 [presidential] campaign. . . . No one who participated in the 1988 DFL caucuses [where Jackson shocked the experts with his strong showing] can doubt that there are definite signs that DFLers are ready to reject conventional politics and conventional politicians in favor of a candidate who is not beholden to the tight circles of greed and power and a campaign that will articulate a vision of the future that Minnesotans can believe in and work for.

The final draft reflected the consensus that Wellstone and Casper had developed on their campus runs: "There was a sea change of public opinion on the horizon about politics and politicians," Casper said.

On April 24, 1989, more than eighteen months before election day 1990, Wellstone tried to catch the first puff of wind from that sea change. He declared his candidacy before an assembly of about four hundred supporters, a crowd that was swelled by carloads from the Iron Range and a couple of busloads of students, farmers, and others from Northfield. Before Wellstone took the stage, the crowd was entertained by a jazz combo, a stand-up comic, a rhythm-and-blues band and a female jazz singer who evoked Wellstone's role in the Jackson campaign with a rendition of "Somewhere over the Rainbow." Strings of colorful balloons arched over the stage to form a rainbow. "We wanted to make it a fun event and a family event, something to bring the kids and grandparents to," said Kris Blake.

When Wellstone spoke, he outlined a guerrilla campaign against incumbent senator Rudy Boschwitz. He renounced Boschwitz's money-and-ads formula and vowed to wage a populist, grassroots crusade. He would reject money from political

action committees outside Minnesota; he did not want to be beholden to corporate and special-interest groups with no connection to Minnesotans. He also snickered at the idea of a television
campaign, saying, "I'm not going to be a made-up media creation."

Mainstream Democrats were not impressed. They foresaw,
at best, a shadowy, marginal candidate rushing around the state
in supporters' battered cars, seldom seen on television, where all
real statewide campaigns are fought. Wellstone volunteer Sylvia
Knutson remembered that a couple of DFL officeholders from
Minneapolis ridiculed the notion of Wellstone's taking on
Boschwitz: at a fund-raiser for a Minneapolis Park Board candidate just a few weeks after Wellstone declared his candidacy,
state representative Peter McLaughlin and Minneapolis City
Council member Tony Scallon told Knutson that Wellstone had
no chance. "They said nobody supports him. Nobody supports
him at the legislature," Knutson recalled. "They were just making fun of him. Definitely at this point nobody was taking his
candidacy very seriously."

D. J. Leary, a coauthor of the newsletter *Politics in Minne-
sota,* confirmed Knutson's impression. Leary told Minneapolis
Star Tribune columnist Doug Grow: "He can't draw the media.
When you can't draw the attention, it's hard to raise the money.
And when you try to live off the land, like he wants to do, you
can't raise the dollars you need to do the television."

Leary's comments were reinforced by the scant attention
drawn by Wellstone's announcement at Sabathani. Neither of
the state's two largest newspapers showed up, and only one television station sent a camera. "We were terribly disappointed,"
said Blake. "That disappointment didn't end with that opening
hit. It was a continuing source of frustration for Paul. [He called
me] just frantic sometimes."

Campaign Themes

Despite the lack of notice, Wellstone remained convinced that his strategy was the only way a Democrat could beat Boschwitz. Democrats had to offer voters a distinct alternative, and Wellstone pledged to make Boschwitz's well-oiled machine—and all the wealth and privilege associated with it—a central issue of the campaign. That, he insisted, would turn Boschwitz's millions into a liability.

"We set out from the beginning to turn that on its head by making it an issue," said Casper. Then, when people saw "one of these smiley, feel-good Boschwitz ads," they would think about the source of the money used to pay for the ad blitz. "From early on we were thinking we would make a point of Boschwitz's money, his preoccupation with fund-raising and his connections with wealthy people," Casper said. "We thought the time might be right."

Everywhere Casper and Wellstone looked, the evidence was building: the public seemed to be ready for a reevaluation of the political system. In the early summer of 1989, for instance, Casper and Wellstone and their wives escaped for a few days to Madeline Island, a jewel off the coast of Wisconsin in Lake Superior. The men rose early one morning while their wives were still sleeping, and as they knocked around the cabin, fixing coffee and rummaging through reading material, Wellstone's eyes lit up over an article in the *Progressive* magazine: a funny-sad story by Ed Garvey, a well-known liberal Wisconsin Democrat, about his fruitless chase for money in a Senate campaign, and his defeat. Casper summarized:

> Garvey wrote about how, early on, he would tell these rich Democratic contributors, but not convincingly, that he could raise the money to win. They told him to come back after he got the endorsement. And then, finally, when he got the party en-

dorsement, he went back to the same people who had told him that it was too early, only now they told him it was too late.

Outraged and amused by Garvey's story, Casper and Wellstone believed that money had so corrupted politics "that the time might be right for running against money," Casper said. "We knew that if we could get some of that sense of outrage going over Boschwitz and money and being completely out of touch we had a chance. We thought a lot in those days about how to turn that money advantage on its head."

That issue—Boschwitz's money, and the power and privilege of the wealthy—dominated the early strategizing and the establishment of themes of the campaign. But there were other issues to think about as well, and the development of Wellstone's agenda also was strikingly different from that in almost all other political campaigns.

The informal Wellstone brain trust in the early days of the campaign was made up mostly of academics: Norman Vig, a soft-spoken, meticulous, gray-haired professor of political science at Carleton; Sy Schuster, the Carleton math professor who had been a key defender of Wellstone during the tenure fight; and Andy Blauvelt, blunt but an incisive political thinker, an assistant professor at St. John's University near St. Cloud in central Minnesota. Blauvelt had written to Wellstone shortly after Wellstone declared his candidacy to say that he thought Walter Mondale should be the candidate. He thought a strong early Wellstone effort might cajole Mondale into running. This hardly qualified him as a true believer, but Wellstone was impressed by Blauvelt's sharpness, and Blauvelt did much of the early research into Boschwitz's voting record and campaign finances.

This nucleus, meeting informally with Wellstone off and on through 1989, soon discovered that it had almost nothing to do. Blauvelt said he spent close to eight hours probing Wellstone to test his coherency and the extent of his development on policy and issues. He came away amazed:

> I have had connections with a number of campaigns over twenty years, and I have to say that Paul Wellstone came to his campaign with more issues, things that he had thought about and made commitments on, than any other candidate I've ever known. . . . Most candidates go through a whole campaign without taking as many stands on issues as Paul had developed before he even ran.

Blauvelt, used to dealing with mainstream Democrats for whom policy development was a chore because they did not really have a strong unifying philosophical foundation, found Wellstone to be entirely different:

> This was not somebody who looked to the left and looked to the right and tried to find something acceptable in the center. His whole campaign actually was based on the assumption that the American people will vote for someone who amounts to a radical once they realize his values are their values and that his concerns to a large extent are their concerns and that he's trying to represent the best of what's in us.

Despite a fairly comprehensive grasp of exactly what legislation Wellstone favored on health care, energy, environment, and tax load redistribution, there were some soft spots in the national game plan, Blauvelt discovered: "He was a little weak, shall we say, on funding mechanisms." The source of revenues for massive investments in health and education programs were not clear in Wellstone's mind. He was notoriously disorganized when it came to something as simple as balancing the family checkbook, which his wife, Sheila, always took care of. This was a paramount concern.

Wellstone's advisers knew that he had to avoid looking like a spendthrift liberal who couldn't balance a checkbook. Even though progressives believed that the massive debts racked up by Reagan and so-called responsible Democrats should have disqualified the guilty parties from making such a charge, the brain trust knew that the media would be susceptible to allegations that Wellstone would "spend the national inheritance," Blauvelt said. So Blauvelt worked with Wellstone to develop a plausible proposal—one that added up, on paper at least—to finance new social initiatives with a combination of defense cuts and much higher taxes on the wealthy, though there was no plan to reduce or retire the deficit.

Other policy positions were settled more easily, Blauvelt said:

> His method was to firmly establish the principle and the direction on a certain issue, then look for the people who were headed in the same direction and pick from proposals they had developed. . . . He had all these contacts, a truly impressive populist-progressive network around the country.

In consultation with progressive doctors and medical experts, Wellstone had already decided to advocate the Canadian-style universal health care system, which at the time was an almost unthinkable position for a major-party candidate. He favored a raft of proposals advocating energy conservation and environmental protection. He himself had been an influential player on a farm-policy approach, the Harkin-Gephardt Bill, that favored smaller farmers through a combination of production controls and higher prices. Opposition to defense spending, weapons development, and military intervention was an easy call and already a strongly developed package. He was ambivalent on trade issues, being both a militant union supporter and an internationalist, but his positions were somewhat more restrictive than Boschwitz's and not a political liability.

Potential internal conflicts were embedded in this agenda— between environmental protections and other players in the coalition, for instance. Auto workers were known to oppose dramatic increases in gas mileage standards for automobiles. Some farmers were nervous about major new restrictions on the use of agricultural pollutants. Wellstone insisted that "environmental imperatives come first," Vig said, and always tried to make a strong case—backed up with extensive statistics, anecdotes, and analysis—that "people were being given a false choice between clean environment and jobs." He tied together the evidence that corporations were abandoning responsibility to both the earth and its workers by fleeing to places like Mexico, with its poor wages and weak environmental standards.

On no issue was Wellstone unopinionated or willing to embrace a policy position simply because his handlers thought it would serve him politically. "He pretty much made up his own agenda," Vig said. Rather than adapting an agenda to the political winds, Wellstone wanted to bring Minnesota around to his views, which he hoped to present with new power and persuasiveness.

The essence, Vig believed, was both abstract and simple:

> He was never much interested in anything but power, who has it and why, and how do people without it get it. He never got involved in any elaborate political philosophy, never really got into Marxist theory, but always adhered to simple populist principles. It wasn't really a philosophy, it was an outlook. How can the poor and powerless organize to get power and social justice, better living standards and material benefits?

Wellstone was neither alone nor a leading thinker or writer in searching for an answer to this question. He was one of thousands of progressive leaders across the country who by the late 1980s developed something approaching a comprehensive fusion of left-of-center politics from a palette of causes and historical strains. His thinking was shaped by a handful of modern progressive writers, among them Saul Alinsky, populist historian Robert Goodwyn, and economist Robert Reich, who would later become President Bill Clinton's secretary of labor. But the thinkers who most influenced him, Wellstone said, were Frances Fox Piven and Richard Cloward, two little-known radical social critics. Their books *Regulating the Poor, Poor People's Movements, The New Class War,* and *The Politics of Turmoil* were influential in shaping and sharpening Wellstone's views during the 1970s and 1980s. What they have to say clearly illuminates Wellstone's core beliefs and the reasons for both his anger and his optimism.

In *The New Class War: Reagan's Attack on the Welfare State and Its Consequences,* Piven and Cloward argued that the 1930s and 1960s were periods of great advances for the lower and middle classes, achieved when they finally broke through cultural barriers and exercised "political rights in behalf of economic rights." The authors charted a history of the United States as a nation in which the capitalist class was more successful than any other in asserting property rights over the "subsistence rights" of lower classes. They asserted that the rich had built "walls" around democratic efforts to spread the wealth, and that for a variety of reasons—including upper-class control of interpretation of the Constitution and the existence of a frontier to absorb the poor—Americans developed a politics of region and ethnicity rather than class, even though the latter would have been in their best interests.

Piven and Cloward further argued that the 1930s and 1960s had changed things forever, and that the Reagan years amounted to a counterrevolution that would fail:

> The once deeply rooted belief that market forces sort out and reward the talented and industrious and punish the untalented and slothful has faded. The doleful justice meted out by the in-

visible hand is giving way to a struggle over justice and injustice meted out by the state.

They acknowledged, however, that Americans "have not changed their views about capitalism and socialism, [and] they do not generally identify with the 'working class' . . . or profess a blueprint for future reconstruction."

At the end of this book, written just one year after Reagan took office, the authors noted that free-enterprise theorists were complaining that people had become ungovernable, that they wanted too much, that their expectations and desires had exceeded the limits of the possible. But, Piven and Cloward wrote, "It is capitalism rather than democracy that has become ungovernable, for it is capitalism that has responded . . . with anarchic disinvestment and speculation."

This view coincided with Wellstone's assertion that the public must have greater control over powerful private interests and a greater share of the proceeds from the nation's economy, but not necessarily outright ownership of the means of production called for by pure socialists. The overarching themes in this theory, themes that came to pervade the Wellstone campaign, are criticism of economic class divisions and repudiation of the notion that the United States is a classless, merit-based society. It is a powerful tool, but a potentially dangerous one in politics.

"The whole theme," said Vig, "was that the wealthy few are controlling our lives, and that was combined with a deep suspicion of the role that politicians (in both parties) play in that. And there really wasn't much inhibition about saying that."

To a European, running militantly against the minority of people in American society who appear to have far too great a share of its money would seem like a sensible proposition. It is, after all, a system in which every adult gets one vote and where most people are not economically secure. But it has not been done very often in American politics, except in the worst of times, for very good reasons.

Wellstone's brain trust was well aware that the fable of a classless society, or at least the notion of a merit-based caste system with open membership and free flow up and down, is a founding belief of the United States, perhaps more powerful than any other, and is embraced by all classes. The shocking disparity in wealth that appalls so many foreigners—the astounding chasm between the South Bronx and the Upper East Side of New York City, between Beverly Hills and south central Los Angeles—can be tolerated only if people believe that the whole system is based on freedom and merit and that people can move at will from one stratum to another. Americans do believe, at least to some degree, that with pluck and true grit, any penniless immigrant or descendant of a slave can become a multimillionaire or a Supreme Court justice, or at least the owner of two cars and a garage to put them in. There is enough truth in the proposition to validate the belief from generation to generation. The middle class has prospered in the United States, even though, ironically, government programs in this century such as GI benefits and Social Security may have done as much to lift the material well-being of the masses as the private enterprise system. Nevertheless, redistributing wealth does not look like such a good idea to those who want to be rich and think they have a fair shot at arriving there.

Among the Minnesotans who recognized how hard Wellstone's politics bumped up against Americans' self-image was Representative Vin Weber, then a leading conservative Republican strategist in Congress. In 1991 Weber offered this explanation of why Democrats have refrained from class warfare tactics and why they work only in times of severe depression or recession:

Americans like to think of themselves as classless. . . . If you validate the notion of class division, you challenge the notion of what America's all about. All these positive symbols of America aren't true. We really aren't the nation where merit and work and effort overcome all previous barriers.

A smart class warrior needed to be careful in 1990. The economy was shaky, but hardly a disaster. Wellstone could only go so far in telling people that the bedrock American virtues of individualism and self-reliance had to be balanced with more universal social entitlements and more equality imposed by government. "We were trying to find apt ways," Casper said, "of describing the situation but not raising red flags . . . to try to tell the truth but at the same time not leave our audience where it wouldn't listen to us anymore."

Critiquing the Eighties

To the relief of the Wellstone campaign, political and intellectual reinforcement began arriving from a variety of sources by early 1990. Some writers and filmmakers already had begun to condemn the 1980s as a disaster; two years later these early prophecies were augmented by many experts who determined that the 1980s were essentially bad for America.

Among the early critics of Reaganomics was Thomas B. Edsall, who wrote *The New Politics of Inequality* in the early 1980s. A few best-selling books and popular movies—Tom Wolfe's *The Bonfire of the Vanities* was both—along with comedians and other ministers of popular culture had begun to ridicule the excesses of Wall Street and the yuppies. Lewis Lapham wrote in his 1988 book *Money and Class in America* that "with the advent of the Reagan administration in 1981 the majority clearly favored the party of self-enrichment and the singing of hymns to Mammon," a cycle he compared to the 1830s, the 1870s, and the 1920s. "The [Reagan] government has been used almost exclusively to the benefit of the equestrian classes," he said, lamenting an emerging emptiness, a "cramped melancholy," in American life growing from materialism and obsession with acquiring and keeping money.

But no writer was more helpful to the Wellstone cause than Kevin Phillips, the Republican author of the visionary book *The Emerging Republican Majority,* which foretold the rise of Reaganism. Early in 1990, Phillips published a tremor-producing book, *The Politics of Rich and Poor,* in which he argued that the nation was poised for another swing of the pendulum, a class revolt and populist rebellion provoked by the outlandish gains made by the wealthy in the "go-go" period of Republican economic expansion.

The book provided Wellstone's issues researchers with a brain-numbing arsenal of statistics that showed the middle and lower classes losing ground or stagnating for the first time in decades. These figures frequently found their way into his speeches. The book was "a Bible for us," said Dean Alger, a Moorhead State University professor and a friend and adviser. Casper said the book was critically important because Phillips was a conservative and enjoyed wide credibility in the media, especially with print reporters and editorialists.

Phillips's statistics showed that per-worker weekly income declined from $366 in 1972 to $312 in 1987. He wrote that there was

> no way to argue with the official government portrait of a shift of income between 1980 and 1988 away from the bottom 80 percent of the U.S. population toward the most affluent fifth. . . . Evidence of a wide range of occupational declines—for manufacturing employees, farmers, people in the oil industry, young householders and the working poor—was more or less irrefutable.

Phillips went beyond just observing what happened to tie the trends directly to Reagan initiatives—tax rate reductions for the wealthy, deregulation of major industries, laxness in antitrust prosecution, and a buildup of debt that resulted in billions of dollars in interest to high-income and foreign lenders. There are myriad ways to look at these income and wealth statistics, and economists will be arguing for years over the finer points. Phillips admitted to having plenty of detractors, and he has said that his book created a "cottage industry" for conservatives who felt compelled to discredit his work.

Essentially, conservatives concede some growth in income and wealth disparities but argue that it was only minimally affected by Republican policy. They see as a more important cause the great, irresistible changes in the character of the economy over the 1970s and 1980s—mainly the integration of the American economy into the world's economy. It was to be expected that the highest-paid manufacturing workforce in the world would lose ground in a more open international economy, and a dynamic, productive system always creates change and discomfort, they argue. And, they point out, the concept of a world economy is hardly a Republican idea. For years, liberals had been pushing for lowering trade barriers in the interest of lower consumer prices, global harmony, and improved conditions for the lower classes in other countries.

At the same time that the economy experienced a sharp growth in low-paying service jobs, it was creating higher-paying jobs in information-based technologies and professions. People with lots of education started making more money than ever before; those with less than a college or high school diploma found the value of their skills plummeting.

Meanwhile, as conservatives see it, the accelerating evolution of social and family structure played a part too. Republicans could hardly be blamed for the sexual revolution, the divorce rate, teenage pregnancies, and the astonishing increase in families headed by single mothers, a major factor in the decline of households on the bottom fifth of the economy. Progressives see some of these "bad choices" made by people on the bottom as more a symptom than a root cause of poverty, but many Americans do believe that people are poor in large part because of their own failures. Feminism and the entry of women into the workforce and better-paid professions resulted in a huge leap in the number of professional couples, whose double incomes also played a part in the widening gulf between families. Many economists think these economic and social factors far outweigh tax law changes and deregulation, or anything else Reagan and Bush might have done, as a factor in widening income disparities.

But the conservative countercritique is complex, and neither Boschwitz nor President Bush nor any other conservative politician in the late 1980s was prepared even to admit that inequality was becoming an issue in America.

Well-armed as they were to press a populist progressive agenda of unprecedented breadth and purity, Wellstone's advisers nevertheless concentrated almost entirely in the 1989 issues planning on three words: *Boschwitz, money,* and *ads.* In honing phrases and themes that they hoped would strip the patina off Boschwitz, Casper produced a four-page manifesto named with the unlikely, Pentagon-style initials SIOP, a single integrated optional plan. Casper wrote:

> It's got to be hard-hitting, undermining Boschwitz['s] phony image. That should be an easy target. Boschwitz epitomizes much of what has gone wrong with American politics. As a legislator, he is a joke, little respected by his colleagues in the Senate. The one thing he does well has nothing to do with representing Minnesotans. He spends most of his time in Washington on reelection politics—raising money for his own and other Republican senators' reelection. In the process, he has become a part of and

beholden to networks of wealthy individual and corporate contributors. . . . How does he get away with it? His political success depends on two things: On Minnesotans not knowing what
he has done in Washington. And on media consultants' creating
a deceptive, positive public image with a multi-million-dollar
television public relations campaign.

The challenge of the campaign, Casper summarized, would be

> turning Boschwitz's television campaign advantage into a liabil-
> ity. Our goals include getting voters to understand where the
> money came from, getting them to see the ads as an attempt to
> manipulate them and to recognize the phony Boschwitz they see
> in the ads as a lie.

In this master plan, Casper also laid out basic tactics for
implementing the strategy, leaning heavily on demonstrating
that Wellstone was a completely different type of campaigner.
Casper proposed acquiring a proletarian symbol, a bus, for going
"directly to the people in a whistle-stop campaign." He suggested
a focus on radio ads rather than television and called for an all-
out effort to acquire as many endorsements from Minnesota-
based groups as possible, reinforcing the image of a candidate
with connections to community, who was perhaps not so radical
after all. And Casper suggested a focus on trying for both newspaper coverage and editorial page endorsement, which would
draw attention to Wellstone as a person of substance in command of the issues.

4

MUSTERING THE CREW

At a news conference in a Minneapolis hotel on the morning of May 26, 1989, Walter Mondale ended the suspense. The 61-year-old former vice president and 1984 Democratic presidential nominee announced that he would not challenge Rudy Boschwitz for the U.S. Senate seat Mondale had once held. In a brief, graceful statement and an extended question and answer session with reporters, Mondale talked about the need for new faces and new ideas in public life. He said he enjoyed his private life, his work at a prestigious Minneapolis law firm, and his "love affair with our lakes, our woods, and our out-of-doors."

Obliquely, Mondale acknowledged that another important factor in his decision was his fear of losing. As a senator, he had seen colleagues run one too many times and become embittered when they lost, he said. In contemplating a race against Boschwitz, Mondale said he worried about the "appropriateness of yet another Senate campaign."

The fact that such a dominant political figure was nervous about challenging Boschwitz on his own turf contributed mightily to the feeling that Boschwitz was unbeatable. As Mondale left the press conference for a fishing trip, a cluster of grim-faced

DFL leaders watched their last best hope disappear into the north woods. Roger Moe, the DFL majority leader of the Minnesota Senate, said:

> I don't think there was necessarily a panic. But when you take somebody of the stature, popularity, and money-raising ability of a former vice president like Fritz Mondale, when you take that out of the equation, obviously it went from a 50-50 or better odds for us to probably significantly less than 50-50 for all the other possible candidates. And well down that list would have been Paul Wellstone.

For Wellstone, Mondale's announcement was a gift, but not an unexpected one. Wellstone's earlier boasts about how he would take on Mondale in an endorsement fight had been fairly easy to make because he didn't think that Mondale would run. Since every Democrat in Minnesota other than Wellstone was waiting for the former vice president to make up his mind, Mondale's announcement left Wellstone as the only declared candidate. Wellstone took advantage of the clear field. Even though he continued to teach at Carleton, he stepped up his campaigning, speaking wherever he was invited—at senior citizen centers, labor halls, political clubs. He popped into cafés, walked in parades, visited county fairs. The long drives—he could not afford to fly—were scheduled for the weekends, when he would head up to the Iron Range or to the flat farmland of northwestern Minnesota.

"Because he was unknown, because he had no money, one of the things he had to do was travel, to be there, to be everywhere," said Jeff Blodgett, a former Wellstone student and one of his chief campaign volunteers at that time. "He had to accept as many speaking engagements as possible."

To keep the Iron Range intimately involved in his campaign, Wellstone held a second kickoff rally there a few weeks after the initial announcement of his candidacy in Minneapolis. The event was held at Mary's Bar, a watering hole owned by Mary Anderson, a member of his Iron Range steering committee. The scene at this potluck affair summed up DFL realists' worst fears about Wellstone's lack of resources. Anderson provided pizza, which turned out to be the delicacy on the menu. Most of the food—sloppy joes, beans, and wieners—was supplied by a dozen women who were members of the low-income support group organized by Pamela Reynolds, a welfare-rights activist and another member of Wellstone's Iron Range steering committee. Bean feeds are classic DFL fund-raising events, and the idea of serving plain food instead of fancy Republican canapés is not new to Minnesota politics. But in this case, virtually all of the women who provided the food were receiving some kind of state or federal economic assistance, and some of the food had been purchased with food stamps. Food stamps! Here was a totally new kind of public campaign financing, Wellstone-style.

"They had never taken part in anything political," Reynolds said of the welfare recipients in her support group. "They were scared. They didn't know any of these people. They had always felt excluded. But this showed that they'll do it if they're touched, if they're given a spark."

For thirty-three-year-old Melody Martin, a mother of two who had just managed to get off Aid to Families with Dependent Children, the small man with the big voice provided that spark. An office worker who still received state medical assistance because initially her paycheck was less than half of her AFDC stipend, Martin had never been to a political event in her life. Like so many others who have heard Wellstone speak, she was captivated when she heard him: "It wasn't any particular thing he said," Martin explained. "He was just such a powerful speaker and I'd never really heard a powerful speaker before in person, only on television. It was personal for me."

First Campaign Manager

Back in the Twin Cities, Wellstone's first campaign manager, Kris Blake, began assembling the structure of the campaign. Blake was a thirty-seven-year-old theater director with a hankering for politics. She grew up in upstate New York and attended Syracuse University, where she met her husband, Paul Brown, while both of them were involved in the theater.

In 1978, Blake and Brown moved to Marshall, Minnesota, where he took a teaching job at Southwest State University. Blake continued her theater work, but she also became involved in local community organizing, working on such projects as pressuring local officials to start a public transportation program and trying to save a historic school from demolition. Blake also started a shelter for battered women, the first in Minnesota outside the Twin Cities. The organizing work soon brought her into the circle of feminists and political activists headed by Polly Mann, a liberal activist for peace and justice who ran as an independent candidate for Minnesota Republican senator Dave Durenberger's seat in 1988.

The more encounters Blake the community activist had with the political establishment, the more she became convinced that injustice and inequality "were based in a political structure [as much as or more than they were] in the hearts and minds of people. [Political organizing] seemed a logical direction to move in if I really wanted to make change." She worked on two unsuccessful congressional campaigns; in one of them, she served as campaign manager for Jim Nichols, a prairie populist, in his 1982 race for the U.S. House. Nichols was a state senator then, and in 1990 he eventually would challenge Wellstone for the DFL endorsement and in the DFL primary.

Blake's campaign work soon led to a job as director of the Minnesota Public Interest Research Group, which she headed from 1984 to 1987, and then she managed the 1988 Jesse Jackson campaign in Minnesota. Blake's work for Jackson had a low-budget start. It began in September 1987, when Blake and two others drove from Minnesota in a van to Raleigh, North Carolina, to hear Jackson officially announce that he was running. One of the riders, an eccentric DFL activist who goes by the sole name Eskit, had compiled a massive list of people who had written letters to the editor that were published in Minnesota newspapers and that showed evidence of a progressive outlook. Eskit brought along his list, phone books, and flashlights. Blake described the trip:

> We'd look up Lorraine, who wrote a letter about education, in the phone book to find her address and phone number. You know what it's like to read phone books at night with flashlights in a bouncing van? We finally had to stop at a rest stop and get magnifying glasses.

One year later, as manager of Wellstone's Senate campaign, she was responsible for "[making] sure we got everything we needed [as long as] it didn't cost a penny," said Blake, who was paid $300 to $350 a week.

Blake was in charge of establishing a campaign logo and printing buttons and literature. Although she was advised by political friends to stick with a patriotic color scheme of red, white, and blue, Blake chose forest green, the color of environmentalists and the European symbol of antiestablishment insurgency. "That set us apart from the crowd. We wanted to be different," she said.

She also began to coordinate a handful of Wellstone's former students and fellow activists to begin the tedious volunteer work of the campaign—collecting delegate lists, booking speaking engagements, making travel plans for Wellstone, and finding other volunteers. Their options limited by a lack of money, Blake and other activists did what they knew best—they began a low-cost, grassroots organizing effort. "We went door to door talking him up," said Blake. Two or three times a week through the spring and summer, eight to ten volunteers fanned out through a neighborhood in Minneapolis, St. Paul, or Duluth, places where they knew support for Wellstone could be found. They knocked on doors to spread his name, to invite people to volunteer, and to sell a button or two for a dollar apiece. "It wasn't much [money], but once you got a dollar out of them it was easier to call and ask them to come and help," Blake said. They also spread the candidate's name at cultural, political, and neighborhood events, including Minneapolis's May Day celebration and St. Paul's Cinco de Mayo festival, where they sold buttons and distributed literature.

The Perfect Volunteer

One of the early volunteers was twenty-two-year-old David Graham. Raised in the tony, Republican western suburbs of Minneapolis, Graham was a product of a private local prep school and Middlebury College in Vermont. As a college student, he earned a summer internship with Amnesty International in Washington, D.C., and when he spent his junior year at the University of Sussex in England, he studied urban unrest in America. It was while he was in England that he first threw himself into activism. His lanky frame, bleach-blond hair, and choirboy face became a regular sight at demonstrations throughout England in support of the Palestinian *intifada,* abortion rights, and gay rights, and against racism. His activism then did not include electoral politics: "I felt that it was too impure," he said. "I wanted to be involved more in issues."

Graham's return to the United States and his graduation from Middlebury in May 1989 coincided with the start of Wellstone's campaign against Boschwitz, whom Graham decided would be his next target. Initially, he thought he would volunteer for Mondale (who had not yet announced that he would not run), but he switched allegiances when his mother showed him an article in an alternative weekly newspaper about Wellstone's candidacy. "My mom said, 'Here's a person more in line with your political values,'" Graham recalled. "I said, 'Yeah, I'd much rather work for someone like this.'"

Beginning in June, Graham tried repeatedly to reach Wellstone. He called the DFL Party's offices in St. Paul, but they had no phone number for the campaign. He even drove down to Carleton, where he left a note at the professor's office saying he wanted to volunteer. But he didn't get a call. For weeks he tried to find what seemed to be a shadow candidate. He finally made contact in late June, after a reporter directed him to a Wellstone supporter who passed his name along to a campaign official. At the time, Graham worked in a bookstore owned by his mother and was a door-to-door canvasser for Greenpeace. Two or three nights a week, he was put to work by a core group of Wellstone volunteers.

Phone calling was done out of the Meridel LeSueur Center, named for a legendary Minnesota poet and feminist. The building houses an assortment of progressive causes, including the antinuclear Freeze Campaign and Physicians for Social Responsibility. The Wellstone campaign at this point was being run out of Blake's house, but she also rented a broom-closet-sized office in the LeSueur building, where she plugged in a computer, a few phones, and an answering machine. The office, shared with the World Federalists, was a place for volunteers to meet at night.

Graham would meet three or four other volunteers at the office to make phone calls to recruit more volunteers and to identify potential contributors and likely delegates to the DFL state convention in June 1990, when the party's endorsement for the

Senate race would be decided. The callers used not only the 1988 state convention delegate list but also membership lists from a number of progressive organizations such as Women against Military Madness, a list of supporters from Polly Mann's 1988 independent U.S. Senate race, and the Jackson campaign's list of supporters.

Graham turned out to be precisely what the campaign needed. He gladly accepted even the most mundane assignments and appeared to be ready to devote himself completely to the campaign. Jeff Blodget, who would soon become the campaign's second manager, told Graham, "You're the perfect campaign worker. You have no life."

After several weeks of dialing phones and doing other chores, Graham was asked to join other Wellstone devotees at a meeting to plan for the Minnesota state fair, held annually at the end of August. "I thought, this is great! I'm invited to a meeting!" Graham recalled dryly. The staff was so small that Graham was handed an important assignment: he was in charge of organizing volunteers to work at Wellstone's booth at the fair.

Graham finally met Wellstone at the fair. Introductions were made hastily, as Wellstone turned to the task of shaking hundreds, perhaps thousands, of hands that day. Later he took Graham aside. "He was really surprised that I was working on the campaign," Graham said. "At that point he pretty much knew everybody who was volunteering. He was kind of surprised that there was someone he'd never met who was willing to put in time on the campaign. He said, 'Why? Why are you doing this?' "

Graham struggled to form an answer because there were so many reasons. He tried to articulate his anger over rising racial tensions and a feeling that things were going downhill in America. Volunteering for a candidate who espoused his values was his way of acting on that frustration. "It wasn't necessarily that Paul was the person I dreamed of working for," Graham said of his answer to Wellstone's question. "It was more issues."

Graham's status quickly grew, and by the fall he was driving Wellstone to speaking engagements around the state. He even tried to dispense advice. During a conversation at the home of state representative Paul Ogren in October 1989, Graham raised the possibility of Wellstone's supporting the legalization of drugs. The thirty-eight-year-old Ogren, who later publicly acknowledged that he had indulged in drug use in his youth, "jumped down my throat," Graham said. "He said, 'No way! We're not going to do that. We're not even going to talk about that at all.' Paul loved it. He was on the floor laughing." (Later in the campaign, Wellstone would reject suggestions that he advocate legalizing marijuana.)

The visit to Ogren's house was typical of the campaign during its infancy, when Wellstone attended countless county bean feeds and spoke at small gatherings in supporters' living rooms. On this Sunday morning in October, Ogren, a high-profile politician, invited neighboring farmers and laborers to his home to meet Wellstone. Graham recounted a story about one of the people who came:

> There was this one guy who couldn't sign his name on the list. I was trying to get him to sign in and he wouldn't. I began to get the idea that he couldn't write. I asked him his name and he told me and I put it down for him. That really gave me a feel for what the campaign was all about.

Second Campaign Manager

In the early days, Wellstone purposely ignored one of the essential tasks of a political campaign—raising large sums of money. It was an activity he would be condemning throughout the campaign, and he knew that few of the party's "investors" would risk backing him. He knew that no matter how much time he devoted to raising money from big donors and political action committees, his efforts would produce few dividends. But even saints need some money, and Wellstone was not quite prepared for the resounding rejections he received.

The difficulty in securing financial support was impressed on Wellstone's advisers when they made a couple of trips to Washington in the summer and fall of 1989. Carlton professor Mike Casper went twice to make courtesy calls at the Democratic Senatorial Campaign Committee, a fund-raising wing of the Democratic Party that could provide large sums of money, in excess of the $10,000 limit on political action committee (PAC) contributions and the $2,000 limit on individual contributions. Casper recalled:

> The striking thing to me when I'd talk to anybody down there was that they wouldn't want to know what [Wellstone] stood for. The first and essentially only question the political professionals wanted to know was how much money could he raise [on his own]. I began to realize what the admission ticket to bigtime politics was.

Refused entrance to the PAC offices and law firms that often bankroll candidates, Wellstone presented his limited options in such a way as to make himself look virtuous. "I can't spend my time trying to raise millions of dollars from wealthy people in boardrooms," he said in an early newspaper interview. "I have to spend my time in neighborhoods, towns, not raising the big money, but raising the big issues."

"We did house parties everywhere," said volunteer Jeff Blodgett. Three nights a week, on average, Wellstone would appear in the homes of supporters who invited friends, relatives, and neighbors to listen to the candidate and contribute to his campaign. As it turned out, Wellstone was not much better at asking for money in living rooms than he was at seeking it in the boardrooms.

Ann Burget, a Dukakis delegate to the 1988 state convention, held the first house party at her Minneapolis home in June 1989, and she recalled how Wellstone shied away from asking for money. Standing on a piano bench in Burget's living room, Wellstone addressed a group of about fifty of Burget's friends, neighbors, and fellow PTA activists. "It was one of his fire and brimstone speeches, about how real people count and real issues count," Burget remembered. When Wellstone finished speaking, David Tilsen, a member of the Minneapolis School Board who had been sitting on a chair beside Wellstone, reached up and tugged on Wellstone's sleeve. "Now you're supposed to ask them for money," Tilsen whispered. Wellstone told Tilsen that he did not know how to ask. "David said, 'If you won't, I will,' and he got up and asked," said Burget. "I think if Paul raised twenty-five dollars, then people probably made contributions I didn't know about. Nobody came prepared to give money. They just came to meet this guy."

Wellstone had more success raising money from Carleton alumni, especially his former students. A letter was sent to about two thousand graduates who had supported campus efforts to force the college to sell its investments in South Africa. During a trip to Washington in the summer of 1989, Wellstone raised a few thousand dollars from about three dozen Carleton graduates at a fund-raiser. "That was big money then," said Blodgett. Wellstone also went to Madison, Wisconsin, for a Carleton fund-raiser and spoke by speakerphone hookup with an alumni group gathered in Michigan. "The Carleton alumni were to us what the Greeks were to Dukakis," said Blodgett.

Wellstone raised just enough money to keep his campaign alive—to pay for travel, leaflets, and phone calls and, beginning in the late summer of 1989, to hire a skeleton staff. The first to be hired then was Blodgett, who took over as campaign manager around Labor Day, when Kris Blake stepped aside to handle scheduling and write press releases. Of the change in campaign managers, Wellstone said:

> There was no falling out of any kind. [Blake's] strength was to make things happen. She is a movement politics person. But Sheila [Wellstone's wife], even more than I, really wanted Jeff to take over. Once it started getting time to put together an organization and structure to win those delegates [to the state endorsing convention], it was a somewhat different challenge. Sheila felt strongly that if Jeff would agree, we should ask him to do it. And I agreed.

This was not the last time that Sheila Wellstone would weigh in heavily on personnel decisions.

Blodgett, then twenty-eight years old, had a youthful, clean-cut look about him, but he was an experienced political operative. As it was for so many of Wellstone's staff, the original connection was a Carleton classroom. When Blodgett took a required political science course, he drew Wellstone purely by chance. He became enthralled by the professor, took a handful of his classes, and chose him as his academic adviser. Wellstone also coached Blodgett in wrestling and trained him as a community organizer. "He turned me on to political activism," Blodgett said. "He encouraged students to go into political or community organizing after school. He saw it as a continuation of real education for students."

When Blodgett graduated in 1983 he became a full-time organizer and advocate for the poor. He was hired by the grass-roots group Minnesota Citizen Organizations Acting Together (COACT), whose staff included a lot of Carleton alumni, most of whom were there because of Wellstone's influence, said Blodgett. The person who hired him was also an ex-student of

Wellstone's. Blodgett was assigned to a new COACT office in Little Falls, a town in central Minnesota, to work on the farm crisis. (Blodgett later organized the farm foreclosure protest at the Paynesville bank that resulted in Wellstone's second arrest for civil disobedience.)

In 1987 Blodgett turned from community organizing to politics. He was recruited by Pat Forciea to work on the Dukakis campaign as a field organizer in Minnesota and spent the year between the Dukakis and Wellstone campaigns working as assistant to the commissioner of the Minnesota Department of Labor and Industry. Those jobs brought him into the state's political orbit.

Blodgett's schoolboy looks were belied by unflinching brown eyes that reflected his toughness. His glare could wilt an offending staff member. "If Jeff gets mad, you'll do whatever he says," said Dick Senese, who organized the Iron Range early in the campaign. "He can blow up, get really angry. You don't ever want to be chewed out by him." Even Wellstone confessed to being occasionally cowed by his one-time student: "He gets this look in his eyes and scares me sometimes," Wellstone said.

When Blodgett took over as its manager, the campaign, like the candidate, had a ragged edge. An example of the campaign's lack of polish is a September trip. Wellstone set out on a blitz across the state to criticize Boschwitz's support of the MX mobile nuclear missile system. The missiles, loaded on railroad cars, would be deployed on railroad tracks that snaked through small towns in western Minnesota, according to a federal environmental impact statement that Wellstone brandished. He traveled through the towns, waving the federal report and telling local reporters that the incumbent was cozy with defense contractors, an arguable conclusion since even by Wellstone's own figures they had contributed a grand total of only $86,000 to Boschwitz since he started running for office in 1978.

From a media coverage standpoint, the trip was botched. There was a modest amount of interest from small-town newspapers, but campaign officials had contacted only one of the two major state newspapers and none of the four major television stations. They had hoped to get a big splash in the single newspaper, but they barely got a ripple. It was a foolish decision to limit coverage of a campaign that desperately needed widespread attention. "We managed to get a lot of people angry at us," Wellstone admitted.

As Wellstone worked out the kinks in his campaign, other candidates were stirring or were ruling themselves out in the face of Boschwitz's advantages. One of the latter was Richard Nolan, a former Minnesota congressman and the associate chair of the DFL Party, who said one of his reasons for not running was the widely held belief that Boschwitz's money made him invincible. "There's a rule in politics that says the one who gets the most money gets the most votes," Nolan said at the time. "You are facing just absolutely impossible odds running against an incumbent with more money."

Even Mark Dayton, multimillionaire heir to a department store fortune who had spent about $7 million of his own money in an unsuccessful U.S. Senate race against Republican Dave Durenberger in 1982, opted out. After taking a poll to assess his chances in the Senate contest, he said he would run for state auditor.

On September 11, 1989, Wellstone got his first challenger for the DFL endorsement: state representative Todd Otis, who also hailed from the party's progressive wing and was closely aligned with labor union leaders. Otis was descended from pioneer Yankee stock, a family that had come to Minnesota in the mid-1800s. His father was a distinguished lawyer and judge, appointed to the bench and eventually to the Minnesota Supreme

Court by Republican governors. Todd Otis was a child of privilege—he graduated from the St. Paul Academy and Harvard University and later got a master's degree in journalism from Columbia University—but he was influenced by the idealism of the 1960s and worked for two years in the Peace Corps in Senegal, in West Africa. In the early 1980s he wrote a book criticizing the safety and efficiency of nuclear power. And in a twelve-year stint in the Minnesota House, representing a strongly liberal enclave of Minneapolis neighborhoods surrounding Lake Calhoun, he became a reliable but low-key advocate for progressive causes.

Unlike Wellstone, however, Otis had ties to the business world, having been a lobbyist for the National Federation of Independent Business and having worked in community relations for the First Bank system. Always neatly dressed and tidily groomed, he presented on the whole a much more moderate, polite face than Wellstone. But he opened his campaign with an attack on Boschwitz that could have been uttered by Wellstone:

> Rudy Boschwitz is running for reelection with a voting record that does not reflect Minnesota's values; a voting record that is out of step with the needs of the people he serves; a voting record that reflects the opinion that Minnesota's politics are for sale to the highest bidder.

Otis immediately claimed the support of state legislators who otherwise might have been Wellstone allies. Iron Rangers Tom Rukavina of Virginia and Jerry Janezich of Chisholm and St. Paul representative Sandy Pappas, all of them strong progressives and labor supporters, threw the support of their individual political operations behind Otis, who ended up with more support among DFL legislators than any other candidate.

(At the very moment that Otis announced his candidacy in

St. Paul, Boschwitz was holding a fund-raiser at the Normandy Hotel in downtown Minneapolis, where he added $6,000 more to his campaign fund.)

In October the field was joined by Tom Berg, a member in good standing of the DFL mainstream. The day he announced, he was flanked by officials of Minnesota DRIVE, the powerful political arm of the state's Teamsters union, which gave him an early endorsement. A successful lawyer, former state representative, and former federal prosecutor, Berg was in many ways a textbook Democratic candidate for statewide office in Minnesota.

Born in the west central Minnesota farm town of Willmar, a descendant of both Norwegian and Swedish immigrants, Berg could hardly have invented a more ideal résumé. On top of the Scandinavian surname, always a plus in Minnesota, his biography was a classic story of achievement through playing by the rules. His father was a postal clerk with a tenth-grade education, and Berg was the first on either side of his family to get a college degree, which he earned by working construction jobs in the summer. After receiving a law degree from the University of Minnesota in 1965, he served briefly with the Army Reserve, and then began to practice law in Minneapolis. At the age of twenty-nine he was elected to the Minnesota House by a solid Democratic district in south Minneapolis made up of affluent lakeside liberals, young renters, and working-class owners of tract houses. Berg was part of a new generation of liberal young DFLers who took control of the legislature in 1970 after years of conservative Republican domination and began to remake state government. He quickly emerged as an important champion of landmark reforms that equalized revenues between rich and poor school districts, put new controls on handguns, and required disclosures and limits in campaign finance.

The consensus was that Berg is a smart, decent, trustworthy man—a good scout in every respect—but his style could not have been a sharper contrast with Wellstone's. Although he was just four years older, Berg essentially sat out the 1960s rebellion. An establishment, by-the-book Democrat, he remembered marching only once in protest of anything—in a march against the Vietnam War. As a legislator, he took controversial stands and got involved in tough fights, but there was no consuming preoccupation with economic and social justice. When he was asked to list his proudest achievements, Berg was likely to mention the millions of dollars he helped free up for replanting the Twin Cities urban forest after devastating shade-tree blights in the 1970s—a relatively modest achievement, but a tangible improvement in many lives. Many people thought Berg was a liberal because it was the right thing to be, not because he was burning to correct injustices.

With his well-tailored suits, preppy glasses, high forehead, and graying hair, Berg looked the part of a corporate lawyer, rather like Georgia senator Sam Nunn, and far more senatorial than Wellstone. Both Berg and Otis could have been models for an L. L. Bean catalog, but even more than Otis, Berg had the contacts and credentials Wellstone lacked.

In fact, although Berg had hinted for months that he would run, he delayed his announcement until November 1 because he was busy with the type of responsibility that was never given to Wellstone. Berg was appointed by Governor Rudy Perpich to chair the Governor's Select Committee on the Impact of Drugs, and the report his commission delivered on October 16 won rave reviews from experts and editorial boards around the state for its recommendations of a judicious mix of law enforcement and treatment and prevention programs. In some ways, the report was vintage Berg: it was carefully and thoughtfully assembled and packaged, but it contained no daring ideas.

In 1980 Berg's good performance in the legislature and his DFL connections paid off in an appointment as U.S. attorney for Minnesota, a post he held for nearly two years. Berg resigned in 1981 and returned to private practice, but he remained visible in legal and political circles. While Wellstone was blocking farm auctions, encouraging strikers in Austin, and organizing welfare recipients to fight proposed stipend reductions at the state capitol, Berg served on a series of blue-ribbon committees. He was chairman of the Minnesota Department of Human Rights Volunteer Attorney Project, a member of the governor's Task Force on the Center for Victims of International Torture, and a member of the St. Paul-Minneapolis Committee on Foreign Relations and the Lawyers Alliance for Nuclear Arms Control. A key credential was chairing Governor Rudy Perpich's reelection committee in 1986, a smashing success that gave him access to and alliances with the state's ruling DFL regime.

Although Berg's background and style differed markedly from Wellstone's, they were not far apart on most major issues. Because of that similarity, and because Berg could raise money easily from the special interests on the left side of the spectrum, he posed by far the biggest threat to Wellstone's endorsement. Berg was the safe, sane choice for mainstream DFLers.

The Senate field was rounded out in November with the announcement by Minnesota agriculture commissioner Jim Nichols that he was running. While Berg's and Otis's base was in the cities, Nichols, forty-three, drew most of his support from the wheat fields and dairy farms in Minnesota's sprawling farm belt, which covers roughly two-thirds of the state, mostly in the south and west. A strapping farmer who stands six feet four inches tall, Nichols fit the original nineteenth-century definition of a prairie populist: a champion for farmers and rural people and a plain-speaking enemy of middlemen and corporations. During the farm crisis of the mid-1980s, Nichols used his post to promote the Harkin-Gephardt Farm Bill, supported by Wellstone, and he became a fixture at rallies and initiatives on debt relief for farmers.

Nichols was raised on farm work, sports, and traditional small-town values in the southwestern Minnesota town of Verdi, a couple of miles from the South Dakota border, where he graduated from high school with only twelve classmates. After graduating from college in 1968 he enlisted in the navy, serving with the Seabees in Vietnam. He returned home an opponent of the war, taught high school for four years, and then bought a farm. Disillusioned with government, Nichols decided in 1976 to challenge the incumbent Republican state senator, so he ran as a Democrat, even though he considered himself a conservative and was a member of the Republican-oriented Farm Bureau organization. He was elected, and on the day he was sworn in at the state capitol, Nichols wore his best outfit—a polyester leisure suit.

Strong evidence of his Republican leanings was Nichols's vote for Rudy Boschwitz in the 1978 Senate race. "I thought this was a Jewish immigrant so he will be a man of compassion. I thought he was a successful businessman, so he will be a successful senator," Nichols explained in a newspaper story in 1990.

Nichols left the legislature in 1980 when a car crash killed his wife and severely injured one of his daughters. The incident made him realize that "nothing is more precious than life," he said, and he switched from advocating abortion rights to opposing them.

After a few years back on the farm, he returned to government when he was appointed agriculture commissioner by Governor Rudy Perpich. Popular as Nichols was with some farmers, his shoot-from-the-hip style and his controversial tenure as agriculture commissioner—he had a tendency toward showboating and rash statements—raised doubts about his judgment. He once described the chairman of the U.S. House Agriculture

Committee, Texas Democrat Kika de la Garza, as "my most bitter enemy in the Congress," hardly the kind of comment to endear him to one of the most influential people in American farm policy. And in December 1988, Nichols led a march of about two thousand American farmers through the streets of Montreal, Quebec, to protest U.S. trade policy because he argued that it hurt Minnesota farmers.

Nichols and Boschwitz clashed over agriculture policy, so much so that at times Nichols seemed to be running because of a personal vendetta against Boschwitz. In true DFL fashion, Nichols sought to piece together a coalition of farmers and laborers, and he was the only one of the Democratic candidates opposed to abortion and gun control.

Although each of the candidates had earned the support of pieces of the alliance needed to win the party endorsement and the election, none could claim as much support from each of the groups as Wellstone could. Berg was popular among liberals and had the backing of some important labor officials, but he lacked connections in rural Minnesota. Otis was well liked by his fellow state legislators and had strong ties to organized labor, but he too was little known outside Minneapolis and St. Paul. And while Nichols had deep support among farmers, his more conservative populism and opposition to abortion rights put off urban liberals and progressives.

Wellstone's activism had put him in the good graces of all these groups. His challenge now was to bring them together under one campaign, to wed the social philosophies of the liberals to the economic beliefs of the populists, progressives, and labor unions.

Focusing on the Caucuses

Once the competition was known, the Wellstone campaign became more focused on its first objective—winning the party's endorsement at the DFL state convention in June 1990. "The campaign was broken down into two stages: the DFL endorsement and everything after that," explained campaign manager Jeff Blodgett. "We knew we had to focus entirely on winning the DFL state endorsement. That was the only way we were going to become a legitimate candidate in a lot of people's eyes."

Earning the party's official backing would not only confer on Wellstone a degree of legitimacy, it also would bring him media coverage and force the party to provide money and volunteers. The first step in securing delegate support would occur on February 27, 1990, when Minnesota's precinct caucuses were scheduled. The controversial caucus system provides an opportunity for voters to gather at eight thousand small community meetings, one DFL and one Independent-Republican meeting in each of the state's four thousand election precincts. These meetings were the first step in the selection of delegates to the state conventions, where Senate candidates would be endorsed. Unlike a primary, where voters can simply cast ballots, the caucuses require a commitment of an hour or more to discuss candidates and issues and to form subcaucuses around either a candidate or an issue or both. Because they demand so much time and personal exposure in front of neighbors, the caucuses are lightly attended. They rarely attract more than 2 or 3 percent of the electorate, mostly party activists and people with a keen interest in politics, a strong view on a single interest, or a strong sense of civic duty.

By their very nature, the caucuses are a good test of a candidate's organizing ability at the local level. It is a system that rewards the idealistic and the committed in both parties—tailor-made, in other words, for Wellstone's grassroots forces. With a strong showing at the caucuses, Wellstone's supporters could dominate the proceedings in the following three months leading up to the state convention. The delegates elected at the precinct caucuses in February would later meet at larger county and legislative district conventions to elect delegates to the congressional district conventions and the state convention. Whoever turned out the most supporters at the February precinct caucuses, in other words, was likely to carry that advantage to the state convention in early June.

Directing the campaign from his dining room table to save money on office rent and phone lines, Blodgett devised a plan to make sure that Wellstone supporters swarmed to the caucuses. That's when the decision was made to put organizers on the campaign payroll, Blodgett said. Shortly after Blodgett was hired in September 1989, he and Wellstone hired five young activists to make the calls and to coordinate the work of dozens of volunteers.

One of the first to be hired was twenty-seven-year-old Dick Senese, who was put in charge of organizing his native Iron Range, Duluth, and the rest of northeastern Minnesota, a critical region for Wellstone. Senese was raised in the small town of Buhl, where his father frequently was on the ballot, running for, and occasionally winning, a city council or school board post or another local office. Senese was imbued with his father's love of politics and activism at an early age. A sixth grader during Watergate, he penned a letter to the *Weekly Reader* calling for Richard Nixon to resign. Frightened by a vacant house he had to pass on his way to elementary school, Senese started a petition to get it boarded up or torn down.

"It seemed like the natural thing," Senese said of his youthful activism. "It seemed that's the way you're supposed to be. You're supposed to be involved in things. Otherwise, it's not a democracy." Unlike most politically active Iron Rangers, however, Senese veered to the Republican Party. As a high school senior in 1980, he went to a Republican caucus and was elected as a John Anderson delegate. He worked on the Anderson presidential campaign, going door to door with petitions to get his independent candidate's name on the ballot and passing out campaign literature at the state fair.

As a college student two years later, Senese was converted to the DFL Party when he heard Wellstone speak during his campaign for state auditor. What impressed Senese was not just Wellstone's speech, but also a gimmick in that speech that became a signature of the campaign.

Although the job he was running for then involved state finances, Wellstone used his platform to advocate a number of social and political causes, and among them was a nuclear arms freeze. To underscore the destructive power of the world's nuclear arsenal, Wellstone asked his audiences to close their eyes and listen carefully. After they shut their eyes, he took out a can filled with about twenty thousand metal BBs. First he would drop a single BB into an empty metal can and explain that the sound represented the destructive power of the atomic bomb dropped on Hiroshima. Next he would tell the audience that they would hear sounds representing all the bombs dropped in World War II, and he would pour a small handful of BBs into the can. Finally, he would say that the next sound represented the destructive power of the world's current nuclear arsenal. Then he would pour the thousands of remaining BBs into the can, slowly at first, then with increasing speed. It would create a stunningly long, loud, and unsettling roar.

"It just seemed to go on forever, this loud crashing. You really got the sense that, my God, we have to stop nuclear weapons," recalled Senese. "I've been impressed with him ever since then." Senese became a devout follower, working with Wellstone on voter registration projects and helping him get reelected to the Democratic National Committee during the floor fight at the 1988 state convention in Rochester. Senese was living in Duluth and working as a chemical dependency counselor and a part-time college teacher in communication and public speaking when he joined the Wellstone staff. He remained in Duluth, organizing the northeastern quarter of the state from his apartment:

> I would sit in my apartment with a cordless phone [and] a TV tray and watch "Duck Tales" [a cartoon] and call people. I was always on the phone. You would make all the local calls during the day and all the long distance calls after five so Jeff [Blodgett] wouldn't yell at you about the phone bill.

Down in the Twin Cities, Scott Adams also was added to the staff. At thirty, Adams was the dean of this youthful staff. Like all the others in the core group, he was raised by politically active parents and was licking campaign envelopes and waving political posters at rallies at an early age. His mother was a "supervolunteer" on the campaigns of Democratic candidates as the family moved from Washington, D.C., to New Haven, Connecticut, and, finally, to Miami. His father was an administrator in local public housing agencies and an outspoken critic of Reagan/Bush policies when he served as president of the National Association of Housing and Redevelopment Officials.

Adams made his way to Minnesota by way of Grinnell College in Iowa. After graduation, he hitchhiked north and joined his brother in the Twin Cities, where he first took a job doing community organizing around local energy issues and then helped organize a door-to-door canvassing program for the Minnesota Public Interest Research Group (MPIRG), one of many environmental and consumer-protection groups spun off by consumer advocate Ralph Nader and the source of much of Wellstone's support. Adams worked at MPIRG for five years, and in the fall of 1987 he was swept up into the Jesse Jackson campaign. He attended one of the earliest organizing meetings, and as the participants discussed the creation of a staff, Adams argued strongly in favor of hiring organizers, "not office managers and supervisors." Adams was asked if he would be willing to do that work, and he quickly agreed. "That's when I made the jump from change politics to electoral politics," Adams said. His work on the Jackson campaign brought him into closer contact with Wellstone, whom he had met several times at labor rallies at the Hormel plant in Austin, at farm foreclosure protests, and through his work on voter registration and other community organizing efforts.

As a member of Wellstone's Senate campaign staff, Adams was assigned to organize the Fifth Congressional District, which includes Minneapolis. With his perpetual five-day beard, his rumpled clothes, and a rusting, ten-year-old Datsun B-210, Adams moved easily in the city's poor neighborhoods and, especially later in the campaign, on the state's Indian reservations.

Although Adams was one of the Rochester campground conspirators who first nudged Wellstone to run, he admitted to being a bit nervous when the campaign actually got under way and he and his compatriots had to prove the efficacy of a statewide grassroots campaign. "I thought, 'Oh my God. Our style is on the line. If we can't do it this time, nobody's ever going to listen to us again,' " he said.

While Adams was assigned a key part of the metropolitan area, Liz Borg was given responsibility for organizing most of rural Minnesota. Like all the others put on the payroll in the fall of 1989, Borg had been a volunteer with the campaign since its inception. The twenty-six-year-old was the one true 1960s-style free spirit in an organization whose lifestyles tended more toward holism than hedonism.

She wore the type of funky clothes—short skirts, low-cut blouses, opaque cotton tights—seen more often in rock and roll nightclubs than in Senate campaign offices. Other Wellstone staffers had their car radios set to Minnesota Public Radio and other news stations, but when Borg sat at the wheel of her Dodge Colt with more than 100,000 miles on the odometer, she punched the buttons for rock music and sang along with the Rolling Stones and Bruce Springsteen.

Borg's assignment to organize rural Minnesota was natural because her politics were shaped in a small town—Ashby, population 450, in west central Minnesota—where her parents owned a small drugstore. The town was small enough to have retained some of the spirit of the pioneer code that required people to help neighbors in trouble. "There's something about growing up in a small town that sets in your mind that you have a responsibility to help other people if they need it," Borg said. "I can remember my dad giving things away. If people didn't have money for medicine for their kids, he'd give it to them. That's just what you did."

Her parents were active in the DFL Party, both of them holding local party posts at various times, so Borg acquired a taste for politics early. As a kindergartner, she went along with her parents when they worked on campaigns, including her father's unsuccessful race for state representative.

After college, Borg held a series of jobs—"Between men and part-time jobs I've lost count at fifty-five," she quipped—that included selling cosmetics in a department store, selling cameras over the telephone, recruiting adult volunteers for the Girl Scouts, and conducting door-to-door canvassing for MPIRG. Through these jobs Borg discovered she had a natural talent for making pitches to strangers. "People like to do things for me, give me things like time and money," she explained. "That's why I'm a good field organizer. The job of a field organizer is to get people motivated."

Borg first tried her hand as a political field worker for Dukakis in October 1987, when she was hired by Blodgett. She directed a phone bank effort in the northwestern Minnesota town of Moorhead before the precinct caucuses in February 1988. After the caucuses, she worked in St. Cloud, in the central part of the state, as the coordinator for one of Minnesota's eight congressional districts. During her work for Dukakis, Borg met Pat Forciea, and at a staff meeting after Jackson dropped out, she also met Wellstone. She had heard plenty about Wellstone from her aunt, who was active in a sometimes violent movement by central Minnesota farmers to block construction of an electric power line in the 1970s. Wellstone and Mike Casper documented that struggle in their book, *Powerline: The First Battle of America's Energy War*, which was sympathetic to the protesters. Several times the professors crossed the line from researchers to advisers, and they became close friends with some of the protesters.

"I just knew he was an advocate for . . . people who were disadvantaged, or who just didn't know how to use their voice yet," Borg said. "He worked on how to help them learn to use their voice by organizing." At the Dukakis staff meeting, "Paul gave this great talk, and I remember thinking, 'I wish every staff meeting would be this exciting,' " she said. But in addition to his speaking ability and his record of organizing the disenfranchised, Borg saw something else in Wellstone that was just as important to her: "He was really nice, too. He was just a really nice person," Borg said.

When Blodgett asked her to work full time on Wellstone's Senate campaign in December 1989, Borg didn't need to be persuaded. For one thing, she craved the fun, excitement, and tension of another campaign, where every day is a crisis. "I like to have that nervous stomach feeling," she said.

Wellstone was delighted to have Borg and her offbeat personality on his team. "She marches to the beat of a different drummer," Wellstone said. "Even when you talk to Liz, sometimes you're not sure she's even in the same room with you." But Wellstone also knew that Borg, through her work on the

Dukakis campaign, had developed a knack for supervising people, had acquired a keen understanding of the state's demographics, and was a tireless worker. "I call her a rural punkster—who does the work of fifty people," said Wellstone.

With full-time staffers being added, the campaign headquarters moved on January 2, 1990, from Blodgett's dining room and the Meridel Le Sueur broom closet into a storefront office on a dowdy commercial strip in St. Paul: 2401 University Avenue, about midway between the downtowns of Minneapolis and St. Paul. It was shabby and bitterly cold at times, and the plate glass window at the front rattled when trucks drove by. The furniture, most of it requisitioned by Scott Adams, who was a master at appropriating free supplies for the campaign, was many times beyond secondhand.

Because money was still short, volunteers and staffers were called upon to lend or donate other necessities, from coffee-makers to Macintosh computers. When a photocopy machine salesman who also was volunteering on the campaign offered to install a photocopier on a trial basis, Blodgett jumped at the proposal without letting on that the campaign could not afford to buy it. "We got that copy machine in our office and we just wore that thing out," said Borg. The salesman "kept coming back and he'd say, 'You probably shouldn't be using it so much.' We just kept making copies."

For all its shortcomings, the $750-a-month office gave the campaign an emotional lift, Blodgett recalled:

> It provided cohesion and a central point to the campaign. It felt good to have a big sign in the window with people driving by. I think it psyched out the other campaigns, too. The three of them did not have very big operations at that point. We had more staff and we had more of a campaignlike feel than they did.

The day the campaign moved into the new headquarters, another young zealot was added to the staff. Dan Cramer's lineage seemed to dictate that he become involved in government and politics. His grandfather was Arthur J. Goldberg, a U.S. Supreme Court justice in the 1960s and later an ambassador to the United Nations. Cramer was raised in the Hyde Park neighborhood of Chicago, and he recalls tagging along with his parents as they backed independent candidates who ran against the Richard Daly Democratic machine. He was a precocious campaign worker, serving as one of fifty volunteer ward coordinators for Harold Washington's 1983 mayoral race when he was just sixteen years old, and volunteering as a precinct captain for Walter Mondale's presidential bid in 1984.

When Cramer enrolled at Carleton College, he was elected to numerous student government posts. "I was, and these are Paul's words, 'a student government hack,'" Cramer laughed. He met Wellstone in his senior year, in 1989, when he took a course Wellstone taught on state government. After Cramer took a second Wellstone class, the two became friends and Wellstone, who was then plotting his Senate campaign, invited Cramer to strategy sessions.

Cramer worked on the early stages of the campaign, returned to Chicago in June to do community antidrug organizing, and came back to Minnesota in December 1989 to work on Wellstone's campaign. The return to Minnesota was the first time Cramer had made a significant decision contrary to his parents' advice. They thought he was leaving a good job and was retreating to Minnesota to work on a campaign that was likely to collapse within months. "I figured it was a no-lose situation," Cramer said. "I always wanted to be involved in politics and public policy, and I knew Paul would be giving me more responsibility than any normal candidate would, given my experience." When Cramer walked into the new office, he took a desk next to

Liz Borg, and the two of them later would be given complete responsibility for the field staff, all the way to election day.

The last hire was twenty-two-year-old David Graham, who had been the hardest-working, most dependable volunteer since he had shown up as a walk-on the summer before and was put in charge of organizing the state fair and driving Wellstone around the state.

These five staffers and Blodgett became an intensely tight-knit group, especially Cramer, Graham, and Borg, all in their early to mid-twenties. Cramer and Graham became roommates out of economic necessity. Their monthly salaries of $400-$500, depending on the amount of cash the campaign had on hand, were barely enough for subsistence. And in Cramer's case, Blodgett failed to deliver on his promise of providing housing. Laughing, Cramer recalled:

> Jeff told me, "We'll take care of housing. It won't be a problem." He was full of shit. There was nowhere for me to live. I lived with friends for four months. A conservative, Rudy Boschwitz-loving couple gave me their spare bedroom. I was feeling guilty about imposing on them, so I went to Jeff and said I needed $600 a month. Then Dave and I moved into a little shithole in St. Paul.

Despite the poverty-level existence, the staffers look back on those days as the best period of the campaign. "It was immediate chemistry. Those seven months between December and June, when we were a small family in the office all the time together, were just wonderful," said Cramer.

Borg regrets that she didn't keep a journal: "I wish I had realized what was happening when it was happening," she said.

5

FERTILIZING THE GRASS ROOTS

When Paul Wellstone declared his candidacy for the world's most exclusive club, he owned just one suit, a seven-year-old light blue pinstriped outfit that he bought when he ran for state auditor. As a college professor Wellstone eschewed ties and suits. Instead, his tastes ran to blue jeans and turtlenecks in cooler weather and to shorts and tank tops or nondescript, permanent-press shirts in the summer. "He cares nothing about clothes. Absolutely nothing," said his wife, Sheila. "He likes to look nice, but his clothes just don't mean a thing to him."

In the spring of 1989, after he had announced his candidacy, Wellstone knew he had to upgrade his wardrobe. Frugal by nature, he was not drawn to fashionable downtown clothiers. Instead, he and Sheila drove to a suburban shopping mall and sought out a discount clothing store. There he picked two suits off the rack and paid a total of $200 for them. Deciding he needed one more suit to fill out his closet, Paul and Sheila marched into a Foreman & Clark outlet and this time he splurged, investing all of $170 for his third outfit. "He had a hard time swallowing that," Sheila said.

Wellstone's new look was completed by Jeff Blodgett's wife,

Emily, who was annoyed that he wore light brown casual walking shoes, a horrible mismatch with his dark blue and gray suits. The clash drove her to buy a pair of dark brown soft-soled shoes. By no means could they be considered dress shoes, but they were less noticeably inappropriate. "Jeff threw them at me one day and said, 'Here, wear these,' " said Wellstone. They were a full size too large, and he regularly stumbled in them, but Wellstone obeyed his campaign manager. This transformation amused Wellstone's younger supporters, but those who were with him in 1982 had seen the change once before: Wellstone caused jaws to drop at the DFL state convention that year when, as a candidate for state auditor, he showed up in blue seersucker.

Wellstone saw the suits as a necessary accommodation and not a real burden. As he would say later in the campaign when a young staffer teased him about wearing a tie, "I'm not going to let a social symbol stand in the way." But his advisers also recognized political opportunity in their candidate's bargain-basement wardrobe, and both they and Wellstone were shameless in alluding to the price tags in talks with reporters. Many reporters took the bait and used the discount clothes as vehicles to reinforce an image of Wellstone as a common man up against Rudy Boschwitz's millions.

Through the summer and fall, Wellstone grew into his new wardrobe and his role as a candidate, refining his message and his attacks on Boschwitz through constant traveling and speaking. "I feel very strongly that politics is not about power games and it's not about money," he said on a trip to the north central Minnesota city of Bemidji in July. "Politics is about making a difference in people's lives." On the Bemidji State University campus he railed against the influence of money in politics and at Boschwitz's fund-raising:

The whole question of the disproportionate amount of influence that money has in politics has become a real ethical issue. I don't want to be beholden to large amounts of money from any well-organized interest group. My goal is not to represent the Rockefellers. It's to represent the little fellas, and the little fellas just don't have that kind of money to give to campaigns.

Over and over again he attacked Boschwitz by pairing Boschwitz's votes against and for different kinds of investments: against adequate funding for schools and in favor of billions of dollars for defense systems; against "fair prices" for family farmers and for a bailout of savings and loan institutions; against a boost in the minimum wage and for tax breaks for the affluent.

In October, in the southern Minnesota town of Mankato, Wellstone stumped for universal health care. "Health care can no longer be a privilege, but must be a right that comes with citizenship," he told several hundred members of a nurses' union, the Minnesota Nurses Association, who were meeting at the Mankato Holiday Inn. Boschwitz, he charged, listened only to the concerns of the medical industry, not to people who forgo treatment because they are not able to afford doctor and hospital bills. "This is not fair," he said. "We can do much better."

And in St. Paul in November, Wellstone issued an analysis of Boschwitz's fund-raising in the first six months of the year that showed the senator receiving more large contributions from Floridians and New Yorkers than from Minnesotans. He also trotted out the names of financiers and millionaires who symbolized the redistribution of wealth in the 1980s, noting that each of them could be found as contributors in Boschwitz's most current campaign finance report to the Federal Election Commission:

It's Donald Trump who gives big money to Rudy Boschwitz, not a schoolteacher in St. Paul. It's T. Boone Pickens from Amarillo, Texas, who gives big money to Rudy Boschwitz, not the farmer

in Rice County. It's Carl Icahn, another corporate raider, who
gives money to Rudy Boschwitz; it's not the steelworker on the
Iron Range.

Wellstone's public attitude was one of confidence, but there
were periods of deep despair by the time Minnesota's fierce winter settled in. He and Todd Otis by this point had formed a close
friendship despite the fact that they were competing for the DFL
endorsement, and they often traveled to distant events together
for the sake of companionship and their nearly bare campaign
treasuries. On those long, late-night drives along snow-swept
county roads, they commiserated about the lack of attention
they were receiving within their own party.

"Those were the most difficult times of the whole campaign," Wellstone said. "You were constantly going at it and
you're wondering where in God's name is it going to go? It's cold
as hell out there. I was starting to get pretty down about it,
about convincing anybody in the DFL Party that it could be
done."

Dialing for Delegates

While Wellstone battled the sense that Boschwitz was unbeatable and struggled to keep his own spirits up, his young, idealistic staff began the tedious task of preparing for the precinct
caucuses. The plan was meticulously crafted by Blodgett, with
help from the staff. "There's no secret to it," Blodgett said. "It's
very systematic. To win at the state convention you need 60 percent of the delegates to vote for you. . . . We were determined to
flood the caucuses."

Recruiting volunteers off a list of Wellstone supporters that
had been compiled from the house parties and the door-to-door
canvassing throughout the summer and fall, the staff organized
phone banks five nights a week—Sunday through Thursday.

With up to ten volunteers each night in the Twin Cities and another handful of callers in Duluth, they began telephoning people who were the most likely to go to the caucuses—the two thousand delegates to the 1988 state convention and the tens of thousands of people who attended the precinct caucuses in 1988. Because the number of likely caucus-goers was so overwhelming, Blodgett decided to focus the phone calling in areas where Wellstone's strength was greatest—Minneapolis, St. Paul, and the Iron Range. During two months of intense telephoning in January and February, the volunteers made thousands of calls and actually reached two to three thousand people and asked them to support Wellstone over the three other Democratic candidates.

"Jeff had one rule on the campaign: from five o'clock till nine o'clock, every night, you're on the phone," Dan Cramer said. "There was no worse crime than not being on the phone during that period."

The staffers tried to bring that same discipline to their supervision of the volunteers. Grateful as they were to have scores of helpers, the staff did not pamper them or let the phone-calling sessions drift into social engagements. There was a rule, for example, against eating supper during a shift. "You don't feed your volunteers because it's time they should be on the phone," Cramer said. "Every phone call is critically important."

The volunteers, however, remember an efficient but not terribly stern organization. And despite the no-eating rule, they also recall bringing vegetarian casseroles and pizzas to share. "The feeling was very warm," said Jo Haberman, director of Citizens for a Better Environment, a Minneapolis environmental watchdog group. She and her partner, Jane Lansing, volunteered about once a week. "The campaign was very well organized, but it was warm and informal," Haberman said. "It was a good feeling. I think it really reflected a lot about Paul and how he was going to operate as a senator."

Haberman had never met Wellstone, but she volunteered after hearing him speak several times. She vividly remembered her first close encounter with the candidate: one evening when she was making calls out of the campaign headquarters on University Avenue, Wellstone burst into the offices, followed by a handful of advisers and supporters. "What impressed me about that moment is he was upset and he was speaking passionately about the issue of U.S. aid to Israel," said Haberman, who was unsure what triggered the episode. "He was livid."

The headquarters had several work areas, but Wellstone stood near the volunteers and brought them into the discussion, Haberman said:

> The people on the phones offered their two cents. He didn't sweep into a back room and close the door to talk. You didn't have to be part of the inside staffer group to be part of this conversation. It confirmed my impression of him as a very down-to-earth, common person.

Some volunteers said that Wellstone's energy was transmitted through them in their phone calling. "I always get my energy from Paul," said Charles Curtis Jackson, a tailor and Minneapolis Park Board youth worker who volunteered three or four times a week. "People loved that on the telephone—that you're enthused about what you're doing. That won over a lot of people."

The phone callers would ask people who they supported in the Senate race and note the answer on the computer printout of names and phone numbers by using a rating system. A person who was solidly behind Wellstone was rated five, a person leaning toward him was assigned a four, an uncommitted person was given a three, a person leaning toward another candidate was given a two, and a person strongly supporting another candidate was awarded a one. To the people who were uncommitted or were favoring another candidate, the volunteer would make a short pitch for Wellstone. "If someone was uncommitted, we would try, if we had money in the budget that week, to send a piece of literature," said Cramer.

Sometimes the organizing seemed easy. Up in Duluth, as Dick Senese called on local party activists, he found an encouraging attitude emerging. When he approached Bill Miller, chairman of the eighth state senate district in Duluth, seeking support for Wellstone, Miller gave it enthusiastically, Senese said:

> [Miller] said if we lose this one [with Wellstone] it'll be nice to go down in a flame of glory rather than just losing. And if we win, there's no one else he would want in the U.S. Senate but Paul. Early on you could see this theme of no mushy middle. That was the big theme of all [Wellstone's] early speeches: This time, stand for what you believe in.

But other times the resistance was strong. Sylvia Knutson, a frequent volunteer who met Wellstone while she lived in North-field before moving to Minneapolis, recalled finding substantial support for Wellstone, but also a "real resignation that Boschwitz was this institution. I remember people saying no one was going to beat Boschwitz," she said.

While the volunteers identified supporters, the staff built up a network of precinct coordinators to make sure those supporters showed up on caucus night. In addition to being responsible for one night of phone calling every week, the coordinators were asked to organize their neighborhoods, get supporters to the caucuses on February 27, and then lead the formation of Well-stone subcaucuses that night. Blodgett estimated that about a thousand precinct coordinators were signed up. In Minneapolis, Scott Adams found captains for about 135 of the 182 precincts in the city. In St. Paul, Cramer filled in names for about 110 of the 139 precincts. "It was just a huge number," Cramer said. "The reason it worked so well is because of Paul. He excites people. He makes people want to get involved. With the campaign, we provided vehicles for them to do that."

Passing the Hat

But that enthusiasm and devotion did not translate into cash. These were worker bees who were backing Wellstone, and they did not have the resources to bankroll a candidate.

By the end of 1989, the campaign had collected $63,487 from 1,110 people, according to Wellstone's treasurer, Rick Kahn, another of his former students. As Wellstone's nineteen-page Federal Election Commission report showed, virtually all of the money came from individuals. Only $85 was attributed to political action committees (PACs). Of that amount, $35 came from the campaign committee of Karen Clark, a state representative from a poor Minneapolis district, but that donation did not qualify as a true PAC contribution; it should have been listed under a different category because it was from another campaign committee, not a PAC. The remaining $50 came from the Dorsey Political Fund, the PAC of a Minneapolis law firm, Dorsey & Whitney, but even that was a speaking fee rather than an outright donation. In other words, Wellstone had to work for his only real PAC contribution.

The house parties, which Wellstone attended throughout the year, continued to be the biggest single source of cash for the campaign. One of those meetings was held in November 1989 at the home of Anita Martinez, a Minneapolis DFL activist. It was attended by about forty-five of Martinez's friends and neighbors, almost all of them middle-class. Most of them shared the feeling prevalent among low-income people that government was irrelevant or, worse, a burden. "My friends were so turned off to politics," she said. Yet she cajoled them to attend by convincing them that Wellstone was different. "I felt really good about some of the people who came. They saw he's really a citizen's politician rather than a politician's politician," she said. The Martinez party raised about $700 that night.

As the Wellstone team worked the phones and passed the hat in living rooms, two of the other Democratic challengers were searching for money and supporters as well, but not nearly so hard. Jim Nichols raised so little money that he was not even required to file a report for the year. Todd Otis, despite his seat in the state legislature and the support of a successful Democratic fund-raiser, lawyer Sam Kaplan, fell way short of Wellstone, raising only $40,135.

Tom Berg, despite his official entry six months after Wellstone declared, topped the Democrats with $80,341. "Our campaign has taken off," Berg boasted when all the reports were in. "In only two months time we not only caught but surpassed Wellstone and Otis. That's a pretty substantial amount of money in just two months. It shows people are willing to stand up and be counted against Boschwitz." Berg also claimed that the "diversity of the list is tremendous. It is a very broad base of people from all over the state."

In fact, Berg's ties to the establishment were evident in the names of people who contributed at least $200, and therefore had to be identified in his Federal Election Commission (FEC) report. These contributors provided $54,865, or 68 percent of his total take for the year. Wellstone, by comparison, received about 28 percent of his cash from donors of $200 or more.

In spite of Berg's claims, the striking thing about his financial report was how limited his fund-raising base really was. Of the 107 individuals listed as contributing $200 or more, 62 were attorneys, 29 of them from his own law firm, Popham Haik

Schnobrich Kaufman Ltd. Big business was represented on the list of Berg contributors by two dozen corporate executives or business owners, including such luminaries as Lawrence Perlman, chief executive officer of Control Data Corp., and John Rollwagen, chief executive officer of Cray Research, a leading supercomputer manufacturer.

While the Democratic candidates competed for dollars and votes at the precinct caucuses, Boschwitz's machine was on cruise control. Boschwitz filed a one-and-one-half-inch-thick, 327-page FEC report that dwarfed Wellstone's, which measured a mere one-eighth of an inch and nineteen pages. Boschwitz's take for 1989 was $3.4 million, or eighteen times the total raised by all three Democrats. Boschwitz hauled in that much despite easing off in the last half of the year, when he knew Mondale would not challenge him. The ease with which Boschwitz collected cash was demonstrated in a single day, when Boschwitz brought in $130,000 at a Minneapolis fund-raiser headlined by former secretary of state Henry Kissinger. With that one event, Boschwitz raised more money than any of the Democrats had in all of 1989.

But Boschwitz's voluminous list of contributors provided some ammunition for the penny-pinching Democrats. Most of Boschwitz's large contributions came from wealthy out-of-state donors. An FEC analysis documented that 75 percent, or $1.35 million, of Boschwitz's large donations—$200 and up—came from people living outside Minnesota. Boschwitz also received $667,651 in PAC contributions, which accounted for nearly 20 percent of his total.

"He's got to raise a lot of money to put up a smokescreen to hide his record," Tom Berg said. Wellstone joined in, charging Boschwitz with "trying to buy this election with money from corporate political action committees and wealthy out-of-staters."

But Boschwitz's campaign manager, Tom Mason, deflected the shots by noting that in addition to his big contributors, Boschwitz also received fifteen thousand individual contributions. Mason accurately argued that the Democrats would "give their eyeteeth" to be able to claim so many supporters willing to donate money.

Squaring Off with the Suits

The Wellstone campaign received its first big break of 1990 on the morning of February 2, when Todd Otis called a press conference in St. Paul to announce his withdrawal from the race. Otis was short on cash—he had only about $2,000 in his campaign bank account—and was frustrated by the defeatist attitude among his fellow Democrats. He admonished them to not concede the race nine months before election day:

> Some Democrats seem buffaloed by Boschwitz, and we should be ashamed of that. He votes against the interests of children, women, workers, senior citizens, veterans, and the environment, and all we can see is his war chest. It is still not too late to turn this campaign around.

On the Iron Range, Otis's withdrawal appeared to help Wellstone more than it helped Tom Berg. Iron Range legislators like Tom Rukavina and Jerry Janezich, who backed Otis because of their friendship with him in the state legislature, jumped to the Wellstone campaign. Five others around the state also endorsed him. But the main advantage for Wellstone was that he now had no competition for the more committed progressive idealists in the party and could position himself as the populist choice.

With Otis out of the race, Jim Nichols showing no signs of organizing, and the caucuses bearing down fast, Berg and Wellstone focused their attacks on one another. Berg portrayed Wellstone as too radical to appeal to the general electorate and as someone who would be incapable of mastering the art of legislating if he ever did make it into the Senate. Clearly taking aim at Wellstone, Berg told a reporter a week before the precinct caucuses:

> I'm not a believer in the idea of just trying to make people feel good or to send a message. What I'm trying to do is to lead our party back into the U.S. Senate. To do that, we have to speak out on progressive issues. I've been trying to do that. I'm hoping that what the [caucus-goers] will look at is who has the ability to get elected. . . . We deserve more than just speeches and talk. I have the best ability of the candidates to appeal to a broad spectrum of Minnesota voters.

Berg acknowledged that there were few differences between himself and Wellstone on the issues, but he claimed that he was the more legitimate candidate because he could raise larger sums of money and because he had the support of twenty of the forty-two DFL state senators.

"I think Paul has got very serious problems getting elected," Berg said. Alluding to Wellstone's activist background, Berg said it would be grist for attacks by Boschwitz. "I think of his past work and his background," Berg said, "and in politics, you have to keep in mind how things will look in September or October."

Wellstone stuck to his script, arguing that unconventional politics would be the winning politics in 1990. He described Berg as the type of tired Democratic offering that voters had rejected in 1988. A week before the caucuses, Wellstone said:

> Tom has his sense of what Democrats should be about. He talks about a middle-of-the-road approach. He talks about raising big money. I say that has been the conventional wisdom and it has failed. . . . It is a euphemism for not taking a position on issues. It is a losing politics. . . . They all go after PAC money.

TV replaces grass roots. Democrats are in retreat. I represent just the opposite.

Faced with the choice between Wellstone and Berg, one key Otis supporter, Todd Rapp, a twenty-nine-year-old legislative staffer on Otis's economic development committee, opted immediately for Wellstone, owing partly to the candidate's charisma, but also to a reasoned hunch about electability. Rapp, who would later become political director of the DFL Party after Otis was elected party chairman, recalled:

> It was partly Wellstone's passion and partly that he was an incredibly sincere person. We have run candidates who believed in what they were saying, but Wellstone took that extra step in dealing with people, so that whether you agreed with him or not, you just know he'd stand and fight for what he believed in.

But the clincher was that Rapp "just didn't think a conventional candidate could beat Rudy Boschwitz. I thought we had run some pretty good candidates, and in the fight for the middle, [Republican senator Dave] Durenberger and Boschwitz consistently captured it." Rapp had no sophisticated analysis for his reasoning: "I'm not that smart; I'm not sure why it didn't work in the past but I thought that with a really different candidate we had a chance, that we could build a totally different kind of excitement with somebody that might capture the imagination. But I also felt there was a risk of being totally blown out." Rapp was enough of an insider, having worked for Otis, to know something about the energy that was going into the Wellstone grassroots campaign.

In fact, the Wellstone forces were pouring far more sweat into this phase of the campaign than any of his opponents. Berg, for example, had only two full-time people, and while all of the other candidates had more elected officials on their side, none

was able to staff phone banks or recruit as many precinct captains as Wellstone. Berg, who kept a diary of the endorsement
campaign, said he tried to get printed material to as many caucuses as possible, but did not push to get people elected to the
next level specifically under the Berg label. "Wellstone did much
more than we did," Berg acknowledged later. And an early entry
in his diary shortly before the caucuses were held betrayed the
midwinter hopelessness of his struggle: "I hear with more fre-
quency that Boschwitz can't be beaten. Very discouraging. Perhaps a head-to-head poll would show something, but we have
no money for a poll. We fight on and hope for a break."

Berg was mounting a conventional effort, giving speeches
around the state and courting leaders of various groups, but he
clearly was banking more on greater name recognition and his
more acceptable image for the June convention than on assidu-
ous organizing. One of his key supporters, Gill Strand, an analyst for a transportation consulting firm, recalled that he phoned
the Berg campaign and volunteered in late 1989 but didn't hear
from anybody for several months. "By the time I got involved, in
March or April, it was over," Strand said.

Wellstone campaign manager Jeff Blodgett's plan involved
follow-up and attention to detail in addition to mass phone calling. Starting two weeks before caucus night, the campaign even
held a series of training sessions for the precinct coordinators.
These sessions were designed to make sure the Wellstone supporters who turned up for the DFL caucuses, especially the first-
timers, were not lost in the complex rules and procedures.

One of these drills was held on February 20, when about
eighty-five precinct coordinators filed into the Minnesota
Church Center on West Franklin Avenue in Minneapolis. Wellstone was introduced by Bea Underwood, a Minnesota member
of the Democratic National Committee and an influential voice
in black politics in Minneapolis who had participated in the

meetings a year earlier that propelled Wellstone into the Senate contest. "I keep hearing how he can't raise the big bucks, how he's not connected," Underwood told the group. "Well, he's connected with the people and it is the people who are going to win this election." Wellstone picked up on that theme in a pep talk to the coordinators, employing the rhythmic speech pattern that was becoming his trademark:

> Rudy Boschwitz has the money. We know that. Rudy Boschwitz is connected to the wealthy and the powerful. We know that. Rudy Boschwitz parlays that into a huge war chest. We know that. But we have the people, the organizers, the creativity, the ideas, the hope, the anger, the solidarity, the mutual support.

Wellstone left the caucus instructions to others and instead threw himself into an animated speech, denouncing the "lost decade" of the 1980s, which saw "the militarization of space and the denial of adequate nutrition for our children." He directly confronted the dicey issue of a proposed constitutional amendment to ban the burning of the American flag. Wellstone said he would not support it. "I don't see the security of our country threatened by people running around burning flags," he declared. "I do see the security of our country threatened by burning cities, by joblessness and homelessness."

But as always, Wellstone wound up on a positive note. First, he insisted that "people are ready for a politics of conviction, for a politics that's not tippy-toe politics, for a politics that's not cynical." Then he worked toward a loud finale in which he ticked off the astounding events unfolding that winter: "If Nelson Mandela can be released from jail, if the Berlin Wall can fall, if they can have real elections in the Soviet Union, then we can beat the oil companies and we can beat Rudy Boschwitz in November!"

Berg, meanwhile, still was doing very little to identify his supporters and bring them to the caucuses. Although he had opened a small office in downtown St. Paul near the state capitol, his effort did not really kick into high gear until after the caucuses. The woman who would become Berg's top campaign administrator, Marcia Krueger, a thirty-seven-year-old feminist activist from the eastern Twin Cities suburbs of Washington County, remembered swinging into action in early 1990 and discovering that Wellstone had contacted many likely caucus-goers, and some of them had been called more than once:

> Our late start was a hindrance. People kept saying that if they had been sent materials, or even gotten a phone call, they might have been for Berg. But they had been asked first by Wellstone and it was too late. We even got calls from people saying "Would you please have [Berg] call me so I can tell Paul Wellstone to leave me alone." He was very dynamic and persistent, but to some it was a turnoff.

Jim Nichols was doing even less than Berg. He already had decided to play to the broader Democratic electorate, knowing that his antiabortion stance would be fatal in an endorsing fight. He didn't even bother to form a campaign committee to raise money until a month before the caucuses, and he hired only two full-time staff members to help launch his campaign.

Nichols adopted the line, a defensible one, that the caucuses were unrepresentative, that they attracted only a tiny percentage of the state's population and produced extremist or elitist candidates. He scoffed at the commitment Wellstone and Berg were making to the caucuses, and he insisted that they were wasting their time chasing potential convention delegates who were certain to vote for a Democrat anyway. He told a reporter days before the caucuses:

> I've been talking to the 40 percent of the people in the middle, neither Democrat or Republican. Those are the people who

don't attend precinct caucuses. I want to reach them through the media. I don't believe in a big staff or fancy campaign office. I believe in the media.

The big night, on Tuesday, February 27, was a typical winter night in Minnesota, subfreezing but not bitterly cold, and not daunting in the least for Wellstone's fervent, well-trained organizers. Several thousand people identified as Wellstone supporters had received at least one phone call from Wellstone volunteers since the previous Friday, reminding them to attend the caucuses. The painstaking preparation paid off. Wellstone backers flocked to the town halls, libraries, junior high schools, and churches where the caucuses were held. Wellstone himself dashed around the Twin Cities to about ten caucuses. At a St. Paul caucus in a shopping center on Selby Avenue, the heart of the city's black community, Wellstone joshed with seventy-two-year-old Helen White, offering her a job on his Senate staff if she supported him. "The best promise you could make is to kick out Boschwitz," White replied.

As Berg raced through fourteen caucuses, he didn't even bother to mention his Democratic opponents' names. He directed all his fire at Boschwitz.

Because of the caucus system's arcane format, it was impossible to tell precisely which Senate candidate "won." Some caucuses formed around the gubernatorial candidates and others identified themselves only with issues, not candidates. There were no "results" reported on this caucus night, but Wellstone claimed victory on the basis of his own straw poll taken by his precinct coordinators at 207 precincts that covered each of the state's eight congressional districts. His results showed him with 43 percent of the delegates, compared to 14 percent for Berg and 7 percent for Nichols. "Based on what came in tonight, we have a decisive lead," Wellstone boasted. "We won this big. We're way ahead. Before this is all over, people are going to love this campaign."

The next morning, Wellstone chartered a small, single-engine plane and flew around the state to declare victory and announce his support for a Social Security tax cut for middle- and low-income workers. Berg resorted to damage control. "This was the night [Wellstone] had to hit a home run and I don't think he hit it," Berg said. "His numbers just aren't accurate. I don't buy that for a minute." In his diary, Berg wrote: "We use his claim [of victory] to undermine his credibility."

Berg said he sampled some large precincts, and his results put him in the lead. But he failed to conduct his own statewide straw poll, so he lacked convincing numbers to contradict Wellstone's claim. This was another example of Wellstone's outthinking and outworking his opponents. Even if they were reported with perfect accuracy, Wellstone's results naturally showed him with a substantial lead because they were taken in precincts that he had thoroughly organized. In the absence of any unbiased tabulations, Wellstone's poll and Berg's defensive response created the perception that Wellstone indeed was the front-runner after the first stage of the endorsement race.

Looking back on the election, Wellstone and his team point to the organizing for the caucuses as one of the most important reasons why he was elected in November. The advantage he gained in the precinct caucuses would carry through to the state convention and help turn the man many considered a fringe candidate into a legitimate contender because he had not only the official backing of the party but also a core of hard-working disciples. Wellstone understood the importance of the caucuses and he spoke about them a week before they were held: "They're crucially important because I'm not independently wealthy. I need a party united behind me to beat Boschwitz. It's important that I win the endorsement in June decisively and in such a way that people are really believing in me as a candidate."

Although in just a few months Wellstone personally would start to devote more of his time to fund-raising and filming commercials and less time to grassroots organizing, the staff would continue to build on the foundation laid during the caucus fight to encourage voter turnout in the DFL primary and the general election. "That commitment to that type of organizing is why Paul's in the senate today," said staff member Dan Cramer.

6

EARNING THE ENDORSEMENT

While the DFLers fought among themselves, to all appearances for the privilege of getting obliterated in November, Boschwitz and his advisers were trying hard not to appear too smug and not to look beyond the election.

Every month during 1989 and early 1990 the Boschwitz brain trust would meet, sometimes in a windowless room in the downtown Minneapolis law offices of Jann Olsten, a longtime friend and confidante, and sometimes in the spacious campaign headquarters near the edge of downtown Minneapolis from which Boschwitz had engineered victories in 1978 and 1984. Boschwitz himself stayed in Washington and seldom attended the meetings, which usually were held after 5:00 P.M. and almost never lasted more than a couple of hours.

"We just wanted to make sure the trains were running on time," recalled Tom Mason, Boschwitz's campaign manager, a big, beefy, cheerful thirty-six-year-old veteran who had served Boschwitz in a variety of capacities for almost a decade.

Boschwitz's fund-raising, telemarketing, and direct-mail juggernaut was running smoothly, practically on automatic pilot. It was considered such a paragon of efficiency and sophistication that Mason found himself frequently responding to requests for advice from other Republican campaigns. "In hindsight, one of the things I wasted my time on was talking to other campaigns, showing them how to set up databases, and giving them other tips. Nobody matched our sophistication," Mason said.

These top advisers were watching the contest among the DFL candidates with almost detached bemusement. "We were a little worried about what Nichols would be like," Mason recalled, "because he was so unpredictable and outrageous. We figured he would either self-destruct or somehow make it interesting." The speculation among Boschwitz's advisers was that Nichols might be able to compete with Boschwitz in his rural southern Minnesota base, among antiabortion forces and social conservatives, while retaining most of the DFL base because it would have nowhere else to go. Wellstone was considered by some in the group to be the least dangerous. "He had a McGovern-type look and we didn't think he'd be able to mount much of a campaign coming just from the left," Mason recalled.

Boschwitz's board of political directors was made up of a handful of highly successful white males in their forties and fifties and one woman, Loanne Thrane, who headed Boschwitz's Senate office in Minnesota. The crew included Bruce Thomson and Jann Olsten, the owner and top executive, respectively, of a fast-growing and very successful photo-developing business; Jerry Pappenfuss, owner of several outstate radio stations; and Mason, the youngster in the core. This was a mature, experienced, sure-handed set of operatives, in sharp contrast to Wellstone's callow idealists. Other than their strong belief in the business imperative and limited government, the Boschwitz trust was not terribly ideological. "Everyone in that group was a Rudy supporter first, and all other political ideals and loyalties were second," Mason said.

Mason's background was middle-class all the way, and like that of many in Boschwitz's inner circle, his involvement in politics was tied to personal loyalty rather than being driven by ideology. He grew up in the comfortable St. Paul suburb of White Bear Lake, originally a summer refuge for wealthy St. Paul residents, and his father was a bureaucrat for the local school district. Mason attended the University of Minnesota, where, coincidentally, a cadre of future Boschwitz aides all worked on the *Minnesota Daily,* the campus newspaper. These included Jay Novak and Bob Anderson, who would join the campaign in the summer of 1990 as communications director and finance director, respectively. Mary Lahr and Tim Droogsma, Boschwitz press secretaries through most of the 1980s, also worked at the *Daily,* a short time after this trio.

Mason and Novak were good friends and their lives at times followed parallel paths: they worked together at the *Worthington Globe,* a daily paper in a southwestern Minnesota regional city, and later in corporate communications in Minneapolis. But it was Mason who became one of Boschwitz's longest-serving and most loyal aides, joining him in 1981 as a press secretary and serving intermittently as a campaign spokesman and an administrator for the National Republican Senatorial Committee when Boschwitz headed that political organization between 1986 and 1988. "We just hit it off; it became a very nice relationship," Mason said of his connection with Boschwitz. That personal appeal and likability were the bonding agents for many of Boschwitz's supporters, rather than a response to a belief system or inspirational leadership.

Mason had been Boschwitz's campaign communications director in 1984. And although he had been the chief of staff to Republican South Dakota senator James Abdnor when populist Democrat Tom Daschle beat him in 1986, Mason had no reason to believe that Wellstone could pull a similar upset. Boschwitz had romped to an easy victory in 1984, defeating Minnesota secretary of state Joan Growe in many urban and Iron Range districts. Since then, Boschwitz had strengthened himself politically and his approval ratings had climbed to a very comfortable level of nearly 70 percent at times. On top of everything else, Boschwitz was treated to extraordinarily favorable coverage in the spring, when he was featured in television broadcasts and in newspaper stories about his emotional return to his birthplace in Berlin shortly after the dismantling of the Berlin Wall.

A new set of poll results before the caucuses gave Boschwitz even more reason to coast. A *Star Tribune*/KSTP-TV Minnesota Poll in mid-February 1990 showed that nearly twice as many people *approved* of Boschwitz's job performance as *recognized* the name of the most widely known DFL candidate. Sixty-seven percent of the respondents said they approved of the way Boschwitz was handling his job. Only 35 percent had heard of Nichols, 24 percent recognized Berg's name, and Wellstone, who had campaigned harder and longer than either of the other DFLers, was known by a paltry 17 percent.

Even more worrisome to the Democrats were the findings that 57 percent of self-identified DFLers, and an unnerving 61 percent of self-described liberals, approved of Boschwitz's performance. With ratings like these, how could any challenger hope to dent the Boschwitz image? Presented with that question, Wellstone would shoot back: "The people haven't voted yet." Only his diehard supporters were convinced.

Later that spring and summer, Boschwitz's advisers would see Wellstone make progress in the polls in name recognition. But for every 10 percentage points of growth in name recognition by Wellstone, they would observe, half of the respondents viewed Wellstone unfavorably. Mason said:

When you got a guy with no name ID, and then half the people who discover him don't like him, it's hard not to become pretty confident. We tried to keep the mentality that we were running behind. But I recall specifically having conversations with reporters who would laugh at Wellstone's prospects. Part of our mindset came from reporters who wouldn't give us the time of day. If we'd mount any kind of effort to make a point or launch an initiative, people would say, "Why are you doing this when you're so far ahead?"

Tom Berg, meanwhile, was greatly encouraged by the Minnesota Poll and relied heavily on it in organizing for the June endorsing convention. But he didn't get the ride he felt he needed from the news media or from party activists. One of his diary entries read: "Minnesota Poll showed that I had 25 percent name ID and good ratings—Wellstone not so good—but party activists don't seem to care. I don't understand." Also that spring, Berg won a straw poll at a meeting of several hundred members of the DFL Central Committee, giving a boost to his hopes that the party regulars would eventually come to their senses.

Berg was frustrated by his inability to get favorable news coverage, in spite of his lead in the polls and his superior fundraising, while Wellstone appeared to get good coverage when he didn't seem to deserve it. For instance, the endorsement of Wellstone by Miles Lord, a former judge and a populist champion with a reputation for headline seeking, got good play in the media. But Berg's overwhelming support among the top party leaders seemed to be overlooked by reporters. Berg knew he was leading in the polls and had raised half again as much money as Wellstone in one-third the time—he had held the standard soirees on St. Paul's elegant Summit Avenue and in the upscale Whitney Hotel in Minneapolis—yet he had no consensus on locking up the endorsement. Berg was convinced that Wellstone had some secret weapon, perhaps Pat Forciea, who still was not involved formally in the campaign, for manipulating the media. "I was doing better than everyone else by all the standards, but I couldn't get that story out," Berg said.

Converting the Kaplans

The first sign of Wellstone's ability to break down the resistance of the party establishment came in early February, when he won the support of Sam and Sylvia Kaplan, influential Democratic fund-raisers who initially had thrown their support to their neighbor Todd Otis. Though the Kaplans had been enthusiastic about Wellstone since a meeting in December 1989, they held onto the Otis candidacy out of loyalty to a close friend. When Otis quit, however, they were free to follow their hearts and join Wellstone.

For the Kaplans, both in their early fifties, politics had been a way of life since the 1960s. Sylvia Kaplan was a Eugene McCarthy delegate to the state DFL convention in 1968 and became active in local antiwar efforts. She also worked on civil rights causes and was a founding member of a suburban civil rights group, the Golden Valley Human Rights Commission. "I thought we were going to change the world—if we could solve the race thing," she said. In 1972 she worked as a speechwriter and press aide to Hubert H. Humphrey during his last presidential campaign, and then was hired to do public relations for the Minnesota Federation for Jewish Service, the preeminent Jewish organization in the state. By the 1980s she was a partner in a chic Minneapolis restaurant, the New French Cafe.

Sam Kaplan was a lawyer and a founding partner of a downtown Minneapolis law firm that counted United Airlines and the Minnesota Vikings among its clients. He was a past president of the Jewish federation, in which Boschwitz also was active. Boschwitz and the Kaplans were good friends: he was invited to their 1974 wedding. But when it came to politics, they parted ways. The Kaplans had always seen themselves as liberal Democrats. Boschwitz "used to refer to us as his best Democratic friends," Sam Kaplan said. The Kaplans were major contributors to DFL candidates and their big home on a parkway next to Lake Harriet in southwest Minneapolis was the site of countless fund-raisers.

Over the years Sam Kaplan's legal career expanded into a string of partnerships and investments in nursing homes, apartment buildings, a bank, and other interests. "I have all the characteristics, businesswise, of a Republican," he said. With a private elevator to his fifty-fifth-floor offices, appointed with Louis XV furniture, Oriental carpets, and oak parquet flooring, Kaplan was the type of Democrat who represented the antithesis of Wellstone's "little fella" campaign. When the candidate first stepped off the elevator into Kaplan's offices in the Norwest Center, with a panoramic view of the Mississippi River and the Twin Cities, he was taken aback by the luxury. "I'd never been in a place like that before," Wellstone said. "I didn't know such places existed."

But it was the Kaplans who were bowled over by the encounter. They met with Wellstone only at the insistence of a mutual friend, Arthur Himmelman, a senior fellow at the Hubert H. Humphrey School of Public Affairs at the University of Minnesota. The Kaplans had heard Wellstone on the radio a few times, and they were not prepared to like him. As they waited for Wellstone to arrive on December 1, they were expecting a wild-eyed radical. "We thought he was to the left of Lenin," Sylvia Kaplan recalled.

Wellstone, too, was dreading the meeting. He did not think he had much chance of enlisting their support and he did not feel comfortable making an appeal to what he viewed as the corporate wing of the Democratic Party. "I did not quite feel that I had sold out, but I groaned about it," he said. "I did not know that community of very well-to-do but progressive people. I had stereotyped them, and vice versa." But when he sat down with the Kaplans, Wellstone charmed and disarmed them. "We don't have any buildings like this in Northfield," he said, breaking the ice. He then employed his first rule of politics: politics is personal.

"I talked to them in very personal terms on why I was running, about what I thought and what I believed in," Wellstone said. He explained that his careers as professor and political activist were focused on "political economy questions." But he surprised the Kaplans by not launching into attacks on capitalism. Instead, Wellstone argued that the growing gulf between the rich and the poor and the Republican philosophy of deregulation were ravaging American society. "He talked about how democracy can't survive if things aren't distributed more fairly and better than they were," recalled Sylvia Kaplan. The Kaplans shared those beliefs, and to their surprise they found Wellstone to be engaging and personable, neither hostile nor condescending. "He wasn't pandering to us," she said.

After Otis dropped out of the race, the Kaplans promised to play a big role in Wellstone's campaign, and three days after the caucuses they took their first public step. In a March 2 letter primarily written by Sylvia but signed by Sam on his stationery, he told his friends about the meeting with Wellstone:

> I wasn't looking forward to meeting with Paul Wellstone when he stopped by my office a while ago. I not only thought that Paul's political view was somewhat different from my own, but, like a lot of other Democrats, I was discouraged by Rudy Boschwitz's war chest and thought I would sit this one out. . . .
>
> I want to tell you that in a short time with Paul Wellstone, I became converted. I began to remember that feeling of excitement I experienced during my early days in the Minnesota DFL

party. We listened to Hubert H. Humphrey and others like him, and we believed that we would make a difference and that we would win even if the odds were against us. Listening to Paul Wellstone, I once again became a believer and it felt good. . . .

I was taken with his intelligence and his understanding of the issues, but it was ultimately the fire and the caring and the pure energy of the man that convinced me. It's been a long time since I've felt this committed to a candidacy.

The letter served as an invitation to a March 28 fund-raiser at the Kaplans' house. Although the custom is to send a check in advance or to write one at the door, many of the people who showed up at the Kaplans' home did neither. Instead, they came armed with suspicions. They wanted to hear Wellstone before they decided whether to contribute to his campaign. And in a scenario that was repeated over and over, Wellstone used the force of his personality to break down the resistance. "They found him to be engaging," Sam Kaplan said. "After they heard him they wrote the check." Until that point, Wellstone's best fund-raising events brought in much less than $2,000 each; the Kaplans' first effort raised $10,000.

"I don't ever want to minimize the importance of the people who sat on the phone banks, doing the grunt work day after day," said campaign manager Jeff Blodgett. "But Sam and Sylvia, in terms of the big picture, were a huge legitimizing factor for us, especially within the DFL crowd and the Jewish community. They were a huge factor in our fund-raising success."

Kaplan's intensity woke up some other Democrats who had been resigned to a Boschwitz victory. His letter "helped give me the confidence to finally get off the fence in the Senate race," wrote R. T. Rybak, a Minneapolis real estate development official, in a note back to Kaplan. "You really are right—we *should* be outraged by Rudy—and angry enough not to concede the election."

Labor Rallies

Soon after winning over the Kaplans, Wellstone scored a key victory among the ranks of organized labor. He had been angling for labor's support since he began the campaign, knowing that the unions could provide the enormous network of volunteers needed to implement his grassroots strategy. But some of the state's labor leaders already had rebuffed him. The Teamsters, for example, were solidly behind Tom Berg from the first day of his campaign. Danny Gustafson, president of the state AFL-CIO and the single most powerful labor official in Minnesota, had not issued a formal endorsement, but it was widely known that he favored Berg. "It was an obstacle that labor itself, as an institution, was not on board," said Pat Forciea, who helped the Wellstone team prepare for the upcoming state convention.

But once again, as with the Kaplans and the wealthy contributors, a guardian angel appeared to help break down resistance. This was David Foster, who had been elected in November 1989 as the director of District 33 of the United Steelworkers of America. Prior to his election in the eight-state region stretching from Michigan to Montana, Foster had worked for sixteen years in a St. Paul steel mill, performing virtually every job in the plant. The third-degree burns on his leg, inflicted by a 1,400-degree piece of steel that shot into his boot, were proof that he had done the most dangerous jobs.

From his position on the steel mill floor, Foster had grown increasingly frustrated over the wage and benefit concessions that left mill workers and miners on the Iron Range earning no more in 1989 than they had in 1982. As the leader of a group of young rebels in the steelworkers' union, Foster challenged and beat an incumbent viewed as too obliging toward management and as an ally of conservative Democrats.

Foster knew Wellstone from his own activism in the DFL

Party dating to the late 1970s. He was a state DFL Central Committee member, had helped organize a liberal caucus within the party, and had worked on Wellstone's 1982 bid to be elected state auditor. Foster and Wellstone were soul mates. While Wellstone tried to push the DFL to the left, Foster tried to stiffen the spine of the labor movement. As Wellstone used his position in the party to promote the candidacy of Jesse Jackson and other progressives, Foster used his prominence in the union to become founder and chairman of the National Rank and File against Concessions, an organization made up mainly of steel, auto, and meatpacker union members who suffered under crushing reorganizations of their industries in the 1980s.

When he took office in March 1990 as the new regional director, Foster immediately began to transform the union into a grassroots political force that would back progressive candidates willing to fight for labor unions. In his first week in office, Foster directed his legislative lobbyist, Bob Rootes, a laborer at an Iron Range mine, to set up a candidate forum for the Senate race for the end of March, with the intention of endorsing a candidate. "I talked to [Steelworker] local leaders about an early endorsement. I decided I was going to play a role in the kinds of decisions that were being made by the party," Foster said. His plan was to counter the Teamsters' support of Berg and to encourage other progressive labor leaders to endorse Wellstone.

"I was determined to stop the steamrolling toward a more conservative candidate," Foster said. He contacted the union's headquarters in Pittsburgh and alerted them that he was about to do something "that in all likelihood would set us at odds with other unions and the state AFL-CIO in the process of making an endorsement," he said. Steelworker president Lynn Williams gave Foster his approval.

On March 29 Wellstone, Berg, and Jim Nichols appeared at the union's forum in the St. Paul Radisson Hotel to debate one another and to take questions from the seventy-five delegates from Steelworker locals around Minnesota who were members of the union's Minnesota State Political, Education and Legislative Committee. Berg and Nichols each stressed their support of union causes, but Wellstone aggressively laid claim to having the strongest labor credentials. Said Foster:

> He reminded them of the many times he had been with them on picket lines from southern Minnesota to northern Minnesota. He was the overwhelming favorite because of his activism. The other two had supported traditional trade union issues. But Paul was so clearly in the trenches with us. He had a wholly different approach to politics that impressed me and our members.

When the forum was over and the candidates had left the hotel, the discussion among the delegates over whom to endorse lasted only a few minutes. "There wasn't much discussion at all," said Foster.

Bob Bratulich, president of the state's largest Steelworkers unit, Local 1938, proposed that the committee endorse Wellstone. When the delegates voted with a show of hands, Wellstone had won the union's endorsement unanimously. That same day, Foster issued a one-page press release announcing the decision. The press release read in part:

> As one of the largest unions in Minnesota (with about 10,000 members), we have taken this step in hopes of giving an early boost to a candidate whose views most clearly reflect the needs of our members. Throughout the 1980's, a terrible injustice was done to the blue collar industrial workers of America. No union felt the loss of jobs in a more devastating fashion than the U.S.W.A. Few communities were harder hit than Minnesota's Iron Range. Today, our membership feels that the proper response to a decade of neglect by the Federal Government to the plight of the working Americans is the election of Paul Wellstone to the U.S. Senate.

The announcement was followed by a $5,000 check from the union's political arm in Pittsburgh, the maximum a political action committee could donate before the primary. Aside from the $50 donation from the law firm PAC, the Steelworkers' contribution was the only PAC money Wellstone received before the state convention.

"That was a very big endorsement," Wellstone said. "Their doing that was key. I think other unions wanted to do it and this helped them." Following the Steelworkers' lead, three other prominent unions also endorsed Wellstone: the American Federation of State, County and Municipal Employees (AFSCME), with 40,000 members; the Minnesota State Council of Machinists, with 20,000 members; and the United Auto Workers, Local 879 in St. Paul, with about 1,850 members.

An Anxious Hierarchy

Because of these inroads, and the slow but steady one-by-one conversion of doubters across the state, Wellstone began closing in on the endorsement. After the caucuses, campaign manager Jeff Blodgett rented a photocopier, and he and other staff members plugged it in at the state DFL headquarters, where they copied the names and phone numbers of the approximately forty thousand delegates and alternates elected to the next level—the county and legislative district conventions scheduled for March and April.

"We spent a week putting them on index cards. Then the phone banks began running again," said Dan Cramer. Once again, the devotion to grassroots organizing paid dividends. In March and April, as county and state legislative district conventions winnowed the delegates down to those who would go on to the state convention, it became obvious that Wellstone's support was strong. The DFL hierarchy, meanwhile, grew increasingly jittery about the prospect of his leading the DFL ticket in November.

On April 25, with all but about two dozen state convention delegates selected, three of the highest-ranking state DFL lawmakers sent a letter supporting Berg to all the delegates who had been selected to that point. The letter, from Senate Majority Leader Roger Moe, House Majority Leader Dee Long, and Assistant Senate Majority Leader Bill Luther, never mentioned Wellstone by name, but it fairly quivered with implied fear. Noting that the entire state legislature was up for reelection in 1990, the authors said it "is critical that we have our most electable candidate on the ticket, particularly in rural and suburban legislative districts where we may only win by a few percentage points." Those were areas where Wellstone was expected to have the least support. "We need a campaign, and a candidate, who will work with us and *raise the funds* [emphasis added]" needed to retain DFL control of both legislative chambers, the letter continued. The letter also was noteworthy for the lack of confidence it placed even in Berg's ability to beat Boschwitz. It never said that he would or could win. The most hopeful statement was this: "Tom Berg can put together our best challenge to Rudy Boschwitz."

That thinking was persuasive for many, but it infuriated those in the progressive wing. On the Iron Range, Bill Ojala remembered a newspaper story in which a Berg volunteer bragged about how the candidate could reach into the "deepest pockets" for campaign funds. "It's those goddamned 'deepest pockets' that have too long controlled everything," Ojala said. "It's the other 99 percent of the pockets that need to have a say in things."

Wellstone over and over again tried to refute the charge that he was too liberal with a simple question: "What issue am I too liberal on?" It was a question that almost always drew stammers or blank stares. For on many major issues, Wellstone and Berg were not far apart: they supported extensive cuts in military spending, were strong advocates of civil rights, proposed major campaign finance reforms, and were ardent environmentalists.

On the criticisms of his tone and style, Wellstone shot back with memorable phrases that implied wimpiness and weakness, accusing Berg of engaging in "tippy-toe politics" and the "politics of no conviction." The charge was a bit unfair. Marcia Krueger argues that Berg was "out there on equal rights, and child care for women long before it was the hot topic for the DFL. He wasn't waving the flag attracting attention to himself and maybe he wasn't able to get that passion going, but he was a good guy." Unfair as the "no conviction" charge was, it crystallized the issue for delegates.

Did DFLers want yet another lawyer with a long and distinguished record of public service? Someone who could attract a significant amount of money, but who had yet to demonstrate that he could motivate supporters and excite the electorate? Or did they want an activist with a record of civil disobedience who had yet to win an election, but whose intensity and stirring orations could fire up a voting public that simply refused to respond to previous DFL campaigns? Those were the choices. Head versus heart. Résumé versus rap sheet. Competence versus chutzpah.

By mid-May, Wellstone staffers had the names of the approximately two thousand delegates elected to the state convention. Although it was clear that Wellstone was the front runner among delegates, the confusing nature of the caucus system made it impossible to count accurately how many delegates were committed to each candidate. Just as they did for the caucuses and the county and district conventions, Wellstone's staff and volunteers returned to the phones to make contact with the delegates, who were lumped into three categories: supporting Wellstone, undecided, and not supporting Wellstone. "We focused on those last two piles," Cramer said.

This time, the staffers called on their best volunteer phone callers. First, a volunteer would call a delegate to ask which candidate he or she supported. Then, Cramer said:

> If a delegate was undecided, a staff person would call them again. And if they were still undecided after that, Paul would call them. That's when I felt we were really moving. The response was great on the phone. The response we were getting from Berg people was they were soft. They were supporting Tom because they had known him a long time. They said they would support him on the first or second ballot, but we felt they would move. It was *our* people who weren't going to move.

Now the trick was not who could make the most calls, but who could be the most persuasive and persistent. "You almost have to do a little schmoozing," explained Liz Borg. "And whether delegates will admit it or not, they love to get calls and to spend time on the phone talking. We had to keep schmoozing them, but there is a fine line between being pushy and not giving up."

As delegates gathered at the brand-new Minneapolis Convention Center on June 8, Wellstone's staff was confident that he had 40 percent of the 1,261 delegate votes locked up. (There were actually 1,372 delegates, but not every delegate had a full vote.) A Minneapolis *Star Tribune* survey of the delegates generally confirmed Wellstone's claim; it found that Wellstone was the first choice of 39 percent of the delegates and alternates who were likely to be seated. That was a clear lead over Berg, who was favored by 30 percent, and Nichols, who had 23 percent. Berg and Nichols had no firm counts of commitments from delegates, but one bit of math remained undisputed: no one had the 60 percent needed for endorsement.

Inside the convention center, the candidates' garish banners, posters, and balloons overwhelmed the convention hall's neutral colors. As delegates found their seats, arranged around long, rectangular school-cafeteria-type folding tables, they found a gift from Berg. His supporters had placed potted fir tree seedlings by each delegate's seat. The distribution of the seedlings, which came from Berg's tree farm in central Minnesota, was an attempt to stress his environmental credentials and to connect with every delegate.

Wellstone's forces took the floor under Blodgett's direction. Combining a little show business with a touch of high-tech gimmickry, Blodgett distributed environmentally correct recyclable paper pom-poms to Wellstone delegates and outfitted his staffers and volunteer organizers with walkie-talkies for instant communication. Blodgett also rented cellular phones, but they turned out to be useless, Dave Graham said:

> I got there and the cellular phones we had didn't work. It turned out that it wasn't a matter of them not working. It was that we didn't know how to work them. And I didn't realize that until later on when we got our own for Paul. We just didn't know how to work them.

By the luck of the draw, Wellstone was the first to address the convention, a distinct advantage because Wellstone's opponents have always dreaded following him at the podium. Sheila Wellstone introduced her husband, and he uncorked a blazing speech, pledging to run a campaign that would focus on grassroots organizing and bring the party back to its roots. He offered delegates the chance to participate in "a progressive, populist campaign in the Hubert H. Humphrey tradition." By invoking Humphrey's name, Wellstone was playing to the deep emotional attachment many DFLers have for the former vice president, who as a young Minneapolis mayor in the 1940s helped forge the coalition of the Democratic Party and the Farmer-Labor Party, the latter having been one of the strongest left-of-center third parties in American history.

"I promise you a campaign that will light a prairie fire that will sweep Rudy Boschwitz and all his money out of office," Wellstone shouted, thrusting himself at the microphone. "It is time to put the government back on the side of people, not on the side of union-busting corporations."

On the floor in the back of the convention hall, Sam Kaplan could not understand what Wellstone was saying because of the poor acoustics that were still being smoothed out in the new center. But Kaplan could tell that Wellstone was connecting with the delegates. "He was great. His passion was so good," Kaplan said. "You couldn't hear a single word. But it wasn't what he had to say. It was the sense that this guy was a believer."

Wellstone wound up with one of his trademark crowd-pleasing lines: "He'll be the senator from Exxon, I'll be the senator from now on." As Wellstone stepped back from the microphone, hundreds of delegates leapt to their feet and the convention floor became a sea of green and white pom-poms.

Nichols, not known as a dynamic public speaker, was next. He told the delegates that "those of you who vote for me are voting for the promise of a better life, a life without Rudy Boschwitz." Nichols's speech was followed by another floor demonstration. Although Nichols's contingent was not as large as Wellstone's, the energy and noise of the demonstration surprised many observers because Nichols had done so little organizing. Nichols recalled being satisfied that his demonstration looked just as powerful as Wellstone's, and that his foe had erred by using pom-poms, which he thought looked juvenile and out of place. "The pom-poms bombed," Nichols said.

Nichols's demonstration also meant that the number of antiabortion activists was larger than expected. That was a troubling sign, because if Wellstone or Berg failed to show any momentum after a few ballots, Nichols's supporters might be able to create a deadlock, resulting in no endorsement. That is precisely what Nichols wanted. Before the convention began, he said he would not challenge the endorsed candidate in a primary if there was a quick endorsement. Nichols defined "quick" as an endorsement within five ballots. But if a divided convention eventually gave a reluctant endorsement, then he would feel free to run in the primary, he said.

Berg was the last of the three to speak, and in an attempt to compete with Wellstone, he added octane to his usual speaking style. He argued strongly for an endorsement of a candidate and against a potentially debilitating primary fight. And he assaulted Boschwitz, calling him "one of the most disgraceful senators in Minnesota's history."

Even one of Berg's most loyal friends and supporters, Sally Chesterman of Albert Lea, later confessed that Berg looked flat and tired next to Wellstone: "As much as I liked Tom, he didn't have that charisma that Wellstone had; it's as simple as that." The floor reaction, a cosmetic but not meaningless final visual test of the candidates' respective strengths, was hardly encouraging. Berg's was clearly not as impressive as Wellstone's or Nichols's.

With the speeches concluded, the balloting began. The delegates cast votes by paper, so all the candidates waited nervously for about forty-five minutes for the first-round results. At national political conventions, the voting is drawn out in full view by a roll call of the states; here, the state convention officials tabulated the written district-by-district results in a curtained area off the main stage and announced only the overall result to the assembled delegates.

When the first-ballot vote was announced from the podium, Wellstone had the plurality he claimed he would have. He won 41 percent of the delegates, a fraction more than he had predicted. Even more encouraging for Wellstone was that Berg had finished 11 percentage points behind, and barely ahead of Nichols. Berg had 30 percent and Nichols won 28 percent. The remaining 1 percent was split among a minor candidate and votes for "no endorsement" and "other."

With the first ballot in, Blodgett's strategy began to unfold on the convention floor. He had meticulously assembled a network of staffers, volunteers, and Wellstone delegates that reached to every delegate table in the convention center.

In a room off the convention floor that served as the campaign's headquarters, Dave Graham was in charge of a team that swiftly analyzed the district-by-district results. Those results were gathered in the curtained ballot-counting area by Wellstone operatives who, along with representatives from the other campaigns, were allowed to monitor the tabulations. A group of about twenty runners raced the numbers from the tabulating area over to Graham's headquarters. Graham's analysts, which included his parents, would identify where each candidate was gaining or losing support, and that information would be relayed to the floor workers.

Blodgett stood in the middle of the convention floor, marshaling an army of Wellstone staff members and supporters. A Wellstone staffer, attired in a homemade green vest, was assigned to each of the eight congressional districts. And in each of the approximately eight state senate districts in each congressional district, Blodgett had recruited a coordinator from among the delegates. These lower-level coordinators were dressed in green T-shirts.

As Blodgett received information from Graham's command post and from the floor workers, he decided where to dispatch

Wellstone, his wife, or a handful of carefully selected advocates. If a rural Berg or Nichols delegate questioned Wellstone's ability to get elected, Paul Ogren, a state representative, was sent to provide an outstate officeholder's assurance that Wellstone could win. Or Pat Forciea, the respected strategist, would go over to a wavering delegate and make a quick sales pitch about how Wellstone could beat Boschwitz.

"Any time a delegate said he didn't think Paul could raise the money, I'd radio Jeff, and [donor and fund-raiser] Sam Kaplan would appear in their face," said Cramer.

When a delegate for Berg or Nichols seemed ready to switch to Wellstone, the candidate himself would be ushered over. "Within two minutes Paul Wellstone was right in front of that person," said Forciea. Because of this superior organization, "Paul was able to hold probably ten to twenty times [more] personal meetings than the other candidates," Forciea said.

On the second ballot, Wellstone gained, but just slightly. He won 43 percent, while Berg slipped to 29 percent and Nichols stayed at 28 percent, reflecting the commitment by antiabortion activists to stick with their candidate. After the second-ballot results were analyzed in Graham's post, the Wellstone team went into action again, fanning out across the floor, searching for opportunities among Berg and Nichols delegates. "The amazing thing was that the Berg people were starting to stand by the Wellstone coordinators to find out what the results were," said Graham.

On the third ballot Wellstone picked up twenty-four more votes, pushing him up to 45 percent. Berg's supporters continued to defect. He lost eighteen votes and fell a notch to 28 percent. Twenty Nichols delegates abandoned their candidate, and Nichols dropped a percentage point to 26 percent. "We were always waiting for Berg to make some big push, for him to do something," said Graham. "But he didn't."

Wellstone continued to widen the gap by topping 47 percent on the fourth ballot. This time Nichols moved into second place by collecting 27 percent of the vote, while Berg's support was down to 26 percent, even though the AFL-CIO and most elected officials remained in his corner.

At about this point, the drama overwhelmed Liz Borg, who was supervising the Wellstone coordinators among the rural delegates. Overwork and a lack of sleep and proper meals in the days before the convention, combined with the tension, made Borg dizzy and nauseous. She stumbled to the women's bathroom, where she fainted and collapsed on the floor. "I was out by the sink," Borg said. "I'm not a big fainter, either. I get woozy every once in a while, but I never really fainted before." Borg was soon revived by a Berg delegate, who wet a paper towel and pressed it against her forehead.

Back out on the floor, it was Berg who was losing control. He was getting dangerously close to being dropped from the balloting. Under the convention rules, a candidate who failed to get at least 20 percent of the vote on the fifth ballot would be eliminated from the endorsement contest. By now it was clear to the Wellstone camp that they would win the endorsement. But Wellstone was worried that if Berg refused to drop out voluntarily, the convention would drag on for several more ballots, thereby giving Nichols an excuse to run against him in a primary.

So after the fourth ballot, Wellstone staff members approached Berg on the floor and asked him to drop out so there could be a fifth-ballot endorsement, thus heading off a primary fight. Berg "reacted with stone silence," according to Forciea.

On the fifth ballot, Wellstone had the support of a slim majority of the convention—53 percent—but he was still short of the 60 percent needed for endorsement. Nichols picked up some of the delegates defecting from Berg, and the agriculture commissioner moved up slightly again, this time to 28 percent, where he was on the first ballot. Berg received only 18 percent, not enough under the rules to advance to the next round. Only when his name was being scratched from the ballot did Berg release his delegates.

Berg's elimination pushed Wellstone over the top on the sixth ballot, giving him 64 percent of the vote and the endorsement. Wellstone's supporters staged a long, raucous celebration on the floor and he encouraged them from the elevated podium, waving one of the green and white pom-poms in circles over his head.

"People will love this campaign because I won't be cynical," Wellstone shouted in his acceptance speech. But on the convention floor, some DFL leaders already were grumbling about the endorsement and predicting doom. "Great. He won't even win 40 percent of the vote against Boschwitz," Allan Spear, a liberal state senator from Minneapolis, complained to those around him. Spear was convinced that Boschwitz was unbeatable, so he supported Berg because he thought Berg "would run a respectable campaign that wouldn't hurt others on the ticket." A campaign for the party endorsement is vastly different from a general election campaign, which is mostly fought on television, Spear explained: "I thought Paul would be too wild on TV, too hot with his arms waving, and I thought he would bring others [on the DFL ticket] down."

The convention victory was the biggest of Wellstone's political career, but it was soured by Berg's refusal to concede until the sixth ballot. That was one ballot too late, for now Nichols felt free to run in the primary. Nichols did not declare his intentions that night, but as Liz Borg, her head now clear, left the convention, she saw a Nichols supporter collecting the candidate's posters. "If you see people loading their signs into a pick-up truck, they're not saving them for posterity or to hand out to friends,"

Borg said. "That was our first clue that it wasn't going to be clear sailing from the convention to the primary."

Wellstone considered Tom Berg's late concession yet another example of sabotage by party elites. "It made Paul kind of angry," Blodgett recalled. "It was a sign that some of the party's mainstream were not going to be very helpful to him, that they resented him more than they were excited by him." Even Nichols recalled being taken aback by the rancor:

> It shocked me how much the Berg people didn't like Wellstone. They viewed Paul as a no-win candidate, no chance to beat Boschwitz, just too radical. Some of them remembered the McGovern days and being dumped by radicals. Paul had done a good job of bringing in new people and that scared them too. Paul built on the [Jesse] Jackson base, new breed, the unwashed. . . . It happens every twenty years or so.

The animosity between the establishment and the populists may have been provoked in at least some small part by the Wellstone campaign's exclusiveness and its stubborn reluctance to embrace the people who had never given them the respect they felt they deserved. Berg supporter Gill Strand said the ill will was palpable, that Wellstone's people

> kind of made it real clear at the convention and afterward that this was their victory and that it had nothing to do with the DFL. They made no bones about it. I remember meeting with some of their people and Marcia [Krueger, a Berg campaign official] afterward. We thought it would be bonding and uniting, but they wanted nothing but our addresses and phone lists.

Krueger corroborated Strand's perceptions:

> In the past it had been normal in endorsement fights for the winner to be inclusive, to offer to put the opponents' staff to work, but the head of his campaign didn't directly contact me. . . . I met with someone who had just joined the campaign, for

lunch somewhere, and there was little concern about where our volunteer staff would go. It was strictly an interest in anything we could do to help them and it was not a good feeling. . . . I see this attitude everywhere in progressive politics, a paranoia about those out to get us. We become overly concerned with differences rather than commonalities and it's a hard thing to deal with. I never ended up doing anything for Wellstone, and never really was asked for it.

Many of the party's mainline leaders, who after all had spent much of their lives fighting what they thought to be righteous liberal causes, were irritated at Wellstone's seeming arrogance and his constant portrayals of Berg as a sellout or a false liberal. "If you looked at Tom's record, it was tough painting him as an archconservative," said Strand. "The irony was that Wellstone's people kept saying 'quit paying attention to image and look at issues,' and they won on image." Berg concurred:

One of the mistakes we made was allowing ourselves to be painted as somehow a conservative because I wore a coat and tie. . . . We didn't do as good a job as we could have in pushing the notion of "results, not rhetoric," that we should get somebody in Washington who could get something done.

These hard feelings and divisions within the party made an impression on Forciea, who joined the Wellstone celebration in a suite at a nearby Holiday Inn. As Forciea drove home in the wee hours of the next morning, he was numbed by the thought of the obstacles ahead. "I remember being tremendously excited for Paul as a friend," he said, "but still thinking, 'My God, how is this ever going to happen?' "

7

HANDLERS AND AD MEN

On the final day of the three-day DFL convention, Greg Frank, political director for Minnesota's Independent-Republican Party, stood at the back of the Minneapolis Convention Center and watched the proceedings with glee. Frank was delighted that in addition to picking a radical like Wellstone for their Senate candidate, the Democrats decided to stick with three-term incumbent governor Rudy Perpich, despite abundant evidence that his public support had deeply eroded after ten years in office.

While Democratic regulars openly feared the damage that a Wellstone candidacy could cause for the party, a number also bemoaned the problems presented by Perpich, whose eccentricities had earned him the moniker Governor Goofy. In his first years in office, Perpich had established himself as an offbeat but refreshing politician who would disappear from the capitol for days without notice and travel alone or with his wife to small-town cafés to take the pulse of the state. But by the end of his third term his populism had worn off. He dyed his hair, wore sharply tailored, expensive suits, was seen less often in public, and reacted fiercely to criticisms of his family's lifestyle at the state-owned governor's mansion.

"Perpich is very vulnerable this year," Frank said. "We feel we'll be strongest running against him."

Perpich won the party's endorsement partly because of the loyalty of the state's top labor leaders, who appreciated his efforts to create jobs and his blockage of legislation that would have reduced benefits for injured workers. The governor lacked the backing of many feminists and abortion rights activists; he was nominally opposed to abortion. Perpich had won a relatively easy endorsement over his former commerce commissioner, Mike Hatch, an advocate of abortion rights. But deep divisions existed within the party over the gubernatorial race, just as it did over the selection of a Senate candidate.

The Democrats appeared to be on the road to self-destruction. Frank and everyone in the convention hall knew that the party was fractured, and that neither Wellstone nor Perpich was likely to win the enthusiastic backing of delegates who had opposed them. He also saw in each candidate a number of weaknesses that their Republican opponents could exploit. Perpich had overstayed his welcome in the governor's office, and Wellstone was a brash leftist, a newcomer—untried and untested— running against a popular, well-funded political veteran.

"He'll pose no threat to Boschwitz," Frank declared.

Asked what he thought of the team of Wellstone and Perpich, Frank said he couldn't be happier. In between licks of a vanilla ice cream cone, he smiled broadly and dubbed the duo the "Tidy Bowl ticket," certain to go down the toilet in November.

While the Republicans gloated, some of the Democratic Party regulars sulked, especially over the choice of Wellstone. "He's unknown, ultraliberal. There hasn't been a history of candidates like that winning in our state," complained Congressman Tim Penny, a conservative DFLer who had backed Nichols.

Eleven days after the convention, Nichols held a press conference at the state capitol to announce that he would run against Wellstone in the Democratic primary in September: "I can win this election because I represent mainstream Democratic-Farmer-Laborites with traditional mainstream values," he said. Nichols also pointed to a recent Minnesota Poll that found that Democrats preferred Nichols as the candidate to challenge Boschwitz. Among the poll respondents who identified themselves as Democrats, 22 percent said they hoped he would get the party's endorsement; Berg was second, with 14 percent. Wellstone was last among self-identified Democrats, with only 10 percent supporting him for the endorsement. Nichols also held a substantial advantage over Wellstone in name recognition: 40 percent said they knew of the agriculture commissioner and only 20 percent said they knew of Wellstone.

Nichols pledged not to run a divisive primary campaign, saying he intended to focus on Boschwitz, not Wellstone. He even volunteered that it was unfair that Wellstone "gets painted with this ultraliberal image." He agreed with Wellstone on most issues, Nichols said, except abortion and gun control.

And it was on those two issues that Nichols expected to cripple the Democratic endorsee. He said members of the statewide DFL Pro Life Caucus, which comprised about 20 percent of the party delegates, had offered to volunteer on his campaign. With the gun issue, Nichols hoped to cut into Wellstone's support among the laborers on the Iron Range, just as Perpich had done in a successful gubernatorial primary campaign in 1982 against the party-backed candidate, Attorney General Warren Spannaus, who also favored gun control.

Wellstone never talked much about guns, but when he was asked he would say he supported the Minnesota law that required a seven-day waiting period and background checks on gun buyers. He was not an absolutist on the subject. He opposed banning handgun sales and did not advocate new laws limiting purchases of hunting rifles and shotguns. It was one of several examples of Wellstone's malleability and his refusal to be hamstrung by issues that were peripheral to his economic message.

Wellstone's strategy for the primary was to expand the grassroots nature of the campaign, particularly in his bases in the Twin Cities and on the Iron Range. But after his convention victory, he also knew his campaign had to be more extensive than a phone-tree operation. Now he was trying to reach all the Democratic voters in a state with a voting-age population of about 3 million, and not just 1,300 convention delegates. And that meant television.

While Wellstone had begun discussions with Twin Cities advertising executive William Hillsman in the summer of 1989, he had neither the money nor the need to air commercials during the caucus and convention fights. Now talks with Hillsman intensified. And although Hillsman's initial response to Wellstone had been lukewarm, the convention victory had impressed him. "I was looking at this campaign with a fairly skeptical eye," Hillsman said. But the convention victory "was a big deal. It said to me that these guys have the organization and the arm twisting they need to win." So Hillsman began recruiting a team that included some of the Twin Cities' best advertising talent, and they started mapping out a strategy.

Third Campaign Manager

In the meantime, Wellstone had to confront the loss of campaign manager Jeff Blodgett, who was scheduled to leave in July on a long-planned, around-the-world trip with his wife. Wellstone decided to turn the campaign over to Dick Senese, who had excelled in organizing the Iron Range and Duluth and had helped Blodgett in preparing the convention strategy. Senese brought a different demeanor to the campaign manager's office. Where Blodgett was high-strung and forceful, Senese was easygoing and quick to laugh. Blodgett ordered Wellstone around when he needed to; Senese was more willing to let the candidate or others decide matters. "Because of my background as a counselor and because of my constitution, I look for consensus," he said.

More importantly, however, Senese lacked statewide campaign experience. His biggest assignment before this was managing a city council race in a small Iron Range town. Although the staff liked Senese, losing Blodgett gave some of them the jitters. "It was confusing," recalled David Graham. "Jeff was leaving. Everyone was nervous."

Besides worrying about the personnel change, Wellstone knew that while he waited for Hillsman to organize the advertising arm of his campaign, he had to do something fresh to draw more attention to his campaign. His friends and advisers at Carleton reached the same conclusion. In the Carleton Stadium locker room after a noontime run around the campus one day in June, physics professor Mike Casper, math professor Sy Schuster, and English professor Ed Sostek were discussing the campaign and they agreed that Wellstone was not getting around the state with enough visibility. Reviewing an old strategy that called for Wellstone to walk across the state, Sostek threw out a new idea. He suggested that instead of campaigning on foot, Wellstone should get a bus outfitted with a platform on the rear that would provide him with the makings of a modern-day whistle-stop campaign. Casper immediately warmed to the idea: "I pushed very hard for a bus. That was something that fit the image of the campaign and was what Paul was all about," he said.

Wellstone had taken a stand against gimmickry in campaigning, but he gave in easily on this one. "I realized issues were not going to be enough. There had to be a distinctive style of campaigning," he said.

Senese and Robert Richmond, a college student who worked on the campaign as a field organizer, located just the right bus one day in mid-July when they got lost in the northern Twin Cities suburbs, where they were searching for a picnic hosted by a local Democratic Party committee. "We got lost as hell, and then Dick started screaming, 'Stop the car! There's our bus!' " Richmond recalled. The bus, painted baby blue, was sitting on a front lawn with a "for sale" sign in the window.

The campaign shelled out a very precious $3,500 for the 1968 Chevrolet school bus, which had more than 200,000 miles behind it. It already had been converted into a camper. The interior was appointed with a sink, a four-burner stove, and a refrigerator, none of which worked. Two lumpy beds were positioned over the rear wheels. The previous owner had fitted a porch onto the back of the bus, behind the rear emergency door, and it was perfect for use as a speaker's platform. Union members helped get it in running order, repainted it with the campaign's green and white colors, and affixed large Wellstone posters to its sides.

"It's Boschwitz's 6 million bucks versus our $3,500 bus," Wellstone shouted to crowds that gathered around the platform as he whistle-stopped through small towns. Before long, as Casper predicted, the green and white jalopy became a symbol for this penny-pinching crusade, an old-fashioned campaign that brought the candidate into towns, neighborhoods, farmyards, and factory parking lots. The bus quickly became such a celebrity in its own right—mostly because of television coverage— that it was in demand at parades and county fairs with or without the candidate.

For all its romantic appeal and strategic value, the bus was a headache. It guzzled gas at a rate of six miles per gallon—an ironic note considering Wellstone's strong energy conservation policies—and it consumed almost as much oil. One day it burned four quarts on the fifty-mile trip from St. Paul to North-field. It spent more time in the repair shop than on the campaign trail. The brakes failed. A piston cracked. The gas gauge didn't work. Fan belts snapped. Diesel mechanics at the mines on the Iron Range and meatpackers in southern Minnesota patched the bus together whenever it broke down in their area, which was often. Still, the repair bills mounted. "We were taking in $3,000 a day (in donations) and sometimes we'd spend $3,000 on the goddamn bus," said Sam Kaplan, now Wellstone's finance chair-man.

The bus was so unreliable that a backup car was assigned to trail it to pick up the stranded candidate and passengers and de-liver them to the next stop. Each lurch, backfire, and odd noise from the bus struck fear in the heart of its first driver, David Graham. He worried that the media would write about the latest breakdown as an indicator of a campaign that was going no-where. In fact, by the end of July, Wellstone, some campaign staffers, and even Senese feared that the campaign was begin-ning to stall.

Media coverage was thin during these summer months and the timing of campaign swings often misfired. The low point came in the third week in July, during a tour of the farthest reaches of the sparsely populated farmland of northwestern Minnesota. The chief destination was the town of Oslo, popu-lation 400, which was hosting a bean feed and parade. Well-stone expected that his visit to an area usually overlooked by major candidates would draw attention from the local reporters and the media in the North Dakota border city of Grand Forks, twenty miles away.

"We got up there and there was nobody at all—no press," recalled Graham. Reporters had been told Wellstone would be there, but no specific appointments had been made. Graham and Liz Borg raced through the town, searching in vain for someone with a reporter's notepad, a tape recorder, or a TV camera. They found no one.

"Paul was really down . . . and he just blew up," Graham said. As he described Wellstone's anger, he imitated the candidate: " 'There's no way we can win this if we keep doing this!' " Graham said. "He was tired, too, but he was getting really angry." There were no media interviews scheduled for the next day, either, so Borg feverishly dialed her local contacts and found someone at a radio station willing to let Wellstone come in the next morning and appear on a talk show.

The Oslo trip was just one of the mounting problems. More campaign workers were being added to the staff, but none had any more experience than the original crew. Nor did they have the proper connections to the party establishment, so there was little help coming from those with influence and money. Lisa Goodman saw this virtually every day when she went to the downtown St. Paul post office, where the Wellstone campaign kept a mailbox. Goodman, a staff member in charge of fundraising, recalled days when there were only one or two checks in the box, usually for relatively small amounts. And on some days there wasn't a single donation. "It was really depressing—just awful," Goodman said.

"This is what I called the black period of the campaign," said Dan Cramer. "It was hell. We didn't know what we were doing for the most part. We were all working incredibly hard, but we weren't moving forward."

The Professionals

Part of the problem, Senese acknowledged after the campaign, was his lack of experience. When he took over as campaign manager on June 11, his twenty-eighth birthday, he had never held an important role in a statewide race. And while he had

proved his skills as an organizer on the Iron Range and in Duluth, he had never expected, when he joined the Wellstone campaign, to be responsible for more than one of the state's eight
congressional districts. When he was suddenly put in charge of
the entire operation, he was unsure of himself. "I did feel a little
out of my league," he said. Rather than expanding and directing
the statewide effort, Senese took the time to organize the campaign's internal structure. He created a table of organization and
put in place payroll and accounting systems. "I probably didn't
involve myself with the political intrigue because I didn't know
how exactly," he said. Compounding the problem was that none
of Senese's staff members was in a position to do better; none of
them had the experience that he lacked.

At home, Wellstone told his wife, Sheila, about the logistical
mishaps and his fears that the campaign was sputtering. Sheila
was not intimately involved in the campaign on a day-to-day basis because she continued to work full time in the Northfield
High School library, to look after their teenage son, Mark, and
to manage the household. But once again, she stepped in to play
a pivotal role in the campaign's events. On July 29 she telephoned Pat Forciea at his home to explain the campaign's
troubles and ask if he could recommend solutions. Forciea had
just returned home from a round of golf at his private country
club, and as he listened to Sheila, waves of guilt crashed over
him.

Forciea had been getting more involved in the campaign
through the spring and summer, attending meetings and talking
frequently on the phone with Blodgett, but he mostly focused on
his job as an executive at a politically connected municipal bond
house, Miller & Schroeder Financial, and tended to his golf
game. He and his wife, Cathy, who also had worked on the
Dukakis campaign staff, had promised each other that they
would sit out the 1990 election cycle for the sake of their sanity

and bank accounts. But at the time of Sheila Wellstone's call, Cathy Forciea was seriously considering an offer from Lou De-Mars to manage his long-shot congressional campaign in Minnesota's Third Congressional District, a Republican stronghold encompassing the suburbs to the south and west of Minneapolis. When Cathy Forciea decided, with her husband's urging, to accept that job, he felt free to join the Wellstone campaign. Pat Forciea recalled:

> Paul told both of us a hundred times all through the fall, winter, and spring that he could understand why we were not getting involved. He went through all the motions of saying the right things. But it got pretty damn hard to look in the mirror in my own case, and actually it was impossible to justify not getting involved.

Forciea remembered Sheila's call as a sincere plea for help, with no hint of recrimination for his modest involvement up to that point. Within twenty-four hours after the call, Forciea had decided to take a leave from his job and join the Wellstone campaign full time as its top strategist, a job he performed without salary.

At thirty-one, Forciea already was considered one of the state's sharpest political tacticians. He grew up in an Iron Range mining town in northeastern Minnesota, where he was reared on hockey and Republicanism. A photograph of Richard Nixon hung over the fireplace in his parents' living room. Forciea turned out to be a fair hockey player—he was a goalie for a second-division college team—and a fiercely partisan Democrat. In his youth, his thin frame and narrow face brought him the nickname of Mouse. A few years and a few pounds were kind to him, and by the time he was in his late twenties, he cut quite a yuppieish figure: wavy black hair, oval wire-rimmed glasses, stylish dark suits or sport coats, and outrageously loud ties.

He had an easygoing, soft-spoken manner in private. In the political arena, he had an air of confidence and a cutting tongue that made people listen. Forciea's most important talents were managing people and manipulating the media; he understood the news business like few other politicos and was masterful in the art of spin-doctoring and news management.

After working for Minnesota congressman James Oberstar in Washington and leading his unsuccessful bid to win the DFL endorsement for a run against Boschwitz in 1984, Forciea spent a few years with the Twin Cities-based bond firm, then broke into presidential politics as a walk-on for the Dukakis campaign. In the spring of 1987, Boston Celtics star forward Kevin McHale, an Iron Range buddy of Forciea's, helped arrange a couple of meetings with Dukakis in Boston for Forciea and his partner in politics, Gary Cerkvenik. The pair convinced Dukakis that Minnesota could be a strategic state in his march to the party's nomination, and Dukakis put them to work. They got an early jump on the other six candidates in Minnesota, and their meticulous planning and organizing produced Dukakis's first primary win outside his native New England. Forciea became something of a troubleshooter for Dukakis and contributed significantly to primary victories in Wisconsin and California.

Forciea and Wellstone had been friends since 1982, and their regard for each other grew during the 1988 presidential campaign, despite the tension of being the state leaders of rival camps for the nomination. Wellstone impressed Forciea because he was the only Jackson advocate and the only DFL Party official to do something virtually every day for the Dukakis camp after the national convention. Forciea felt that Wellstone had matured as a leader and as a spokesman for progressive causes. He also was convinced that he had a political future. That's why Forciea, during the meetings in January and February of 1989, had frowned on the idea of Wellstone's challenging Boschwitz: "I feared what a loss would do to that future. It seemed like such a risky thing to roll the dice on. . . . Why throw away twenty or thirty years of opportunities for him for this incredible long shot?"

By the summer of 1990, Forciea was more optimistic about the odds of Wellstone's winning. He was impressed with each victory the campaign scored. Through his work on the campaign, he saw firsthand the energy and zeal of the staff and volunteers. And he knew that more than anything else they needed a seasoned hand to guide them.

Like the recruitment of Sam Kaplan, the addition of Forciea gave the staff an enormous boost of confidence. They knew of his successes in the Dukakis campaign and they knew he could pick up the phone and reach the major donors and other party heavyweights who were not returning the campaign's calls. "People were more impressed with Forciea than with Paul," said David Graham. "We knew how well he ran the Dukakis campaign. He was on television all the time. He was this mystical kind of figure." Forciea was, in Liz Borg's unique phraseology, "a celebutante."

Sheila Wellstone's call to Forciea was made without Senese's knowledge. But Senese himself had been talking frequently with Forciea and he welcomed the reinforcement that Forciea represented. "I never questioned the move," said Senese. "I thought it was great to call Pat."

One of the first moves Forciea made was to bring in another veteran campaign worker. Within days after Forciea signed on, thirty-three-year-old John Blackshaw packed up his Jeep Cherokee 4x4 and left his law practice in Los Angeles to join the Wellstone team. Forciea had met Blackshaw during the 1988 Dukakis campaign, when Blackshaw was a top field director for the California primary and an advance man on the national staff.

Forciea had a number of motives in hiring an outsider to take over as Wellstone's press secretary. A friend of Wellstone's, Moorhead State University journalism professor Dean Alger, was in charge of press relations, but despite his academic expertise in the field of journalism and politics, he had never managed the press side of a statewide campaign. Wellstone had grown increasingly frustrated at the lack of press coverage, partly because his expectations about media interest during that stage of the campaign were unrealistically high, but also because scheduling lapses convinced him there were problems within his own operation. Forciea recognized the problem too, and he knew Blackshaw had had extensive contact with the press during the Dukakis campaign.

Forciea had another reason for bringing Blackshaw to Minnesota. During the Dukakis campaign, Blackshaw had met Cathy Forciea's sister, Barb Lawrence, who volunteered for the California primary. They began dating, and when Lawrence returned to her teaching job in Minnesota, the two continued a long-distance courtship. Blackshaw was drawn to Minnesota by two kinds of romance, the conventional kind and the adventure of a long-shot campaign, which he preferred to his corporate law practice.

Blackshaw had been involved in California campaigns since Robert F. Kennedy's fateful race in the 1968 Democratic primary. By 1980 he had worked his way to Capitol Hill, where he was a member of the staff of liberal Senator Harrison Williams of New Jersey. He joined Williams's office one month before Williams was indicted in the Abscam scandal. When Williams resigned in May 1982, Blackshaw left the Senate, too. He marked time for a year in Washington, mostly working as a waiter and as a volunteer at the National Zoo, where, as part of its Panda Watch, he was a scientific voyeur who peeped in on the pandas to observe their mating habits. He also jumped into a congressional race in Virginia.

Blackshaw returned to California to attend law school and was doing corporate litigation when Forciea called in July 1990. Three days after he left Los Angeles, the vegetarian lawyer reported for work as the campaign's press secretary. Wearing a suit, he walked into an office where most people were dressed in jeans and open-collared shirts. Was he the type of "slick handler" from whom Wellstone said he would never take directions? Others had been working on the campaign for more than a year, and now Blackshaw was being brought in as a top official.

Although Forciea engineered Blackshaw's hiring, it was done with the approval of Dick Senese and Jeff Blodgett, who had interviewed Blackshaw by phone a few weeks earlier. The two not only liked what they heard on the phone, they were impressed by Blackshaw's credentials. So was Wellstone, who said he was not at all bothered by bringing in an outsider.

"I didn't frankly give it a second thought," Wellstone said. "Pat thought very highly of him, and we needed additional help. His presence didn't automatically make us slick. He was counterbalanced by plenty of people who were new at it."

Forciea warned Blackshaw that he would have to move slowly, and Blackshaw recognized the delicacy of the situation himself. "I was a complete outsider," he said. "I was this hired gun and there were these devotees of Paul Wellstone who had been with him for a hundred years and they're willing to die for the guy. So I had to be very sensitive to that."

Although Blackshaw sensed the tension, nothing was said overtly to him, and he immediately established himself with a mixture of strong guidance and deference. "He was very open about the fact that he was new and didn't know the state," said David Graham, who was one of the first to become acquainted with Blackshaw when Blackshaw joined him and Wellstone on a campaign swing to northern Minnesota. "He was very open about the fact that that was our expertise, and we needed to share that with him." Blackshaw's ignorance of Minnesota was captured and turned into a running joke when, during a scheduling meeting, he mistakenly called the Fargo-Moorhead area "Margo-Forehead."

Rather than being jealous, Graham and the other core staff members were relieved by the addition of Blackshaw to the team. "It was a comforting thing for me," said Graham. "Here was someone who knew about the media. Here was this new blood, someone else to look up to" besides Forciea.

The hiring of a second seasoned pro only days after Forciea had signed up was a fortunate move for the campaign. Together, Forciea and Blackshaw supplied the maturity and experience to harness the energy of a fuzzy-cheeked staff.

The Ad Man

In contrast to the dewy-eyed twentysomethings who pervaded his staff, Bill Hillsman at thirty-seven was a hardened pragmatist. Even when he was a student at Carleton College, he took a dim view of the activist politics that consumed Wellstone. When Wellstone and other teachers canceled classes, held teach-ins, and staged other events during a Vietnam War moratorium action, Hillsman skipped the protests and used the free time to play softball and drink beer. "For me it was basically passé," Hillsman said. "The whole world wasn't exactly watching what was going on in the middle of farm country in Minnesota."

If anything, Hillsman reacted to the Vietnam protests like a love-it-or-leave-it conservative. When students held a Ho Chi Minh victory party at a college rathskeller, Hillsman thought it was an affront to those who had lost loved ones in the war, so he showed up with a few beefy football players and told the revelers that he had a brother who died in Vietnam. It was a lie, but it had its intended effect. "The party pretty much died down after that," he recalled.

Unlike the other Carleton alumni who joined the Wellstone team, Hillsman never took one of Wellstone's classes, and he did not idolize the professor. They did become fairly good friends, though, through two of Hillsman's best friends who were close to Wellstone, and they saw each other often even after Hillsman graduated in 1975. "He was very committed in the right way," Hillsman recalled.

When Wellstone went shopping for advertising talent a couple of months after he declared his candidacy, he turned to Hillsman because he was the only person he knew in the field. As a vice president of Kauffman Stewart Advertising in Minneapolis, Hillsman conducted business with legendary bluntness and a self-confidence that bordered on arrogance. He earned this reputation by leaving an ad firm when he became convinced that the company was compromising its integrity to retain a $30 million account. Hillsman grabbed the largest layout pad he could find and scribbled this message: "This place sucks! I quit!" Late on a Friday night, he propped the pad on his boss's chair and walked out.

Hillsman was open to the idea of working on Wellstone's campaign, but first he gave the candidate a dose of reality. Wellstone would need at least $2 million to $3 million for advertising alone, he said, an amount the campaign would never come close to raising in total, let alone for advertising. In a December 1989 letter, Hillsman also impressed on Wellstone that he had no intention of joining him on a quixotic journey:

If you aren't in this for the duration, if you harbor any ideas that your campaign is worth it just to spotlight and open up new issues for discussion, I and the people I would be able to bring into the campaign are not interested. It is not in our nature to open up new areas of discussion; we are trained to get results.

Hillsman held off committing himself to the campaign until the spring of 1990, when he became convinced that Wellstone's candidacy and his campaign organization were legitimate. As Wellstone moved closer to securing the Democratic endorsement, Hillsman began enlisting about two dozen colleagues from the Twin Cities ad industry to collaborate under the umbrella of his freelance business, North Woods Advertising. While a handful joined Hillsman because of their commitment to liberal causes, many signed on because they were flattered to be selected for his all-star team. Once Hillsman got signs of interest from the creative talent, he invited them to meet with Wellstone. "The key recruiting tactic I used was to get Paul in a room and talk to them," Hillsman said.

Judy Wittenberg, an executive producer at the Minneapolis ad firm BBDO, attended one of those sessions not out of interest in politics, but because she felt honored to be invited. She became a believer after listening to Wellstone explain his issues and his belief that politics was relevant to everyday life. After the meeting in a conference room in Sam Kaplan's law offices, Wittenberg approached Wellstone and told him that she could tell he was sincere. "She told me, 'If you stay that way you have a chance of winning,' " Wellstone remembered.

"It was his passion for what he was doing that really hooked me," Wittenberg said. "I couldn't believe I had met someone in politics who spoke like a real person and meant it."

Once Hillsman had assembled his team, he gave the members

copies of Ronald Reagan's 1984 presidential campaign ads and Rudy Boschwitz's ads from his first Senate campaign in 1978. Hillsman believed that both ad campaigns were masterpieces.

In 1978, Hillsman told the team, Boschwitz effectively portrayed himself as an outsider—which, ironically, Wellstone was now doing twelve years later. Despite his personal wealth, Boschwitz cultivated the image of a common man. He wore casual clothes in his ads and projected friendliness and freshness.

Produced in close consultation with Baltimore ad executive Robert Goodman, who would direct Boschwitz's 1984 and 1990 ad campaigns as well, the ads played heavily on the I'm-on-your-side theme. In 1978 Goodman skillfully showed Boschwitz listening and talking to real Minnesotans in classic settings: with dairy farmers in southern Minnesota, a snowplow driver in northern Minnesota, a feed store operator. There was even a Boschwitz song, "Gather Round Minnesota, Gather Round," a country-and-western type ballad that gave Boschwitz a kind of mythic image as a champion of the people.

As good as Boschwitz's 1978 ads were, Hillsman said he considered the spots produced by Reagan's so-called Tuesday Team in 1984 to be

> the high-level mark for political advertising. It was outstanding work. Totally inaccurate, but outstanding work. It was propaganda in the ultimate sense—the "Morning Again in America" theme. The bear in the woods ad. That was a brilliant ad. They tapped into this idea that people didn't just vote with their head. There's a lot of emotion. Their ads looked like ads; they didn't look like political ads.

That was Hillsman's sacred principle: if a political ad looks like a political ad—too preachy, too serious, too cautious, and, worst of all, dull—then it is a failure. He knew that nothing will make a TV viewer run to the kitchen or the bathroom faster than the sight of a politician in a suit boasting or lecturing.

"I cannot think of a body of work that's more hated than political ads, except maybe car dealer ads," said Hillsman. "Political ads don't give you anything back."

When Hillsman went to work after the state convention, party members and even Wellstone's own teammates were in a dither over the candidate's 17 percent name recognition. "People were just panicking about that," Hillsman recalled. "They were yelling, 'The sky is falling.' " Hillsman was undaunted: Wellstone, after all, was a product that had not yet been marketed through the mass media. "All the people in the party were more concerned about Paul than they needed to be, because nobody outside the party knew him," Hillsman said. "We had a blank canvas to work with."

With the first commercial Hillsman began to fill in that canvas. He wanted the first ad to serve two purposes. It would introduce Wellstone and give viewers a feel for his unconventional campaign, and it would warn people to look with suspicion on Boschwitz's commercials. "We wanted to get Paul's face, his name, and his personality out there, and we wanted to get his message out and to keep harping on this money thing," Hillsman said. "So every time someone saw a Boschwitz commercial, it would reinforce what we were trying to lay the groundwork for: he's trying to buy the election."

On a bright August morning, exactly one month and one day before the primary, Wellstone found himself surrounded by the image makers he so often claimed to despise. Lugging storyboards, waving microphones, and pointing a film camera, they came to Northfield and took control of his life for two days. The candidate, who had publicly sworn on the opening day of his campaign that he would not be a video-created creature and would not run a television-dominated campaign, had given himself to the marketeers. It was a moment that Wellstone later described as inevitable. "I never dreamed we'd be able to win without any ads," he said. "I knew we had to have a presence on TV. The question was what kind of ads. I didn't want them to be hack attack ads. I didn't want them to be manipulative."

Wellstone saw most political advertising as "simple jingo crap" that pitched candidates as if they were soap or breakfast cereal. The inherent limits of television advertising reduced complicated issues to thirty seconds of drivel and corrupted attempts to foster a meaningful discussion of ideas. At their worst, Wellstone said, political commercials were "morally reprehensible": they distorted an opponent's positions and exploited voters' fears and prejudices.

The producer on this first day of shooting, Judy Wittenberg, sensed Wellstone's wariness and deliberately egged him on by referring to him as "the product":

> In the ad biz, every commercial has to have a shot of the product, no matter what it is. It's always the part of the commercial that the client loves, but it's usually the dullest part. . . . This time we were selling Paul Wellstone, so he was the product. I'd say, "It's time for the product shot. Bring the product over here." I never did let up.

Wellstone knew she was kidding, but he was not amused. "I didn't like it one bit. It really pissed me off," he said.

"You could just sort of see him bristle each time she said it," said Hillsman. "I'm sure that didn't help Paul's feelings about the whole deal."

The "product's" suspicions were soon heightened by Wittenberg's zany directions. Against backdrops that included his family, his house, his son's farm, a stream, a hospital, a school, a fac-

Wellstone joins nurses on the picket line while campaigning in southern Minnesota during the primary. His long record of supporting striking workers earned him the ardent backing of many rank-and-file union members. (Photo by Richard Sennott © 1990 *Star Tribune*/Minneapolis-St. Paul)

During the primary, Wellstone bought a beat-up bus to give him added visibility. Here, he campaigns in Duluth with state representative Willard Munger. (Photo by Terry Gydesen)

Rudy Boschwitz talks to voters at the Minnesota State Fair in late August or early September 1990. (Photo by Terry Gydesen)

Wellstone and his wife, Sheila, wave from the back of the campaign bus in Rochester, four days before the election. Wellstone traveled by bus that day to draw a contrast between his $3,500 vehicle and Air Force One, which that day brought President George Bush to Rochester for a Boschwitz campaign rally. (Photo by Charles Bjorgen © 1990 *Star Tribune*/Minneapolis-St. Paul)

Wellstone's first and strongest base of support was on the Iron Range, where residents liked his aggressive populism. Here he shares a laugh with residents in Hibbing. (Photo by Terry Gydesen)

Campaign Manager John Blackshaw *(left)* and top strategist Pat Forciea *(right)* confer on the front steps of the Minnesota State Capitol in St. Paul after a Wellstone press conference. (Photo by Terry Gydesen)

Wellstone addresses his staff and volunteers in his run-down campaign headquarters in a blue-collar section of St. Paul. (Photo by Terry Gydesen)

Wellstone visits a commodities distribution location in north Minneapolis. He had strong ties to Minnesota's black communities because of his work on Jesse Jackson's presidential campaign and his long history of advocacy for poor people. (Photo by Terry Gydesen)

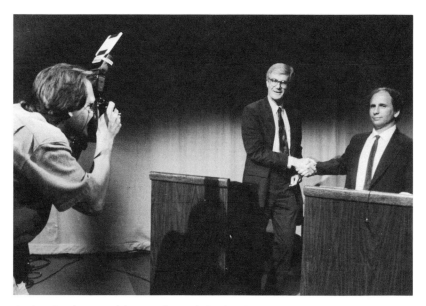

A relaxed and overconfident Boschwitz shakes hands with a pensive Wellstone before their first debate, which was held in Washington, D.C., because congressional gridlock delayed Boschwitz's return to Minnesota. (Photo by Joey McLeister © 1990 *Star Tribune*/Minneapolis-St. Paul)

Wellstone Field Director Liz Borg and Deputy Field Director Danny Cramer spend a late night on the phones in campaign headquarters. (Photo by Joey McLeister © 1990 *Star Tribune*/Minneapolis-St. Paul)

With Wellstone closing in on him in the polls, Boschwitz delivers his most
spirited performance during a debate broadcast on WCCO-AM Radio on Halloween.
(Photo by Joey McLeister © 1990 *Star Tribune*/Minneapolis-St. Paul)

Thousands of volunteers worked through
the night before Election Day, distributing
literature throughout Minneapolis and St.
Paul. Here volunteers check a map of
Minneapolis before heading out. (Photo
by Terry Gydesen)

Surrounded by his family, Wellstone soaks in the applause and cheers shortly after midnight, when news media were projecting him to be the winner. (Photo by Joey McLeister © 1990 *Star Tribune*/Minneapolis-St. Paul)

Wellstone, accompanied by Sheila and Marcia, waves from the back of his bus as it departs from Minnesota, heading for Washington, D.C., and Wellstone's inauguration. (Photo by Terry Gydesen)

tory, and city hall, Wellstone was told to walk into the camera frame from the left, pause, quickly utter a few words, and then rush out of the frame to the right. When they were set up in front of a factory, Wittenberg told Wellstone to walk past the camera quickly, without stopping to say anything.

"Our children were lying on the sidewalk laughing," said Sheila Wellstone. "They thought it was the funniest thing they'd ever seen, with Paul running around in front of the house."

Off camera, Wellstone quietly stewed and wondered whether he was participating in precisely the kind of advertising he abhorred. He had only a vague idea of what the ad would look like because no one had shown him the storyboard—the handful of sketches that act as a sort of visual script for the spot. Wellstone wasn't shown the boards because Hillsman was afraid he would refuse to go along. "We thought he'd say this is crazy and ridiculous," said Hillsman. After lunch, when Wellstone was shown the storyboard, his suspicions were not entirely abated. He worried he would look silly, but he continued to follow orders.

While Hillsman, Wittenberg, and their crew wrapped up the location work and went back to the editing room, another set of Wellstone ads was being produced by Gerald Austin, national campaign manager for Jesse Jackson in 1988. Austin had called Wellstone in July from Columbus, Ohio, where he ran a national political consulting firm, and volunteered his help free of charge. Hoping to offset Wellstone's ultraliberal image, Austin's ads focused on Wellstone's family—especially his wife, Sheila, and their twenty-one-year-old daughter, Marcia.

On August 28, Hillsman previewed a rough cut of his ad for Pat Forciea, John Blackshaw, and Austin. Hillsman knew that the offbeat ad, which he called "Fast-Paced Paul," represented a breakthrough in political advertising. He assured Wellstone's advisers that it would wake up television viewers.

"I was pitching this to them, and they didn't have much to say," Hillsman recalled. "It was pretty much silence. They were saying semi-nice things and you knew they didn't believe a word of it." He was right. Forciea thought the ad, which had cost about $9,800 to shoot and edit, was terrible. "I was scared to death we had made this incredibly huge investment, and it had been a waste of money," said Forciea.

Hillsman refused to back down, and Forciea consented to let him finish the editing. A week later, Hillsman delivered the final version to Forciea, who instantly recognized the improvements. But he was paralyzed over whether to actually put it on the air. The ad was unconventional, witty, and unlike any political advertising Forciea had ever seen.

The ad begins with Wellstone standing outside in short-sleeved shirt and tie. Addressing the camera, he immediately takes on Rudy Boschwitz instead of Jim Nichols, his Democratic primary opponent. "Hi, I'm Paul Wellstone," he starts, "and I'm running for the United States Senate from Minnesota. Unlike my opponent, I don't have $6 million, so I'm going to have to talk fast."

Then Wellstone literally races through the commercial, stopping for a breather and a few words, such as "I'll lead the fight for national health care," in front of an appropriate backdrop before he rushes off to the right and enters again from the left for the next scene. By the end of the thirty-second spot, he's running across the screen at fast-forward speed. He looks like a blurred hybrid of Harpo Marx and a Keystone Kop as he jumps into his campaign bus, which speeds away as the narrator says, "Paul Wellstone won't slow down after he's elected."

Forciea showed the spot to his political friends, who were aghast at its undignified nature. Pat Milan, a former television political reporter who was press secretary to Minnesota attorney general Hubert H. Humphrey III, said, "I loved it when I saw it, but it sacred the hell out of me." Milan showed it to other aides in Humphrey's office, and the overwhelming reaction was that the ad was funny, but they disapprovingly warned that Wellstone didn't "look senatorial."

"I don't know how many times I heard that line," Milan said.

Forciea received the same feedback. Many Democratic operatives were certain that Wellstone had no chance of winning, so they hoped that at least he would not embarrass the party. Political insiders said that Wellstone's advertising group, composed of political neophytes, might know how to sell snowmobiles, airlines, and other goods in the marketplace, but they knew nothing about selling a candidate in the political arena. To the regulars, this ad was heresy.

For seventy-two hours after the tape was placed in his hands, Forciea did nothing. It was now only a week before the primary, and newspaper polls showed that the race with Jim Nichols was tight. In one newspaper poll, Wellstone trailed by 6 percentage points.

Finally, Forciea bought air time for "Fast-Paced Paul," but at the last minute he panicked. "There were several points in the campaign where I was arriving at forks in the road, and this one fork looked like it went right over the cliff," Forciea said. "I was just uptight about how unorthodox it was. It was a difficult decision and I also didn't want to anger Paul"—who also argued against using it.

In place of "Fast-Paced Paul," Forciea ran considerably less risky spots created by Austin. But these pieces, featuring Paul, Sheila, and Marcia, did not seem to have any real impact. The only thing they did was push Hillsman to the brink of resignation. He was expecting to see "Fast-Paced Paul" air, and he was stunned to see one of Austin's ads.

"I was at home watching television, and my jaw falls through the floor," Hillsman recalled. For the next two hours, he received calls from Wittenberg and others on his team, whom he had assured that he had been given complete control over the advertising. "When these commercials started appearing, I got pretty upset," he said. "It was destroying my credibility with the people I was recruiting."

When Hillsman drafted a resignation letter and threatened to quit, and when Wellstone showed no sign of moving in the polls, Forciea reversed his decision. He took to heart a discussion he had had in a bar one night with Milan and Austin. According to Milan, "We said we don't have a chance in hell of winning [against Boschwitz], so let's just break all the rules."

On the afternoon of September 5, with Wellstone on his way to campaign on the Iron Range, Forciea decided to run the ad that night on the six o'clock news, during *Wheel of Fortune,* and on the ten o'clock news. He didn't tell anyone but Blackshaw—not even Wellstone.

"When it ran, BOOM!" Forciea recalled. "The phones went off."

While Vanna White was still turning letters on *Wheel of Fortune,* Forciea's friends were on the phone telling him it was not only the best political ad they had ever seen, but the best ad, period. "It had the impact of a knockout punch," Forciea concluded.

The Primary

A knockout punch was desperately needed: until the ad ran, Wellstone was trailing Nichols on the official scorecards—the media polls—despite the fact that his quirky opponent was barely bothering to campaign. Nichols continued to work full time as agriculture commissioner. While Wellstone knocked around the state in his bus, Nichols was confined to the state capitol for most of each week, leaving only nights and weekends to chase votes. He visited the county fairs or parades that could be reached on a weekend's drive, but he was rarely seen outside the metropolitan area.

For a campaign staff, Nichols continued to rely heavily on his wife and daughters, who ran the operation out of the family room of their home in a St. Paul suburb. When it was time to assemble more lawn signs, the work was done in the garage and driveway. Instead of committing himself to a full-fledged campaign, Nichols was relying on the power of Minnesota Citizens Concerned for Life (MCCL), the state's largest and best-organized antiabortion organization, which had a grassroots base that far exceeded the reach of all the state's abortion-rights groups. He was also counting on the fact that he was better known than Wellstone.

Despite Nichols's half-hearted effort, his strategy seemed to be paying off. In one survey of likely primary voters, Nichols had a 29 to 23 percent edge over Wellstone; a whopping 45 percent were undecided. Regardless of who was favored, political writers interpreted the poll as a sign that both candidates had failed to excite voters and that neither had a chance against Boschwitz. Faced with this discouraging news, the Wellstone campaign stepped up its efforts to reach voters.

Scott Adams, who had helped start the canvassing operation for the Minnesota Public Interest Research Group, argued that the campaign should launch a similar door-to-door effort. Several dozen people, some of the most energetic community organizers in the state, were hired in August to carry Wellstone's message to the front porches of Minneapolis and St. Paul residents. Day after day they promoted Wellstone's name, recruited volunteers, sold buttons, and begged for donations. Although they occasionally returned with a substantial check, most canvassers brought back fistfuls of one-, five-, and ten-dollar bills.

The canvassing caught Boschwitz's attention. After Adams placed ads in Twin Cities newspapers to seek canvassers, Boschwitz dashed off a note to Wellstone saying he was tempted to apply for one of the jobs. Boschwitz's comment was relayed around the office, and it confirmed what many staff members suspected. "Good," Scott Adams said when he saw the note. "He's even more arrogant about it than we thought."

After surveying the scene for a few weeks, John Blackshaw gradually began to assert himself. In addition to arranging press conferences and campaign swings designed to draw media attention, he started making decisions on field operations and on Wellstone's schedule. "I was a little concerned at one point about how in the hell we were going to get this done," he said.

About two weeks before the primary, concerned that the organizing in northeastern Minnesota was not as strong as it needed to be to overcome Nichols's strength in the rural areas of the state, Wellstone asked Senese to return to Duluth and take over the field operations there until the primary. Senese agreed without complaint, even though he recognized "that things are shifting" at campaign headquarters and that his absence would give Blackshaw even more freedom to direct the campaign.

As the September 11 primary approached, Wellstone's grassroots organizing began to pay off. His staff began to track a big swing in the electorate, and they were convinced from their telephone calling that they were going to bury Nichols, contrary to what the polls said. Their candidate's message was getting through, and his supporters were promising to go to the polls and vote.

In the closing stretch, Nichols turned increasingly to the antiabortion movement for support. On the Sunday before the primary, MCCL volunteers swept through church parking lots and the streets around churches. The flyers they slipped under car windshield wipers urged antiabortion voters to defeat pro-choice candidates like Wellstone.

Wellstone, who lives only two blocks from a Catholic church, found one of the flyers on his car that morning. "When I saw that flyer on my car, ohhhhh," he said, clutching his chest, "my heart went to my stomach, because I figured a whole lot of people saw that flyer on their cars everywhere."

They did, and on primary day antiabortion groups turned out in force, defeating abortion-rights candidates in both guber-natorial primaries. In fact, Republican gubernatorial endorsee Jon Grunseth, a conservative, overcame double-digit deficits re-ported by opinion polls in August to defeat Arne Carlson, a moderate Republican who supported abortion rights.

In the wake of the U.S. Supreme Court's *Webster* decision, which put greater power to regulate abortion in the hands of states, the MCCL had stepped up its activities, focusing on the Republican and Democratic gubernatorial primaries and a handful of state legislative races. The effect did not spill over into the Senate primary, where Wellstone appeared to have bro-ken the pattern of Minnesota Democratic politics. To the sur-prise of everyone but his staff, Wellstone's strong showing in the Twin Cities and the Iron Range carried him to an astounding 60 to 35 percent margin over Nichols. Wellstone received 226,306 votes to Nichols's 129,302; a third candidate, Gene Schenk, got 19,379. It was the first time Wellstone had ever won a statewide election.

Wellstone's coalition of labor unions, liberals, progressives, environmentalists, and supporters of abortion rights finally pre-vailed over Nichols's line-up of supporters—the antiabortion advocates, opponents of gun control, sportsmen, and farmers who typically have played a key role in deciding Democratic pri-maries.

In addition to taking the Iron Range by a margin of more than four to one, Wellstone won with big spreads in places like the East Side and North End of St. Paul, in blue-collar, Catholic, white neighborhoods that had not been friendly to liberal candidates in the past. In precincts in North St. Paul, for example, where Boschwitz beat Democrat Joan Growe in 1984, and where Republican senator David Durenberger beat Democrat Hubert H. Humphrey III in the 1988 Senate race, Wellstone defeated Nichols by margins of nearly three to one. Ramsey County, comprised of St. Paul and its northern suburbs, which Boschwitz carried in 1984, went for Wellstone over Nichols by a two-and-a-half to one margin. Wellstone scored well in the suburbs and also in rural areas. In the northern suburb of Anoka, for example, Wellstone defeated Nichols by nearly a two-to-one margin despite the community's blue-collar makeup and the fact that it had a record of electing Republicans and conservative Democrats to the state legislature. Of the seven counties that make up the Twin Cities metropolitan area, Wellstone won six and lost the seventh by only fifty-four votes.

And while Nichols won the farm vote, Wellstone actually stole a handful of rural farming counties, including Clay and Clearwater in the northwest and Goodhue, Olmsted, and Blue Earth in the south and southeast. Those were places where Wellstone could not expect to win against Boschwitz, but he had to get enough votes there to make his lead in Minneapolis and St. Paul and the Iron Range stand up on November 6. The primary returns were tremendously encouraging in that regard.

The fact that Wellstone was the only pro-choice candidate to survive the primary captured some attention, but the power of his grassroots organizing was overlooked in most analyses. The pundits did not realize that his energized forces were going door to door not just to drop literature, but also to engage people in conversation and to make arrangements to get them to the polls.

In parts of the state his supporters organized as thoroughly as if they were running a city council race in a small town.

Political insiders attributed Wellstone's landslide to the fact that Nichols never organized a serious campaign. Like most other political pros, Boschwitz failed to comprehend the excitement and energy of Wellstone's supporters or the significance of his coalition. The morning after the primary, knowing he was going to have an underfinanced liberal college professor as his opponent, Boschwitz brimmed with confidence. "Paul is certainly not as strong a candidate as might have been fielded," he said in a speaker-phone call from Washington, D.C., to a roomful of cheerful Republican legislators gathered at the state capitol. At one point, Boschwitz was bold enough to suggest that a twenty-point margin in November was likely.

A few minutes after the Republican press conference, Wellstone and his bus rattled up to the capitol steps. The new Democratic nominee for the U.S. Senate stepped off the bus and greeted and joked with an assembly of reporters. When he was told of Boschwitz's boast, Wellstone became indignant. "Boy, he's making a mistake," he shot back. "This is going to be a very serious race, and we're going to win it."

Fourth Campaign Manager

Wellstone spent the rest of the day flying to three cities to meet with reporters and generate some publicity. Forciea accompanied Wellstone and assured him that the margin of victory, as much as the victory itself, would give him a big boost. "The important thing about the size of the margin is the impact it has on political insiders," Forciea said to the political science professor. "If you beat Nichols by 2 percent, people would be saying, 'How are you going to beat Boschwitz?' "

As the chartered plane made its way from St. Paul to Duluth,

Forciea assessed the dangers of working with two advertising teams. "We're going to keep going with both, but it's a risky thing to pull off," he said. "We can't afford to make any mistakes. Every ad has to hit its mark. We're sitting here with a slingshot and we can't afford to miss once, because it's money down the drain."

On each leg of the flight, Forciea offered suggestions about themes Wellstone should stress on this day. As the plane lined up to land at the Duluth airport, on a high plateau overlooking the Duluth harbor, Forciea urged Wellstone to attack. "You cannot be too tough on Rudy Boschwitz up here," he said. "There are parts of northern Minnesota that don't even exist in Rudy Boschwitz's mind."

Midway between Duluth and the flat farm country around the twin border cities of Moorhead, Minnesota, and Fargo, North Dakota, Forciea advised Wellstone to offer a stronger-than-usual dose of class-rooted populism. "I think we have to push this millionaire business," he said. "I don't think you can say *millionaire* too many times out here. . . . I would do more of this than the issues today."

Wellstone dutifully obeyed. "I'm not a millionaire and I won't take money from the oil companies," the candidate said at a press conference at the Fargo airport. "I don't have to be a millionaire with all that money to win," he added, repeating *millionaire* or *million* four more times.

That evening, after the plane returned to St. Paul, Wellstone and Forciea drove back to campaign headquarters for a staff meeting and to deal with a delicate personnel matter. Before the meeting began, Wellstone asked Dick Senese to take a walk around the corner with him. As they walked, Wellstone explained that while Senese had done an admirable job guiding the campaign through the primary, he wanted a more experienced professional to take over as campaign manager now.

Having been reassigned to Duluth shortly before the primary, Senese was not entirely surprised by Wellstone's decision, and he did not object to the shift. "There was a sense of relief," Senese said. "I had no hard feelings. I think it was a good decision." Wellstone asked if he would like to be the campaign's finance director, adding that Forciea had noted that Senese had done an impressive job of keeping money in reserve for television ads at the end of the primary race. Senese, who thought he might be happier and more effective as a field organizer, told Wellstone that he needed time to think about it.

But when they returned to the offices and the staff meeting began, Wellstone announced that Blackshaw would become campaign manager and Senese would be finance director. The announcement angered Senese because he had not agreed to accept the finance director position. "When he did that I became incredibly irate," Senese said. "I felt I was put in an awkward position."

Nevertheless, when Wellstone finished speaking, Senese told the staff that he thought the new assignments would make the campaign team even stronger. "I understood group dynamics and I knew what I had to say," Senese said. Although he was hurt, he put aside his pride and his momentary anger with Wellstone because the campaign "wasn't about my becoming campaign manager. It was about electing Paul to the Senate."

8

WASHINGTON WOES

As Paul Wellstone delivered a fiery victory speech on the night of the Democratic primary, Jay Novak listened on his car radio. Heading west into the comfortable lake-district suburb of Wayzata, the forty-year-old Novak was a bit unnerved as he heard the attacks on his new employer, Senator Rudy Boschwitz.

A tall, dark-haired, youthful-looking journeyman reporter and former editor of a Minnesota business magazine, *Corporate Report,* Novak had joined the Boschwitz campaign just a few weeks earlier. Given the job of press secretary, Novak took his place in a campaign that he expected would run flawlessly to election day.

But almost immediately, Novak began to feel uneasy. As he wrote and released 150 pages of "white papers" detailing Boschwitz's new statements on agriculture, nutrition, and the environment, nobody in the political press corps seemed interested. Instead, reporters called almost every day for responses to Wellstone's potshots. At the same time, Republicans took a relaxed, confident approach to the Senate race, committing most of their attention to the gubernatorial candidacy of Jon Grunseth.

On primary night, Novak tried to force himself to accept that a sober review of the situation led to only one conclusion: the radical Wellstone had no chance whatsoever of beating Boschwitz, the most popular and well-endowed politician in the state. Still, as he listened to the car radio, and to Wellstone's assaults on Boschwitz and the monied classes, he feared that they would create a momentum of their own and leave the Boschwitz team in an entirely defensive posture.

"It was a little like playing goalie with no forwards," Novak said, using the ice hockey imagery that most Minnesotans understand. "We were taking an awful lot of shots, and blocking almost all of them, but some are going to get through. Even if you're way ahead in the game, it creates an uneasy feeling."

Nevertheless, Boschwitz staffers found comfort and reassurance in their bank account. While Wellstone boasted of his grassroots organizing, Boschwitz countered with an overpowering advantage in fund-raising. Each time Wellstone portrayed Boschwitz as the agent of a corrupt elite who filled his campaign coffers, Boschwitz cited the donations he had received from 70,000 people, a staggering display of support.

As his second term drew to an end, Boschwitz relished his reputation as one of the most prolific and unapologetic fund-raisers in the nation. "Ask for it. Make the calls," Boschwitz replied when, in August 1990, he was asked to explain his golden touch at raising cash. Boschwitz was not timid about prying open wallets because he did not view fund-raising as a distasteful, seamy necessity. The senator compared his political fund-raising to his extensive work on funding drives for charities like the American Cancer Society and the Kidney Foundation. And in reply to Democratic critics who said there was something morally wrong about his delight in asking donors for money, Boschwitz used the issue to draw attention to his own philanthropy. "Most of these guys are ill at ease because they don't give [money] themselves," Boschwitz said. "I give quite a bit of money."

Despite the public stance that there was nothing improper in Boschwitz's fund-raising, there were some concerns within the campaign. In fact, Boschwitz had so much on hand in the summer of 1990—about $1.5 million—that his campaign manager, Tom Mason, was wary of piling up much more. Nevertheless, many national campaign experts and academics were impressed by the Boschwitz machine. Boschwitz employed every known technique for raising money: big-ticket parties; small gatherings; celebrity fund-raisers that featured presidents, Arnold Schwarzenegger, Jackie Mason, or Tom Clancy; special-access clubs and gimmicks; house parties; and personal telephone solicitations.

The most important elements, the ones that helped build the list of small contributors, were direct-mail and telephone marketing—a computerized operation that rivaled any mail-order outfit in the nation in sophistication. The core of this machine was a huge list of contributors who had supported Boschwitz over the course of two previous campaigns.

The computer entry for each "customer" contained all kinds of useful information. A few strokes on the keyboard could sort out an endless variety of special audiences—by age, occupation, geography. This wealth of information allowed Boschwitz to target groups from the elderly to licensed aviators with special appeals.

Boschwitz's operation was considered by some to be a model of the future, not only because of its raw horsepower but also because of features that allowed him to deflect criticism. Chief among these features was a huge list of what he called "skinny cats," contributors of less than $100. Campaign finance consultants and academics agreed that Boschwitz had the largest in-state contributor lists in the nation. If the day ever comes when political action committees (PACs) are banned, they said, Boschwitz would have an enormous list of native-grown contributors ready to tap.

"That's smart," Tom Mann, who studies Congress at the Brookings Institution in Washington, D.C., told a reporter. "Boschwitz appears to be way ahead of the curve."

Larry Sabato, a professor at the University of Virginia who studies political fund-raising, predicted in October 1990 that other candidates would emulate Boschwitz. "Boschwitz is not only blazing a new trail, he's blazing a superhighway," Sabato told another reporter.

A second redeeming fact was that Boschwitz collected more than 80 percent of his money from individuals and only about 15 percent from special-interest PACs. (The remaining 5 percent came from Republican Party groups and other campaign committees.) Other senators reaped an average of about 25 percent from PACs. And, finally, Minnesotans accounted for 60 percent of the contributions and more than 80 percent of the contributors. Their average donation was about $60.

Two days after his primary victory, Wellstone stood unbowed beneath the overhead storage compartment on a jet that would take him to Washington, D.C. The flight was delayed and as it stood at the gate, Wellstone took the opportunity to shake the hands of a few passengers. The businessmen in the first row of the coach section greeted him warmly, but one suggested that he had a tough race ahead of him. "Hey, I'm tall, blond, blue-eyed," Wellstone joked. "What else do I need?"

This absurdity brought howls of laughter. Basking in the size of his primary win, Wellstone was smiling and enjoying himself. But a few hours later the plane landed in Washington and Wellstone was off on a demoralizing search for something he truly needed—hard cash.

He fared poorly on the trip—financially, emotionally, and physically—because he was out of his element. Most politicians profess to dislike this chore, but Wellstone abhorred it so much that he failed to conceal his contempt from his political patrons. And while most Senate challengers had made repeated fund-raising trips to Washington already, Wellstone stayed away longer than most.

Wellstone unequivocally agreed with what by 1990 was a growing body of critics—including former *Wall Street Journal* reporter Brooks Jackson, author of *Honest Graft*—who lambasted the American system of campaign finance. Jackson's inside look at congressional fund-raising revealed a legal and open system of trading money for access and influence.

Campaign finance reformers, energized in 1990 by the savings and loan scandal, suddenly looked more credible than ever before. The senators who had intervened to help contributor Charles Keating had just illustrated the reformers' main point: special interests do get something—action or inaction—in return for the hundreds of millions of dollars they pump into campaigns. That money, after all, enables the ascent and ensures the very survival of the nation's most powerful politicians.

In his appearances across Minnesota, Wellstone frequently described the campaign finance system as one that sets up two elections, one in which the wealthy and powerful determine who the candidates will be, then one for the general public. As he arrived in Washington he knew that to mount a serious challenge against Boschwitz he had to play a game that he considered essentially corrupt, without being corrupted himself.

From the airport, Wellstone and campaign manager John Blackshaw took a taxi to the Connecticut Avenue apartment of Steven Emerson, an investigative reporter and author and a former student of Wellstone's. After depositing their luggage in

Emerson's living room, they left for their first appointment, a dinner with their D.C. pollster, Diane Feldman.

Feldman was a partner of Feldman, Lester and Associates, a political research, consulting, and polling firm that had worked for many liberal and progressive candidates from the municipal level to presidential races. Feldman had done polling for Michael Dukakis in New York, for example, and had worked on national polling projects for the Democratic Senatorial Campaign Committee.

At dinner, Feldman and Blackshaw prepped Wellstone for the centerpiece of the trip—a gathering sponsored by the Democratic Senatorial Campaign Committee (DSCC). An offshoot of the national Democratic Party run out of the party's headquarters at the foot of Capitol Hill, the DSCC is the Senate Democratic Caucus's fund-raising arm. Incumbents typically receive the majority of DSCC distributions, but the committee also backs Democratic-endorsed challengers and invites them to Washington to be looked over by scores of executives from many of the nation's richest political action committees.

These events, referred to by the participants as "cattle calls," serve as a kind of one-stop shopping opportunity for both candidates and contributors. If a candidate impresses these people, then sizable checks—the legal limit is $10,000—will land in the campaign treasury. But as Wellstone learned from his advisers, a candidate's stand on issues usually matters less than perceived electability, as determined by polls and the ability to raise money. The PAC heads keep score on hundreds of congressional races each year, and they pay attention to a challenger only when a successful fund-raising program already is in place and polls show the incumbent to be at least within striking distance.

"You've got to convince them that we're going to win this thing in November," Blackshaw told Wellstone. Feldman urged Wellstone to emphasize that he could raise money successfully.

"One of the things holding them back is Larry [Harrington, the DSCC political director] saying, 'I'm not going to finance a whole campaign,'" Feldman explained. "You've got to convince them you're on your way to raising $800,000."

But Wellstone could not make a convincing case that he was likely to beat Boschwitz or that he was a talented fund-raiser. Instead of talking to the PAC leaders about polls and money, Wellstone said, he wanted to "tell them about my coalition of liberals and working-class people. That didn't happen in '84," he said, referring to Boschwitz's last election. "When I got support on the East Side of St. Paul, when I got the support of the Building Trades [union], I knew something was going on."

As the discussion continued, Wellstone pecked away at a bowl of crab soup and a salad, and then he finally exploded. "I don't look like their candidate. I don't talk like their candidate. I don't act like their candidate," he fumed, his voice raised. "I want to say, 'I'm tired of coming here and begging.'"

"Don't get angry," Feldman cautioned as she and Blackshaw exchanged silent glances.

"No, but I'll say, 'We can beat him. It's up to you,'" Wellstone replied.

Again, Feldman advised him to be circumspect. "Don't get that blunt. Tell them they can help you," she said.

"Say, 'You're going to help us make it happen,'" added Blackshaw.

Finally, Wellstone calmed down. "I won't be angry," he said, his voice lower. "But I want to be honest."

Despite his disdain for the process, Wellstone understood the need to swallow his objections and participate. He didn't expect much from the PACs, but the DSCC, even more than the PAC managers, could make or break his campaign. The DSCC had control of a chunk of money he absolutely had to have. Under federal law, which allows political parties to contribute more money than PACs, the DSCC was permitted to donate directly to Wellstone up to $17,500 in cash, and to spend on his behalf an additional $300,000. That was about one-third of the total amount Wellstone could expect to raise from all sources under the most optimistic projections.

Cattle Call

The next morning, when Wellstone and Blackshaw arrived at Democratic headquarters they were joined by Feldman and Norm Kurz. A former press secretary to representative Les Aspin of Wisconsin, Kurz started a two-person fund-raising operation in 1987 that primarily worked for progressive candidates. He was recruited to help Wellstone by Feldman, who made the "candidate and the campaign sound intriguing and [full of] possibilities," said Kurz.

Wellstone and his team filed into a first-floor meeting room along with dozens of PAC executives. As he helped himself to a buffet table heaped with doughnuts, muffins, bagels, coffee, and juice, Wellstone saw the name tags that identified representatives of the American Israel Public Affairs Committee (AIPAC), the Letter Carriers, the Human Rights Campaign, and politically active law firms. Like a schoolboy at his first dance, Wellstone stood against the wall, visibly uncomfortable.

At this gathering, Wellstone was on review along with two other Senate hopefuls—Harvey Gantt, a former mayor of Charlotte who was challenging Jesse Helms in North Carolina, and Josie Heath, a Boulder County commissioner running for an open seat in Colorado against Hank Brown, a five-term congressman.

Gantt, who was participating in an obscenely expensive race that eventually would cost a total of $26 million, the most in the nation in 1990, addressed the meeting first. In a calm, unemotional manner, he stressed that his race was a dead heat. The latest poll showed him with a 2-point, 46-to-44 lead over Helms. Gantt's focus on the winnable nature of the race and his easygoing manner brought a favorable reaction from the crowd.

Heath delivered a lighthearted talk in which she humbly begged for money. "This is where I feel like Tammy Faye," she said, referring to Tammy Faye Bakker, wife of televangelist Jimmy Bakker, serving time in prison for defrauding followers. "This is the worst. I need you to write that check. . . . For the few of you who have already given to my opponent, there's still time for redemption. And I'm not proud." Although Heath smiled as she said it, and the PAC executives chuckled, her comments perfectly captured the essence of the event. Heath lacked Tammy Faye's tear-streaked mascara, but the relationship between candidate and contributor was tawdry and exploitative.

When Wellstone stepped to the lectern at 8:45 A.M., he gave a rousing stump speech that jolted the PAC men and women. Like most people who hear Wellstone for the first time, they were mesmerized. In a seamless ten-minute spiel, Wellstone focused on his role as an underdog. He told how he surprised pundits with his enthusiastic, grassroots campaign, which now was moving from a sweat-drenched "three-shirt-a-day campaign to a ten-shirt-a-day campaign."

Unlike Heath, Wellstone never directly asked for money. In fact, he ripped into the PAC-candidate relationship when he called Boschwitz "the senator from Exxon" and implied that he would not answer to PACs that contributed to his campaign. He came close to saying he didn't expect to receive their money and didn't want it when he added: "I've said it in Minnesota and I'll say it here. I don't plan to match Rudy Boschwitz pollster for pollster, image maker for image maker, $6 million for $6 million."

The PAC leaders did not need to hear that from the candidate to know it was true. They merely had to look at the fact sheet the DSCC provided. The summary of the Minnesota race listed the cash each candidate had on hand. Boschwitz, despite running television ads since June, still had $1.03 million. Wellstone had $66,036.

Wellstone clearly was asking for high-risk venture capital, the political equivalent of junk bonds, but with the outrageous, up-front pledge that no return on investment would be forthcoming if he won. Still, the PAC leaders greeted his presentation politely. They smiled when he quoted an incredulous rabbi commenting on the fact that two Jews were running against one another for the Senate for what might have been the first time in American history: "In Minnesota?" And to the delight of Blackshaw, Feldman, and Kurz, the audience erupted in laughter and applause when they were shown "Fast-Paced Paul."

"We win on that ad," Wellstone boasted over the noise.

Then, amazingly, with the audience primed for the sale, Wellstone beat a hasty exit, hardly stopping to chat and shake hands with the dozens of PAC directors who milled about after his presentation. His shocked advisers chased him out the front steps of the Democratic headquarters, where they chastised him for his failure to even try to cozy up to the PACs.

"Paul, can I yell at you?" Feldman began in a tone that made it clear she was going to whether or not he allowed it. "You've got to schmooze better. You can't look like you want to kick them in the balls."

"I mean Ashland Oil is here," Wellstone replied, contempt dripping from his voice with the mention of an oil company. "Looking at these [name] tags—these aren't my people. I don't like cattle shows and I'm not going to beg them and I'm not going to kiss their ass. I'm not so constituted."

Wellstone then was reprimanded by Kurz, who saw him frittering away an important opportunity. Kurz told Wellstone that he didn't have to like the PAC managers, but "you've got to connect on a personal level." Kurz urged Wellstone to talk to Kentucky senator Wendell Ford, who was in the audience, and ask him to come to Minnesota to campaign with him.

"I want to know where he stands on issues," Wellstone demanded. "Let me ask you, what's his position on choice?" Kurz, who was familiar with Minnesota politics, countered by noting that Wellstone had campaigned with Governor Rudy Perpich even though Perpich was against abortion. Wellstone shot back that Ford was from a tobacco state and was probably a defender of tobacco companies: "Then he's the last person I want coming to Minnesota."

The heated exchange lasted several minutes but ended on a friendly note. "I do sort of think these things through in my own strange way," Wellstone said, smiling. He hugged Feldman and promised, "I will be good from now on."

The argument over, Wellstone and his crew went back inside and met with the DSCC chiefs, Louisiana senator John Breaux and political director Larry Harrington. The DSCC officials promised to send $17,500, the maximum the organization could donate directly to Wellstone's campaign, but there was one condition: Wellstone must squeeze $10,000 out of his supporters to buy a table at the Democratic Party's annual black-tie fundraising dinner in Washington two weeks hence.

Begging in Georgetown

The Wellstone campaign was strapped for cash, but Blackshaw and Kurz did not think it would be a problem to raise the $10,000. They were satisfied with the deal, accepting the $17,500 as a down payment on what they hoped would be a much bigger commitment later in the form of "soft money," which the DSCC could spend or donate to other organizations for Wellstone's benefit. After the agreement was completed, Wellstone's anger flared again on the way to his next appointment. "They have no sense of possibilities," he said, a phrase he would repeat many times about groups that ignored him. "They're stuck in the mud."

With Kurz as their escort, Wellstone and Blackshaw were taken to a Georgian mansion in the Georgetown section of Washington. The mansion was owned by Elizabeth and Smith Bagley, among the most prominent Washington socialites. Smith Bagley, the grandson of tobacco tycoon R. J. Reynolds, split from the family business and came to Washington from Winston-Salem, North Carolina, with Jimmy Carter. He was an early Carter supporter and the former president's friend.

Democratic congressional leaders dined frequently at the Bagley home, which also was the site of innumerable political fund-raisers. The Bagleys were among the biggest fund-raisers for Dukakis in 1988. Elizabeth Bagley was Dukakis's finance chair for Washington and also went to California to work for him. Smith Bagley was one of forty-four Democrats who pledged to raise $500,000 apiece in "soft money" for the presidential campaign.

The door to the Bagleys' house was answered by Lilly, a maid whose salmon-colored uniform matched the hue of the marble in the foyer. Lilly escorted the threesome into the wood-paneled library, where Rembrandt's *Portrait of an Old Man* hung above the fireplace. After a few minutes, Elizabeth Bagley came in. She sported a deep tan acquired on Nantucket Island, where she and her husband had just vacationed. They had socialized with Senator Ted Kennedy and, ironically, Boschwitz, who also summers there.

Wellstone, who wore soft-soled shoes and an ill-fitting suit, began the meeting with an optimistic recap of his campaign, stressing its grassroots nature and his progressive politics. He had been told by Kurz that the Bagleys liked to back progressives. As if on cue, Bagley responded to Wellstone's remarks by saying, "We're progressive, even liberal. I would even use that word."

Nevertheless, Wellstone found her a hard sell.

"So what's your pitch, other than you're a progressive and Boschwitz is not?" she asked at one point.

Wellstone fumbled, dodging the question by repeating his commitment to his community-organizer approach to politics. "We'll use money we raise for ads, but I'm not giving up on this grassroots campaign," he said.

Then Bagley probed to learn how much effort Wellstone had devoted to mining traditional sources of money, and she quickly uncovered the truth. She named at least a dozen prominent Democratic donors, including Kate Michelman, executive director of the National Abortion Rights Action League, and asked if Wellstone had contacted them. Wellstone and Kurz, who had been hired only about three months earlier, were forced to admit with a mixture of sheepishness and frustration that most either had not been contacted or would not return the calls. "Most of these people have never heard of Wellstone," Kurz confessed. "It's almost October and they've never heard of him."

Bagley then confided that when Kurz telephoned to ask for an audience, she was not thrilled. "I thought, 'Oh God, do I really have to talk to one more person?' I really have never even heard your name. Whose fault is that?"

Wellstone did not answer her imperious question directly, but he displayed mild irritation. "I haven't been in a café in Minnesota in a year and a half where there hasn't been thirty to thirty-five people, sometimes a hundred, not for a rally, just to talk about issues," he shot back. "Then I come here [to Washington] and it's always, 'I don't know your name.'"

"It's a cynical town," Bagley said. "And you're one of many, too."

Things obviously were not going well. The most Bagley offered in this meeting was to make a handful of calls on Wellstone's behalf. She would put in a word with Kate Michelman, who thus far had not returned Wellstone's calls, and also promised to speak with the Holywood Women's Political Caucus, among other groups. She did not say whether she would write a check herself.

As the conversation wound down, Wellstone offered to show Bagley "Fast-Paced Paul." She led the group downstairs to a family room where there was a videocassette player and a large-screen television. On their way, they walked through an enclosed courtyard and down a flight of stairs lined with pictures of the Bagleys posing with Michael and Kitty Dukakis and of their eight-month-old daughter being bounced on Jimmy Carter's knee. At the bottom of the stairs was an indoor swimming pool, lined with glass and marble columns, patterned after a pool at the Mandarin Hotel in Hong Kong. After the visitors ogled the sumptuous surroundings, Bagley led them through an exercise room with mirrored walls and a ballet barre.

In the family room, they were joined by Bagley's next appointment, Gail Leftwich, a former Dukakis volunteer and the development director of the Joan Shorenstein Barone Center on Press, Politics and Public Policy at Harvard's Kennedy School of Government. Bagley was a member of the center's board. Leftwich's arrival was another of those lucky breaks that seemed to help the Wellstone campaign at every turn. It turned out that she was a close friend of Jeff Blodgett, Wellstone's just-departed campaign manager. Bagley watched as Wellstone fell into an animated conversation with Leftwich about their mutual friend.

"Gail's arrival played a significant role in Liz Bagley's warming up to Paul and in some of the things we were trying to tell her—that this guy has a fire in his belly. That's something that you can't see in Washington—what's happening on the real grassroots level," said Kurz.

After Bagley saw the ad—she said it was "cute"—the group began the return journey upstairs. In the exercise room, Wellstone was so engrossed in conversation with Leftwich that he walked straight into one of the mirrored walls.

"I just spent an hour and a half trying to impress this woman and then I walk into a mirror and I almost break my nose," he said, laughing in spite of himself when he was back on Georgetown's cobblestoned streets. "I'm not used to being in places like this."

Despite the roughing up he had gotten from Bagley and her mirror, Wellstone did impress her. She said later that she sensed his positions on issues were deeply held and were not offered merely to satisfy her. Also, his awkwardness "was actually endearing," she said. "Most of them are so slick. They walk into your house like they own you. Paul wasn't your average politician. He wasn't cocky. Well, he was cocky in his own way, about his grassroots operation and what he could accomplish with it."

By the end of a day of trying to raise money from PACs and wealthy individuals, Wellstone wanted to go home that night instead of the next morning, as scheduled. At the Washington Hilton, where he moved among friends at a meeting of the Democratic National Committee, Wellstone complained that he had a headache and the chills. Blackshaw thought Wellstone looked tired and sick.

"I feel like I'm trapped in an elevator," Wellstone said as he stood in line for a buffet dinner at a reception given by the Democratic Hispanic Caucus.

Blackshaw was not able to get seats on a flight to Minneapolis that night, so Blackshaw and Wellstone took a cab back to Steven Emerson's apartment. There, the candidate and his campaign manager slept on a mattress on the floor like a couple of college kids stretching money on spring break.

"I've never shared a bed with the candidate before," Blackshaw commented the next morning. "There are a lot of firsts in this campaign. But that's the engaging part."

9

THE SMELL OF MONEY

On the Sunday after the primary, Wellstone and nine advisers and campaign staff members kicked off their Nikes and Reeboks to plot campaign strategy in a Duluth bed-and-breakfast called The Mansion, on the shore of Lake Superior. The big-game trophy heads mounted on the walls and the overstuffed furniture in the room overlooking the lake were reminders of the environmental and economic plunder of the robber baron era, an ironic setting for the work in progress that day.

Wellstone settled into a chair and looked at the people who would surround him through election day. Pat Forciea and John Blackshaw would make most of the important decisions. Forciea would focus on the campaign's broad strategies and themes, coordinate the advertising, and keep in touch with Washington. On weekdays he would rise by 5:00 or 6:00 A.M. to fax newspaper stories and other information to *The Hotline,* a daily newsletter on national politics. Each day would end around 11:00 P.M. or midnight, usually with a long phone call with Wellstone, recapping the day's events and planning the following day.

Blackshaw would help implement Forciea's strategies by directing the day-to-day activities of the staff, supervising the field operations, setting Wellstone's schedule, and calling press conferences. Also present in Duluth was Liz Borg, the funky field director who had impressed everyone with her skills in turning out the vote for Wellstone in the primary. Wellstone's old friend Mike Casper was there, too. Forciea also had invited state representative Paul Ogren and some staffers from Governor Rudy Perpich's reelection campaign.

Sitting on the floor, Forciea led the discussion, first recounting the trip to Washington, then reviewing the surprising success of Bill Hillsman's advertising team. Next he focused on the mechanics of the field operation—recruiting precinct captains, establishing phone banks to call voters, mailing persuasion literature to undecideds, and printing and distributing lawn signs.

"We need a big lawn sign presence," said Forciea. "By the tenth or fifteenth of October, we need to see thousands of lawn signs." Liz Borg assured him that the planning already was under way. "Two thousand people have already asked for signs," she said.

Forciea then laid out the vote totals that Wellstone needed to achieve in order to win on November 6. "We need 60 percent in the fourth, fifth, and eighth" congressional districts, Forciea said, referring to St. Paul, Minneapolis, and Duluth and the Iron Range. "We need to get into the mid- to high forties in the sixth," a predominantly blue-collar district made up of the northern Twin Cities suburbs. "And we need to avoid being beat more than 60-40" in the state's rural congressional districts, he said.

"That gets us to 50.001 based on the '86 and '84 vote," Forciea concluded.

The response to "Fast-Paced Paul" had erased Forciea's earlier doubts about Wellstone's chances of winning. Now he saw how Wellstone could pull it off, but he still was concerned about the young staff's inexperience. They were so young, in fact, that as he celebrated Wellstone's primary victory in a Minneapolis hotel suite along with the rest of the staff, Forciea had worried that some of the staff members drinking beers were under the legal drinking age of twenty-one.

"We're thin on older people," he told the group. "No matter how skilled our younger people are, they're going to have trouble being accepted when they go see legislators x, y, and z."

Forciea also knew that Boschwitz's team of veteran political professionals had no such weakness. "That is an intimidating group of guys," he said, referring to Boschwitz campaign chiefs Tom Mason, Jay Novak, and Bob Anderson. "I disagree with what they do, but boy do I have a lot of respect professionally for [campaign manager] Tom Mason. . . . These guys have been playing golf for eighteen months, waiting and getting ready for these next couple of months. . . . It's the ultimate white-boy brigade—men in their thirties and forties, from successful families, successful careers. They are experts at, among other things, class warfare."

Yet Forciea could not figure out Boschwitz's strategy in these first days following the primary. Why had Boschwitz not already started bombarding Wellstone with negative television ads? "I cannot believe he's not snubbing this thing out right now," Forciea said. "This mega-million-dollar outfit is choosing not to bang on us. I sense a high degree of overconfidence. If this race ever tightens up and we win, it will be because of this."

As the discussion touched on Wellstone's advertising, preparation for the debates, and lines of attack Wellstone might use against Boschwitz, one overriding theme emerged: Wellstone was so far behind that he had to take enormous risks. "You've got to roll the dice and come up with some big-time gimmicks," said Paul Ogren.

Many in the group thought the key to defeating Boschwitz was to hammer at the issue of money—the size of Boschwitz's campaign treasury, who his contributors were, the economic philosophies of the 1980s that he championed. "RudyBoschwitz cut taxes for the rich," Ogren bellowed. "Every rich person in the United States is twice as rich today [as] twelve years ago because of Rudy Boschwitz. It's basic pocketbook politics and Democrats for the last ten years have been afraid to go after the issue."

In fact, Wellstone would pursue that issue aggressively. The tone that was set in this strategy session lasted throughout the campaign. It would be a campaign willing to take tremendous risks and to attack vigorously, an attitude captured by Forciea's partner in politics, Gary Cerkvenik. Tall and lanky, Cerkvenik walked around the room in his stocking feet, settling for a few minutes, then shifting to another spot like a lion stalking prey. "I think we should rip this guy's head off," he said. "I'm a real advocate for tearing this guy's heart out."

The Boschwitz Machine

The attack required a detailed analysis of Boschwitz's millions. Relying on newspaper articles, staff research, and Boschwitz's own words, Wellstone had plenty of ammunition. While Boschwitz tried to deflect criticisms by making a big fuss about all his mom-and-pop contributors, Wellstone pointed to a *New York Times* article that reported that in 1989 the incumbent raised $1.8 million from individuals who gave $200 or more, more than all but one of the thirty Senate incumbents who were up for reelection in 1990. Of the $1.8 million, Boschwitz raised $1.35 million, or nearly 75 percent of the total big-donor haul, from non-Minnesotans.

Illustrating the impersonal nature of the national fund-raising game, the *Times* quoted a Tucson, Arizona, auto dealer who had given $250 to the senator from Minnesota: "I don't know a thing about him. . . . Never heard of him. I don't know whether he's tall or short or wears red socks."

A *Washington Post* report showed that Boschwitz was no slouch when it came to soliciting PACs, either. The *Post* reported in June 1990 that Boschwitz ranked seventh among senators in total PAC contributions, having raised $790,535 between January 1, 1989, and March 31, 1990.

The notion that Boschwitz was preoccupied with money was reinforced by his two years as chair of the National Republican Senatorial Committee. As chair, he was intimately involved in raising $70 million for other Senate Republicans. He was, his critics implied, the bagman for the whole Senate. Although the job also entailed working with issues and strategy, Boschwitz's phenomenal ability to haul in cash was the most talked about aspect of his tenure.

Boschwitz was so convinced of the efficacy of his electronic juggernaut that he let it take the place of the human element, cutting the complement of campaign field coordinators from twelve in 1984 to four in 1990. While Wellstone was building sweat equity, Boschwitz was letting his own human resources depreciate. The dramatic drop in the number of field coordinators also signaled Boschwitz's earnest belief in the value of contributors as an army of advocates and word-of-mouth supporters. The letters Boschwitz sent to his contributors, he believed, built a feeling of ownership in the Boschwitz enterprise, and he always urged them to spread the gospel. That function of the "skinny cats" was at least as important in Boschwitz's eyes as what they offered in money and political cover. Smart politicians have always known about this phenomenon: givers become investors and advocates. The concept that people feel kindlier toward those who owe them something is at least as old as Machiavelli, who wrote, "It is the nature of man to feel as much bound by the favors they do as by those they receive."

While Boschwitz openly embraced the small contributors and used them to rebut charges that he catered to the financial elite, his professional staff was well aware that the small donations were the least efficient. Campaign finance director Bob Anderson acknowledged that it cost the campaign fifty cents to raise every dollar from contributors of fifty dollars and less, while it cost only twenty cents to raise money from those who gave more. The small donors became important not just for their word-of-mouth advocacy, but also for statistically offsetting the large contributions from PACs and wealthy individuals. Boschwitz would do anything he could to build his contributor lists with even one-dollar and five-dollar givers to bring his average contribution down.

Despite the potential trouble inherent in raising money on a grand scale, Boschwitz was careful enough to avoid scandals like the ethics charges brought against senators who intervened on behalf of contributors involved in the savings and loan bailout. But he was not unscathed. The high volume of fund-raising resulted in a few lapses that could be exploited by an aggressive adversary like Wellstone.

Boschwitz, ever the retailer, could not resist providing some sort of tangible benefit for his contributors. He set up clubs and a hierarchy of direct services for donors at varying levels. For the smallest contributors, his so-called "skinny cats," Boschwitz offered invitations to Rudy's Annual 50th Birthday and Polka Celebration. To attract larger donations in the mid-1980s, Boschwitz offered a more valuable reward. Contributors willing to give $1,000 or more were offered membership in his Washington Club, which entitled them to a three-day trip to the nation's capital. Offered at cost but arranged by Boschwitz, the trip included meetings with the senator and other public officials as well as "briefings on current issues."

As an extra perk, the *St. Paul Pioneer Press* revealed in 1986, Boschwitz issued club members a batch of blue stickers, which he imprudently called "special access stamps." Stamps also were issued to Skinny Cat Club members, defined as those who pledged to give up to $100 per year for five years. Placing the stickers on a letter to the senator would "expedite your mail to me through my Senate office," Boschwitz wrote in his "annual report" to his donors.

When the special preference for donors was disclosed, Boschwitz was inundated with criticism and ridicule from campaign reform groups, editorial writers, and ordinary citizens. *Common Cause Magazine* described the setup as an example of how trading money for access had become "much more open." Writing one's congressional representatives is a hallowed tradition in representative government, and the notion of letters from well-heeled donors being culled from the mail sack for faster service infuriated many Minnesotans. Although Boschwitz initially claimed that all citizens got prompt constituent service, he eventually backed down and stopped dispensing the stamps, but did not discontinue many of the club's other services.

In at least three other cases Boschwitz was accused of behavior bordering on impropriety, or of being more responsive than was seemly to contributors. In 1986 Boschwitz was featured in a front-page *Washington Post* story about heavy-handed tactics by the Israeli lobby. In a room off the Senate floor, Boschwitz introduced Senators Phil Gramm of Texas and Dan Evans of Washington to Michael R. Goland, a wealthy backer of Israel who had figured prominently in the defeat of former senator Charles Percy of Illinois. Goland described the kind of ad that might be used against the two senators if they approved a pending arms sale to Saudi Arabia. The senators were outraged.

Boschwitz apologized, but the furor resulted in quite a bit of inside-the-Beltway finger pointing. Syndicated columnist Mark Shields called it a case of "intimidation by big money" that had "all the subtlety of a knee to the groin."

And *Common Cause Magazine* reported in 1990 about a Rabbi Milton Balkany, a Brooklyn operative who mastered the art of "bundling" hundreds of thousands of dollars from Orthodox Jews and funneling the campaign contributions to Republican candidates. Boschwitz was one of the biggest beneficiaries of Balkany's largesse, and the senator admitted to pulling strings for Balkany's pet foreign aid projects in Israel, schemes that were criticized by other members of Congress as inappropriate targets of aid.

Finally, the *Nation*'s David Corn assailed Boschwitz for taking about $30,000 from the Chemical Specialties Manufacturers Association and then leading a fight to weaken state standards on chemicals and pesticides. Boschwitz claimed that the contributions from political action committees that truly had an interest in the issue was overstated. While conceding that public safety should be the paramount concern, he claimed that small companies needed protection from state legislators who were "trying to outdo themselves to look like environmentalists."

While Boschwitz's money offered Wellstone a clear line of attack, the challenger could not generate much excitement in the first few weeks of September. He spiritedly jabbed at Boschwitz, holding press conferences and making statewide tours dedicated to various themes—the savings and loan bailout and Boschwitz's acceptance of money from related interests, Boschwitz's votes against Democratic programs for children and child care, and his poor ratings on environmental scorecards. But despite these targets and his old-fashioned bus trips across the state, Wellstone's candidacy was not picking up speed. Instead, the campaign was following familiar rhythms: the challenger trying desperately to get on the front pages and the ten o'clock news, usually without success, and the incumbent reposing statesman-like in Washington.

Two weeks after the primary, the *Star Tribune*/KSTP-TV Minnesota Poll found that Boschwitz led Wellstone by 15 percentage points, 55 percent to 40 percent, which both campaigns interpreted as favorable news. While the gap seemed huge, Wellstone found solace in the fact that it was down considerably from the 33-point spread (60-27) that his own pollster had measured in mid-July. In the Boschwitz camp, many expected the 15-point lead to grow now that the incumbent could concentrate on battling a single opponent rather than a crowd of DFL contenders.

Meanwhile, the Republican team of Boschwitz and gubernatorial candidate Jon Grunseth reached a high point when President George Bush visited the state on September 27 for an orgy of fund-raising at the Hyatt Regency Hotel in Minneapolis. Boschwitz basked in warm praise from Bush during a breakfast speech—and the senator deserved it, having voted with Reagan and Bush 80 percent of the time. But more important was the fact that in a series of three quick fund-raisers before 9:00 A.M., Bush raised almost a million dollars for state and national parties and candidates.

A Wellstone radio ad attacked the assemblage of well-heeled donors. The narrator says Bush is

> not here to visit our award-winning schools. He's not coming to meet with farmers and workers hurt by the Reagan-Bush economic policies. No, he's coming to raise money for Rudy Boschwitz. Why, Rudy, you've already raised over $6 million for your campaign. Do you really need more money?

On balance, however, the Bush event was a big plus for the Republicans, who shrugged off the criticism and banked the money.

PAC Problems

While Wellstone was ceaseless in his attacks on Boschwitz's campaign finances, he was hardly pure when it came to money. The day he announced his candidacy, Wellstone tried to distinguish himself by promising he would not accept money from out-of-state PACs. "I'm not going to sell my soul or mortgage my vision for corporate PAC money," he said. He repeated that vow frequently in the early stages of the race.

By eschewing groups based outside Minnesota, Wellstone said, he would be free of the corporate interests that dominated many of them. The only PACs he would take money from were those that had offices in Minnesota and thus, he reasoned, were more likely to represent the interests of Minnesotans. Initially, it must have seemed an easy sacrifice to make. Wellstone knew that corporate-connected PACs for defense contractors, medical industries, and a host of other big businesses would not contribute to him no matter how loose his fund-raising rules were. Wellstone would never be "the senator from Exxon" because Exxon would not have him.

What Wellstone did not understand was that he also would forgo contributions from dozens of natural allies, including political PACs like Democrats for the '90s, the National Committee for an Effective Congress, the Americans for Democratic Action PAC, and other national groups that favor liberal and progressive Democrats. Donations from some Minnesota labor PACs come only through their national offices.

In developing his initial position, Wellstone showed a surprising ignorance of how the PAC game is played. For all his attacks on the role of money in politics, he did not truly understand how money flowed. Here was a political science professor who had made a colossal miscalculation of how political campaigns work. "I didn't understand the way they were structured," he conceded. "I should have, right? I was teaching the stuff."

The reality crashed up against the principle in May 1990 when the United Steelworkers of America wanted to make a $5,000 donation, the first big PAC contribution of the campaign. The Minnesota Steelworkers had endorsed Wellstone in March, hoping to give him an early boost, but all political donations had to be sent from the union's headquarters in Pittsburgh, not from the local district offices. Suddenly, the campaign faced the loss of a desperately needed $5,000 because local union officials did not have check-writing authority.

Wellstone reconsidered his policy and modified it. He would accept donations from PACs located outside Minnesota, but only if they raised from within the state at least the amount of money they wanted to contribute. "The Steelworkers union members of Minnesota had donated at least the amount we were being given from the national. The money came from Minnesota, so we felt it was keeping in the spirit" of Wellstone's original position, Dick Senese said of the change.

The flip-flop gnawed at Wellstone as his campaign bus rolled across the flat farmland of southern Minnesota on a warm early-October afternoon. Before a handful of reporters on board, Wellstone raised the issue in a confessional tone. "That'll be a weakness for me," he volunteered. "I'm faulting myself for it."

Indeed, Boschwitz's campaign directors soon called attention to Wellstone's change of heart. They charged that his PAC guidelines were more show than substance. "We've heard a lot of phony rubbish from him for a good long time," Boschwitz's press secretary, Jay Novak, told a reporter. "He is sanctimoniously denouncing Boschwitz for taking PAC money but he has taken a great deal." Novak also pointed out that most of Boschwitz's PAC receipts would qualify as clean under the loopholes Wellstone had opened for himself.

Of the approximately $58,000 Wellstone received in PAC contributions in the first half of October, more than $50,000 came from groups outside Minnesota. And only a few PAC donations were refused because the donor could not prove that the dollars were raised in the state. Moreover, Wellstone's PAC receipts through mid-October actually added up to a slightly greater percentage of his total contributions, 18 percent, than Boschwitz's 16 percent.

If accepting a substantial percentage of PAC money made a candidate beholden to special interests, as Wellstone argued in his attacks on Boschwitz, then Wellstone, too, owed favors. Instead of being influenced by corporate-related and conservative PACs, as Boschwitz was, Wellstone was indebted to the labor unions whose PACs dominated his campaign finance reports. "Paul Wellstone condemns all political action committees except those who give him money," charged Tom Mason. "Only his hypocrisy allows him to do that."

But Boschwitz and his staff were not in a position to exploit Wellstone's vulnerabilities. While Wellstone had a higher percentage of PAC receipts, his collections from these groups totaled $283,539. Boschwitz took in more than four times that amount, a total of $1.32 million. Repeating a line that he used in the first debate, Wellstone said, "For him to criticize me for accepting PAC money is like Goliath calling David a bully."

Wellstone's willingness to amend his PAC policy was not his only compromise in fund-raising. He also engaged in the legal but unchaste practice of raising "soft money"—money from PACs and wealthy individuals that is contributed to and spent by third-party groups to help a candidate. This path allows donors to legally exceed federal contribution caps.

Mark Dayton, an heir to the Dayton-Hudson department store fortune and himself a former U.S. Senate candidate in Minnesota, contributed the maximum individual donation of

$2,000 directly to Wellstone's campaign. Then, at the request of Wellstone and Governor Rudy Perpich, he wrote a $25,000 check to the state Democratic Party and its coordinated campaign fund. That was on top of the initial $25,000 he had donated to the party's coordinated campaign fund, which organized a voter identification drive, polling, and get-out-the-vote calls for the entire DFL ticket.

Similarly, Wellstone coaxed a total of $35,000 from the American Federation of State, County and Municipal Employees—$10,000 for his campaign (PACs could donate up to $10,000) and $25,000 for the party's coordinated campaign. Wellstone said he had no choice but to engage in the very activities he despised. To do otherwise, he said, would amount to "unilateral disarmament." Said Dick Senese:

> You could not take any PAC money, not take any soft money, not take contributions from individuals of over $500. You could do all that and you wouldn't be able to print five hundred bumper stickers. What's the use of that? You would never be able to reform campaign finance laws because you could never get into the Senate to do it.

Though the campaign diligently worked to squeeze money from Minnesota labor unions and from $10 and $20 contributors, the inner circle's eyes were always cast toward Washington and the Democratic Senatorial Campaign Committee (DSCC). After the primary, Forciea spent money as fast as it came in, trying to keep Wellstone on television and close in the polls. He did not plan to hold anything in reserve for advertising in the final, crucial two weeks of the election. Forciea's go-for-broke game plan depended on the DSCC's coming through with a major donation, and he was assured by DSCC officials that this was the correct strategy.

Late in September, Wellstone and Forciea went to Washington to attend the DSCC annual dinner and to meet with some wealthy individual donors and a few PACs. The trip brought mixed results. Wellstone's national fund-raiser, Norm Kurz, and Elizabeth Bagley, the Washington socialite and political activist whose elegant Georgetown home Wellstone had visited, helped open the doors to some big contributors. Bagley herself contributed $1,000, which was matched by her husband, and she had phoned leaders of progressive and liberal PACs and urged them to at least listen to the candidate. Among those Wellstone met with on this trip was Pamela Harriman, the highly influential chairwoman of Democrats for the '90s, who wrote a $2,000 check. He also had an appointment with the National Abortion Rights Action League PAC, which had previously ignored him.

Wellstone also was invited, along with other Senate challengers, to meet with the DSCC Leadership Circle, about 150 members who had given $10,000 or more apiece to the Democratic Party. After the Leadership Circle meeting, he was presented at the DSCC's black-tie dinner, which he attended in his bargain-rate business suit.

But for each check and word of encouragement, there was an irritating or infuriating setback. When he and Forciea showed up at the Washington Hilton for the meeting with the Leadership Circle, Louisiana senator John Breaux, who as DSCC chair was greeting people at the door, did not recognize Wellstone. They had to be reintroduced. During the reception, when Breaux formally presented the candidates to the donors, he mispronounced Wellstone's name, calling him "Paul Westone."

"You could hear the teeth grinding from the other end of the room," Forciea said of Wellstone's reaction. Though the gaffe was corrected at the dinner that followed, the incident did not boost Wellstone's or Forciea's confidence that the DSCC would help when needed. To make matters worse, the Wellstone camp had not held up its end of the deal struck with the DSCC immediately after the primary; it had fallen short of its promise to raise $10,000 for a table at the dinner.

The worst disappointment on this trip was a meeting with the Council for a Livable World, a nuclear arms control organization that administers the PEACE PAC. Besides offering campaign contributions, the council serves as a "bundler" for its nationwide network of about 100,000 supporters, sometimes providing tens of thousands of dollars to a candidate. Given the council's record of helping challengers plus Boschwitz's reputation as one of the most dependable Pentagon supporters in Congress, Wellstone figured his loud calls for cuts in military spending would earn him substantial help from the council.

But the council's president, Jerome Grossman, offered what Forciea felt was the most stunning rejection of the campaign. Grossman told Wellstone, Forciea, and Kurz that giving money to an underdog with so little chance of winning would not be a good investment. Grossman explained that he had a "fiduciary responsibility" to his members and therefore could not foresee a contribution for Wellstone, Forciea recalled. "Their attitude was the most arrogant of any groups we dealt with, this so-called liberal organization," he said. The council eventually sent a $1,000 check five days before election day—a fraction of what the group could have provided and what Wellstone's advisers felt he deserved.

When he got home from Washington, Wellstone told staff members about the trip. Rather than recount how much money was raised or which group promised help, he adopted an incredulous tone and with exaggerated gestures summed up his disgust for the Washington money game. "Here's how you introduce yourself in Washington," he told his issues director, Ellen Anderson. " 'Hi, I'm Paul Wellstone. I'm only 15 points behind.' That's what works! It's incredible."

Debating the Debates

As Wellstone grew increasingly frustrated by snubs and set-
backs, an unusually intractable deadlock between Congress and
President Bush over the federal budget began to dominate the
news in early October, a development that would prove to be of
immeasurable help to Wellstone. The stalemate, replete with the
class warfare theme—Bush refused to tax the wealthy to help reduce the federal deficit—made all incumbents look bad, but the
Republicans looked worse. Bush's approval ratings in the polls
began to drop. Boschwitz was slow to realize it, but the dormant
volcano of anti-incumbency was rumbling to life.

Meanwhile, almost as soon as the primary results were tabulated, Wellstone's team had begun negotiations with Boschwitz's
campaign chiefs over a series of debates. The debates were considered essential to Wellstone's attempts to make up ground
against the incumbent. "Our only chance to trip up Boschwitz is
at the debates," Forciea had told Wellstone after the primary.
"It's the single most important event in the campaign."

Negotiations with Boschwitz campaign manager Tom Mason and press secretary Jay Novak were entrusted to the Wellstone team's two lawyers—finance chair Sam Kaplan and campaign manager John Blackshaw, who pressed for a series of eight
debates, one in each of the state's congressional districts.
Boschwitz agreed to only three, two of which could be televised.

The first debate would be on a Sunday night, October 14,
and would be televised during prime time on an independent
Twin Cities station, KMSP-TV. The second would be a noon debate on Minnesota Public Radio, broadcast statewide, on October 23. The final debate would be held on Halloween night on
WCCO-AM, the state's dominant radio station, with the strongest signal and most listeners. This schedule meant far less exposure than Wellstone had hoped for, but it was all Boschwitz

was willing to offer, so Kaplan and Blackshaw accepted the package.

Novak recalled the debate negotiations as not nearly so tense and important as Kaplan and Blackshaw remembered them, and as Blackshaw portrayed them to the press at the time. Novak said:

> I remember one day we went to discuss debate preparations, they didn't argue with us about our limit of three meetings, and they seemed resigned and looked defeated. Afterward, Bob Anderson and I took a walk to the Dairy Queen. . . . Bob said they had spent all the money they had, had gone from 15 points to 18 points behind, that they looked dispirited, and that now was the time to attack, time to finish them off. At another point, I remember somebody in the campaign quoted Ray Kroc [founder of McDonald's restaurants] as saying that when a competitor is drowning, stick a hose down his throat.

But the attack was held off, according to the grand design, because Boschwitz still seemed to be gaining. Instead, and not surprisingly, it was Wellstone who continued to press the attack.

Bill Hillsman's second ad was ready. By now it had become clear that television advertising would be given a higher priority in the campaign than Wellstone had anticipated on the day he announced his candidacy. But because Wellstone lacked the financial resources to compete with Boschwitz in the battle of the airwaves, Hillsman designed a strategy that depended on the commercials getting attention in the news.

Here again, Wellstone was helped by events outside his control; he deliberately and deftly took full advantage of them. In 1990 news organizations across the country were examining and revising their political coverage in response to charges that they were manipulated during the 1988 presidential campaign. Virtually every major news outlet in Minnesota decided that one way to improve coverage was to scrutinize the most important way candidates deliver their message—the TV commercials. The

St. Paul Pioneer Press and the Minneapolis *Star Tribune* regularly described and analyzed the ads of every statewide candidate. And even as the ads ran during commercial breaks on the six o'clock and ten o'clock news, TV reporters alerted viewers when to beware of false or misleading advertising.

"We knew the media was going to be, in essence, reviewing the commercials this time out," said Hillsman. "For us, that was great news. We knew we were going to have better commercials." Indeed, Wellstone's ads manipulated the media in their own way. Boschwitz followed the time-honored tactic of saturating the airwaves with his ads. Wellstone took the limited-edition approach to advertising. His ads ran so infrequently that they gained a sort of mystique and very nearly became collectors' items.

When a new ad was ready, Forciea called reporters and usually personally delivered copies of the tapes for them to preview. Reporters coveted the videocassettes of each new Hillsman production, and they were eager to do stories about them. National media such as the *New York Times* and the *Washington Post* also noted Hillsman's work, and CNN played excerpts from the ads.

Wellstone's strategists were hoping for precisely this kind of attention. Because of the campaign's budget constraints, each ad had to be given extra media exposure for it to be successful. "Every time we looked at the tapes," Pat Milan said, "that's what we assessed: What would the reporters think about the ads?"

In addition to drawing laughs, Hillsman's first three ads sold selective Wellstone traits—his agreeable personality, his energy, his prankishness, and his willingness to make fun of himself. The goal was to show that Wellstone had a wife, a happy and intact family, a modest home, and a sense of humor. If Hillsman could make that portrait stick, then it would be more difficult for

Boschwitz to paste the ultraliberal label on him later in the campaign.

The ads also expanded and honed a strategy that had been in place from day one: turn Boschwitz's money against him. "Fast-Paced Paul" touched on Boschwitz's money advantage in its opening lines ("Unlike my opponent, I don't have $6 million") and the ensuing ad, "Faces," was devoted exclusively to that issue. In this ad, photographs of Wellstone and Boschwitz, both sporting expansive smiles, are interchanged as Wellstone explains in a voice-over that viewers will be seeing a lot more of Boschwitz's face in the coming weeks than they will of his. The reason is that Boschwitz has $6 million, and

> unlike Mr. Boschwitz, I didn't take money from out-of-state special interests like Exxon and Reynolds Tobacco. So when you get tired of seeing this face [Boschwitz's], just imagine it was the face of someone who was better prepared and in a better position to represent your interests.

Boschwitz's photo fades into Wellstone's as Wellstone delivers the punch line: "Not to mention better looking."

While he was taping the voice-over, Wellstone expressed doubts about the last line. "I don't know about this business of better looking," he said.

"Women dig you," Jarl Olsen, the author of the script, said. "That's what the polls said. . . . The thing people don't expect in political advertising is a sense of humor. The thing about Rudy Boschwitz that my mother doesn't like is he's one humorless S.O.B."

That was not true at all: Boschwitz had a fine sense of humor. One of the first billboards he leased for his plywood business in the early 1960s declared, "Keep Bullfighting out of Minnesota." This was a "public service" campaign, Boschwitz said at the time, and a similarly offbeat style pervaded much of his early commercial advertising. But his political ads in 1990 were either schmaltzy or strained to present a dignified, influential persona. Boschwitz's polling showed that Minnesotans thought he was a nice guy but that he had not accomplished much.

The taping finished, Wellstone started to leave the studio when he spun around and rushed back inside. "I see what you're getting at," he said excitedly. "If I *was* good looking, then it would be a problem. But since I'm *not*, it's not a problem."

Others, however, thought it was indeed a problem. David Lillehaug, who would coach Wellstone for the debates with Boschwitz, wrote in a memo to Wellstone that the punch line was counterproductive. His assessment reflected political insiders' continuing anxiety about Wellstone's increasingly off-the-wall television campaign.

The "Faces" ad probably was the riskiest of Hillsman's offerings, flirting with the possibility that the punch line would be interpreted literally and as a personal attack against the senator, but it did not create the furor that Wellstone feared. In a fit of nervousness, he ordered that the ad be taken off the air, and then he received positive responses to it, including praise from a pair of nuns and a $100 check from a businessman he met on an airplane. Wellstone immediately gave Forciea permission to put the ad back on.

Looking for Rudy

"Faces" primed the television audience for the next Hillsman ad, a masterpiece called "Looking for Rudy" scripted by Bob Barrie and Jarl Olsen, the same pair that created "Fast-Paced Paul." The two-minute spot was patterned after the 1989 hit documentary *Roger & Me* in which director Michael Moore sets off in search of an audience with General Motors president Roger Smith, to ask him why he is laying off thousands of workers in

Flint, Michigan. This time Wellstone was not at all reticent to follow Hillsman's directions in a piece of guerrilla theater.

In fact, the candidate was open to the idea of seeking interviews with Donald Trump, the chairman of Exxon, and other high-ranking capitalists. One scheme was to approach Trump, who was in deep financial trouble, to ask if he needed help in retrieving the thousands of dollars he had donated to Boschwitz. Another idea was to ask the Exxon executive if the oil company felt it had gotten its money's worth out of Boschwitz. But budget and time constrictions did not permit out-of-town trips, so the group had to settle for filming in Northfield and the Twin Cities.

"Looking for Rudy" opens with Wellstone chatting with a shopkeeper, an auto mechanic, and a mother with preschoolers, all of whom say they would like to see debates between the Senate candidates.

"Getting hold of the person I had to debate, however, proved easier said than done," Wellstone says as he begins his search for Boschwitz.

His first stop is the senator's campaign headquarters—not a movie set, but the real thing in downtown Minneapolis. Wellstone passes a BMW in the parking lot and says under his breath, "Nice car!" Then he barges into the office and surprises two young, tall, white-shirted campaign workers who look and act like bouncers. With their hands out in front of them, they block Wellstone's path and one says, "We don't like strangers walking around." Like other Boschwitz employees who show up in the ad, the young men unwittingly serve as perfect foils for the friendly, joking Wellstone.

Wellstone asks if he can leave a message, and obligingly scribbles his home phone number on a piece of his campaign literature.

"I'll make sure that he gets this, and we'll get back to you, uh . . ." Boschwitz finance director Bob Anderson says, trailing off.

"What do *you* think?" Wellstone asks. "Do *you* think we should have debates around the state? So that people can see . . ."

Anderson interrupts. "I'll get the message to him."

"What do *you* think?" Wellstone asks again.

Curtly, Anderson shoots back, "Glad to meet you."

With a broad smile, Wellstone gently presses the point. "No, but about these debates?"

"Thanks for coming down," Anderson gamely replies.

Breaking into a laugh, and shaking hands with the Boschwitz workers, Wellstone backs down. "OK, OK, all right. I'll see you all."

Next, Wellstone visits Boschwitz's Senate office in St. Paul, where an aide stiffly informs him that the senator is not there; he's returning from Milwaukee.

"No luck," Wellstone says in a voice-over.

Again, Wellstone jots down his home phone number and then admires the pen in his hand.

"Is this your pen?" he asks.

"I'm not sure," the woman replies as she leans forward to look at it. "Probably not."

"Oooooo!" Wellstone coos admiringly. "It looks like a nice one. Well, I don't have a lot of money, so I'll keep this for our campaign." He flashes an enormous grin and turns to leave.

The commercial then follows Wellstone's efforts to track Boschwitz by phone. He asks his staff if Boschwitz has returned the calls. Naturally, he has not.

"I tried everything; I mean everything," he says, exasperated. The ad concludes with Wellstone on the phone, calling directory information for Boschwitz's home number.

"In the meantime," Wellstone concludes in a voice-over, "if

you see a silver-haired gentleman in a plaid shirt, mention I'm looking for him."

For weeks after Hillsman had filmed "Looking for Rudy" in August, he pressed Forciea for the money to edit it. Before the primary, cash was too tight to spend on the expensive two-minute spot. When Wellstone's primary win brought in more money, Forciea provided Hillsman with the funds he needed to prepare the ad for airing.

As it turned out, the timing was propitious. When Hillsman's team completed work on "Looking for Rudy" on October 2, Boschwitz was stuck in Washington for the budget debate. Boschwitz's absence from Minnesota provided the perfect justification for the daring ad.

Forciea stirred up interest among the political press corps by calling reporters and telling them that another Hillsman gem was in the offing. On October 3 he personally delivered copies of the ad to reporters, hoping they would do stories about it. Forciea's plan worked brilliantly.

Television reporters showed the ad before the campaign had spent a penny for air time. In fact, by the time "Looking for Rudy" ran that night in its commercial slot at 9:58 P.M., it had already been shown on the early-evening newscasts as part of their reports on the campaign. There was still more coverage on the ten o'clock news. "Looking for Rudy" was run even on TV stations from which the campaign did not buy commercial time; Forciea made sure that reporters at those stations had the tapes.

The success of "Looking for Rudy" gave Wellstone an enormous boost. During a campaign swing the next weekend, he was delighted to hear people ask over and over, "Have you found Rudy yet?"

As it turned out, Wellstone had to make another trip to Washington to find Rudy to debate him. Hardly were the debate negotiations concluded when Tom Mason hinted that Boschwitz might be too busy to return to Minnesota for the first debate because of the deadlock in Washington over the federal budget. In reply, John Blackshaw dashed off a tongue-in-cheek note to Mason on October 8. Remarking that Boschwitz had found time in his schedule to fly home for the September 27 fund-raiser in Minneapolis with President Bush, Blackshaw suggested that Mason schedule more fund-raisers in conjunction with the debate.

"Perhaps they may serve as incentives for Senator Boschwitz to return to the state," Blackshaw wrote. He also jokingly offered an alternative: Wellstone would travel to Washington for the debate.

The next evening, a letter from Mason rolled out of the fax machine in Wellstone's campaign headquarters:

> Thanks for Paul's offer to debate Rudy in Washington this Sunday. As you know, Rudy has been working long hours, often late into the night, as Congress has wrestled with a solution to the budget crisis. It appears that the Budget Committee will be meeting this weekend, and that weekend sessions of the full Senate are quite likely. We therefore would be pleased to accept this change of venue.

Mason also replied to Blackshaw's suggestion for arranging fund-raisers with his own touch of humor: "Thanks, too, for the advice to conduct fund-raisers with the debates. We'll pass, however. We believe we are adequately funded."

To the Wellstone camp's amazement, Mason had accepted their joking offer to move the debate to Washington. "Our initial reaction when Pat [Forciea] and I talked about it [Mason's letter] was they called our bluff," said Blackshaw. A check with Democratic leaders in the Senate disclosed that no weekend meetings had been scheduled. Wellstone was outraged. "Why are we letting them get away with this crap?" he said.

After the shock subsided, Blackshaw and Forciea concluded that the change of venue was to their advantage because it would focus more attention on the event. "We take these jabs and these incredible risks and they keep working to our advantage," Blackshaw said, shaking his head at the luck that was breaking Wellstone's way.

10

CRAZY BOUNCES

"Looking for Rudy" disturbed the Boschwitz camp's equanimity and forced his advisers at last to respond harshly to Wellstone, the first clear sign that damage had been inflicted. Boschwitz's brain trust saw the ad as misleading, if not downright inaccurate. The commercial ran after Boschwitz had already agreed to three debates; all that was left to be negotiated was the time, location, and ground rules.

Sam Kaplan and John Blackshaw, who were negotiating on Wellstone's behalf, were convinced that Boschwitz's aides were stalling and were trying to make the debates as meaningless as possible, so Wellstone had no qualms about letting loose with "Looking for Rudy." Moreover, while the ad may have left the impression that Boschwitz was refusing to debate, the script carefully avoided any direct misstatements. In fact, one of the concluding lines was, "Rest assured, there will be debates on the key issues of this campaign."

The ad's real impact was to portray Boschwitz as remote and haughty and his retinue as snooty yuppies. Insofar as it created the impression that Boschwitz was somehow avoiding engagement with his puckish challenger, it was defensible. For months,

Boschwitz himself almost never responded to Wellstone's attacks, and his strategy was built squarely on running as if Wellstone did not exist.

Now this annoying opponent had to be dealt with. Spokesman Jay Novak unleashed three carefully chosen epithets in interviews with the Minneapolis *Star Tribune*. He called Wellstone an "Abbie Hoffman-type character," a "leftist hustler," and a "self-promoting little fake."

Long after the election Novak revealed that the terms were crafted and approved by Tom Mason, and that part of the strategy was to damage Wellstone's credibility among mainstream DFLers: "The Abbie Hoffman comparison was for the legitimate left, for those who remembered Hoffman as a kind of a show-biz character rather than a serious reformer. The attack was really aimed at the serious liberal."

Novak recalled indignation in the Boschwitz camp at "Looking for Rudy" and a genuine feeling that Wellstone was seriously alleging that the senator was refusing to debate. The disclaimer that "there will be debates" was seen as a claim by Wellstone that he would force the debates to happen.

But Novak's put-downs of Wellstone struck many observers as spiteful and humorless, and as a sign that Wellstone had scored a direct hit. Pat Forciea snapped back with a classic put-down of his own, one of the most devastating one-liners of the campaign: Novak "should buy some looser underwear," he said, magnifying the ad's portrayal of the Boschwitz campaign as uptight and humorless. The ad, which appeared on October 3 and 4, also served as a warning that this campaign was not going to be the routine slam dunk that Boschwitz had anticipated.

As the date of the first debate—October 14—approached, the Wellstone camp saw it as a make-or-break opportunity. Blackshaw begged Wellstone to have a professional barber tame his frizzy hair. "I gave him the finger," Wellstone said, laughing.

Since his marriage twenty-seven years earlier, he had never gone to a barber; Sheila always cut his hair at home. Wellstone finally relented, and an appointment was arranged for him at a downtown salon the day before the debate. He stood up the barber and got a trim from his son's girlfriend instead.

Wellstone was more agreeable to submitting to two days of intensive preparation at the hands of David Lillehaug, one of the few DFL insiders who committed to Wellstone's campaign. Lillehaug had been Walter Mondale's executive assistant during Mondale's 1984 presidential campaign, a role that qualified him for inclusion in what Atlanta mayor Andrew Young once called Mondale's club of "smart-ass white boys." Now thirty-six years old and graying prematurely, he practiced corporate law in a prominent Minneapolis firm. But Lillehaug craved a good political fight, and at the state convention he told Forciea that he would be glad to help Wellstone prepare for debates against Boschwitz. Lillehaug had been a supporter of Tom Berg, whom he had known for years through legal and political circles, but when Berg lost the endorsement contest, Lillehaug did not hesitate to offer his help to Forciea. "Candidate debate preparation is the political activity I most enjoy," he said. "For me it was like candy."

The opportunity to work with Wellstone was especially appealing, because as Lillehaug watched Wellstone deliver his rousing speech to the convention, he wondered whether he could channel the candidate's hot public speaking style into the cool medium of television without robbing him of his passion. And, unlike most of the DFL regulars, Lillehaug was drawn to Wellstone out of party loyalty. "I wanted to make sure that he did well and that what he did reflected well on the party," Lillehaug said.

As a latecomer to the campaign and as a representative of the Democratic Party's establishment wing, however, Lillehaug was resented by some of Wellstone's academic friends and advisers. To them, he was symbolic of the cancer of modern politics—an upscale handler who focused on style and appearance instead of issues. "I think it would be fair to say we detested each other," said Andy Blauvelt, a professor at St. John's University in Collegeville, Minnesota, who clashed repeatedly with Lillehaug during one of the debate preparation sessions.

But Lillehaug was in tune with Wellstone when it came to class issues, and he offered the candidate good advice and sharp phrases for prosecuting the case. The debate training sessions were held in the downtown Minneapolis office where Lillehaug practiced law. First he showed Wellstone excerpts from a handful of political debates, including one of Boschwitz's debates against his 1984 opponent, Democrat Joan Growe. He also brought in a podium and a video camera to tape Wellstone in dry runs and in a mock debate with Sam Kaplan.

Lillehaug reviewed with Wellstone the mechanics of the debate—which clothes he should wear, what he should do with his hands, how to tell when a camera pointing at him was actually on. Most importantly, he stressed that Wellstone had to stoke the anti-incumbent sentiment by continually blaming Boschwitz for the gridlock in Washington and weaving into his attacks the powerful pocketbook issues that Wellstone had been championing throughout his campaign. "I want you to ring that anti-incumbency bell every time you can," Lillehaug said. "If you can ring that bell every thirty seconds, then the debate will be a success."

When the coaching session turned to taxes, Lillehaug reassured Wellstone that the tax issue was an asset. "For the first time in twenty years, the word *taxes* out of the mouth of a questioner will be beneficial to you as a Democrat," he said. And again, when they reviewed the budget stalemate in Washington, Lillehaug told Wellstone: "This is obviously fertile ground to ring the [anti-incumbency] bell. If there's a single question on the budget where you don't ring the bell, I'm going to take my television and throw it across the room."

Boschwitz was preparing too, and his campaign was keenly aware that Wellstone was an unpredictable challenger. Campaign manager Tom Mason recalled in a postmortem on the election that he wrote for *Minnesota Monthly* magazine that after an afternoon of debate preparation, Boschwitz, his wife and staffers went out to eat at a Chinese restaurant in McLean, Virginia. Boschwitz's fortune cookie told him: "You'll soon be looking for a new job." Mason recalled that the "diners laughed nervously . . . but nobody thought it funny."

The opening camera shot of the debate showed the two candidates standing side by side at their podiums, the difference in height between them spectacular. Despite the fact that Boschwitz was nearly a foot taller, Wellstone had refused offers from the producers to provide him with a hidden riser to stand on to eliminate the glaring difference. "As long as I can see over the podium," Wellstone said, "I want to take him on my own terms."

Wellstone's first words betrayed a nervousness that only those in the tiny studio could truly appreciate—they could see his hands shaking uncontrollably—but he warmed up quickly. His rhetoric and his body language were combative as he hammered on the fact that Washington was a mess and Boschwitz was at the scene of the crime.

"I can see why you might not have wanted to come home, considering your role in this budget mess," Wellstone said in his opening statement. His sentences were peppered with words and phrases like "Washington happy talk," the "terrible decade of the eighties," and "incumbent."

Wellstone's better moments came when the debate turned to domestic issues. One of his best lines (the real credit goes to

Lillehaug) described the extra $75 that Medicare recipients would have had to pay as a result of a recently failed budget summit agreement. "That may be lunch in Washington, D.C., but that's a lot of money to Medicare recipients," Wellstone said. At another point, Wellstone put his case succinctly: "Poor people are poorer and the wealthy are getting away like bandits."

Boschwitz fought back with his trademark statistic on how the bottom 50 percent of taxpayers pay less than 5 percent of taxes, but he failed to refute convincingly many of Wellstone's biting attacks on Reaganism. Boschwitz argued that the 1980s had brought an end to inflation and high interest rates, and he observed that Wellstone seemed to want every federal program but defense to "grow and grow and grow."

Much as Wellstone had looked forward to the debate, it was hardly a critical or defining moment in the campaign. The consensus among political observers was that the debate was a draw, which was good for Boschwitz. The senator maintained his composure, and he did look more senatorial than Wellstone. Wellstone came across as a well-informed if unpolished character who at most could hold his own against the incumbent. Many local political experts felt that Wellstone would have few chances to really damage Boschwitz, and that he failed to do so this time. Chuck Heineken, a Twin Cities financial planner who was interviewed by the Minneapolis *Star Tribune* as part of a focus group of independent voters, said the debate actually moved him from leaning toward Wellstone to leaning toward Boschwitz. Heineken said Wellstone was "too belittling" and spent too much time complaining about having to hold the debate in Washington. "It wasn't relevant," Heineken said.

The Swimming Pool

The debate was quickly overwhelmed by a story that would engulf the rest of the 1990 Minnesota election in confusion. For the next week and a half, Wellstone's campaign would be muted by the most sensational allegations anyone could remember in the state's politics.

Moments before the debate began, as Forciea and Mason sat side by side in the studio, Forciea leaned over and whispered cryptically about a tip he had picked up about the gubernatorial race: Grunseth . . . nude . . . swimming pool . . . teenage girls . . . newspaper story . . . he's finished. Mason tried to make sense of it as the debate began, and then he pulled up short. He thought Forciea might be trying to rattle him so he wouldn't pay attention to the debate, so he put it out of his mind and returned to matters at hand.

Later that evening, however, Mason realized Forciea wasn't playing mind games. He learned from a reporter that a major scandal was about to break, and on Monday morning the whole state was steeped in it.

Two young women, Liane Nelson and Elizabeth Mulay, had provided the *Star Tribune* with sworn affidavits that late at night at a July 4 party in 1981, when both were in their early teens, an inebriated Jon Grunseth, now the Republican gubernatorial nominee, had jumped nude into a swimming pool with them. They said Grunseth encouraged them to take off their suits, and even tried to pull down the top of Mulay's suit. Questioned and cross-examined about their motives, the young women said they had not stepped forward earlier because they did not think Grunseth would win the gubernatorial primary. After he won, they decided they had to speak up to warn voters of Grunseth's character and for their own peace of mind, they said. The young women, both of whom were then out-of-state college students, Nelson in Massachusetts and Mulay in California, struck many voters as credible.

Grunseth—tall, handsome, lantern-jawed, deep-voiced—until that day looked very much like Minnesota's next governor. Grunseth had secured the Republican Party's endorsement and swept to a surprising primary election victory with a strong appeal to party idealists—abortion opponents, gun-control opponents, free enterprisers, and social conservatives.

Unlike Wellstone, Grunseth had never run for statewide office and he had not been very active in party politics for at least ten years. He was vice president for public relations with a well-known company that made cleaning and lawn chemical products, but most of the political world knew next to nothing about him. His critics said he was an empty shell, a fellow who looked and talked like a governor, but whose real essence was a mystery. There were also rumors about his lifestyle, a messy divorce, a period of "booze and broads," his press secretary would later admit in a revelatory and damaging article in the *St. Paul Pioneer Press*.

Weeks before the primary, some of these rumors already had begun circulating. Reporters checked the stories and did not find much of substance. DFL governor Rudy Perpich had tried to make an issue out of Grunseth's messy divorce and his refusal to pay a small portion of a child support payment, but that controversy appeared to hurt Perpich almost as much as Grunseth. When the Nelson-Mulay allegations surfaced, however, the media leapt at the story.

Partygoers from the July 4 event were rounded up by the Grunseth campaign, and they submitted affidavits affirming that they did not see Grunseth in the pool. Other people corroborated the girls' accounts. Grunseth in his interview with the *Pioneer Press* did confess to a swinging bachelor's lifestyle and to being a "warm-blooded American male" in his "wild years" between marriages, giving credibility to numerous rumors about womanizing and carousing, but he categorically denied the swimming pool charges. He secretly took a lie detector test and later released the results, which supported his version of the events.

The whole state was abuzz with this spectacular political soap opera. Jokes like this one proliferated: "Q: What's the difference between Elvis Presley and Jon Grunseth? A: Jon Grunseth is dead." And there were many who found it not funny at all. Legislators campaigning for reelection reported that citizens were angry. They also detected that the Grunseth-Perpich debacle was intensifying an already prevalent anti-incumbent sentiment.

Wellstone was angry too. Already convinced that the media had ignored his campaign, he saw the virtual blackout of the Senate race as its death knell. What really irritated him was a *Star Tribune* Minnesota Poll story on October 18 that found Wellstone 18 points behind Boschwitz, 56 percent to 38 percent. That was a slippage of 3 points for Wellstone since the last poll about three weeks earlier. (Wellstone's own internal poll showed the gap had narrowed to only 7 points.) The demoralizing poll story, which ran on the front page of the metro news section, was the best play he had received in the paper in weeks. Although the story did not explicitly say so, the clear message was that his campaign was hopeless. The story infuriated Wellstone, who had long griped that the paper devoted more time to conducting and publishing polls on the Senate race than it did to covering the substance of his campaign. His advisers were actually afraid that Wellstone might go to the newspaper office and take a swing at the managing editor.

Settling for a more civilized approach to gaining media coverage, Wellstone called a press conference for Monday, October 22, when he tried a combination of wisecracks and goading to get back in the news. "I've never been swimming in my life, not by myself or with anyone else," he joked to reporters. He welcomed them back as if they were prodigal children, saying, "I want you to be able to tell your grandchildren that you covered this race."

Wellstone gamely tried to sound upbeat about his chances of defeating Boschwitz. What he did not know then was that he would be vindicated on the very next day, when the clouds would part and give him one of the most glorious days in his eighteen-month quest.

Round Two

The second debate was scheduled for October 23, and the logistics of this one, like those of the first debate, were altered by Boschwitz's insistence that he had to stay in Washington to work. So while Wellstone sat in the Minnesota Public Radio (MPR) studio in downtown St. Paul, Boschwitz joined the debate from Washington.

In the hour-long debate, the senator was subjected to some of Wellstone's most spirited and sharpest attacks. Wellstone was energized by the news that a *Star Tribune*/KSTP-TV Minnesota Poll rated him just 3 points behind Boschwitz, 45 percent to 48 percent. The poll would not be reported until KSTP's ten o'clock news show that night, but word of the results reached the Wellstone camp early that morning.

Wellstone's inner circle was jubilant. Pat Forciea and John Blackshaw knew that this could be a turning point in the race, a development that would immediately transform Wellstone into a legitimate candidate. The poll would help Wellstone overcome the media's preoccupation with the Grunseth intrigue, and it would draw desperately needed campaign donations. Best of all, it would give the campaign a sense of hope.

"We've climbed on top of Goliath's $7 million and we're staring him right in the face," a newly confident Forciea said.

"This thing is going to go through the state like electricity." As he drove Wellstone to the debate, Forciea made light of Boschwitz's public statement that he was suffering from a prostate problem. "How do you think his prostate's feeling right about now?" Forciea smirked.

Out of Wellstone's earshot, however, Forciea confided that the campaign was on the ropes financially. Just a week earlier, shortly after Boschwitz reported that he was sitting on a mountain of cash—$1.1 million—the Wellstone bank account was down to $7.15. Dick Senese, then the campaign's finance director, had ordered that the campaign payroll be delayed for a few days because he knew the checks would have bounced. With the final weeks of the campaign approaching, and with other campaigns quickly buying up the prime times for TV ads, Forciea had no money to reserve time for Wellstone's ads.

"The reality is we have no money to make our buy Friday—none," Forciea said as he trailed Wellstone into the MPR building. "We've been counting on the DSCC [the Democratic Senatorial Campaign Committee] to buy the last two weeks of ads. We have to put $40,000 down Friday and $50,000 down Monday and we simply don't have the money."

Inside the MPR studio, Wellstone knew none of the details of the campaign's money problems. Fueled by news of the poll results, he tore into Boschwitz. The debate, which also was filmed and shown on public television that night, began with Boschwitz making small talk about what a tough budget debate he was involved in and how it might be best if "we just shut 'er [the federal government] down" to force an agreement. Wellstone immediately struck back and blasted Boschwitz's recent lobbying at the White House against a tax hike on the wealthy:

You and the gang of sixteen other senators went in and told the president, "Don't raise the tax rates for wealthy people." For the top 1 percent. And I think that it's come to the point in the history of our country where people are just tired of it. Middle- and working-class people are really being squeezed and people on the top [are] getting off like bandits, and the poor poorer.

Boschwitz responded with a statistic-laden defense of the justice of the income tax system:

> Please don't say that the income tax system of this country is unfair. As you know, the top 5 percent of all taxpayers pay 45.9 percent of all the income taxes. The top 10 percent of all taxpayers pay 57 percent of all income taxes in this country. The income tax system in this country is fair. After the 1986 tax bill . . . you've read no articles about the rich escaping taxation. They do not escape taxation. We closed all the loopholes. . . . The income tax system really does nick the wealthy.

Boschwitz also tried the gloom-and-doom theme, a favorite of conservatives, when he chided Wellstone for being "so downbeat on America."

"I'm not quite so sure that I think the eighties were such a dismal failure," Boschwitz said when Wellstone tried to pin a share of the blame for the federal debt on him. "In the 1980s we had seven and a half years of economic growth unabated," Boschwitz continued. "It was the longest period of economic growth that this nation has ever had." Boschwitz noted that there were spending increases, even accounting for inflation, for many social programs. One by one, Boschwitz ticked them off: the school lunch program doubled in the 1980s, the food stamp program jumped from $9 billion to $16 billion annually, and Head Start programs, which prepare disadvantaged preschoolers for kindergarten, "have gone up very nicely in the 1980s— almost doubled."

Wellstone countered with a vengeance. "No, I'm sorry," he said. "I can't let you get away with this, I really can't. This is a bunch of Boschwitz." Wellstone pointed out that the demand for those programs had grown faster than the increases. He charged that Boschwitz had voted for the chintzy alternatives on decisions affecting poor women and children, yet almost always embraced the most expensive options when it came to defense spending. These were "mean-spirited votes," he said, suggesting that Boschwitz, the millionaire Washington insider, simply had not associated with the people who were hurting. "You need to be there with people to know what's happening," Wellstone said:

> The Head Start program is reaching only one out of four eligible children. The WIC program [which provides prenatal care and nutrition help for women, infants, and children] is only serving about a quarter of children who are eligible. And in case you didn't notice it, Rudy, in our state there was a study done by the Urban Coalition that something like a third of children from low-income households in Hennepin County [which includes Minneapolis] are going to school hungry. . . .
>
> You try and tell all of us here that there's been all these great things done for child care, all these great things done for investment in education in children. It has not happened. We've abandoned our children during this decade of the eighties. And we're not going to have real security until we invest in our children. That's a big difference between the two of us.

After the debate, Wellstone joined Forciea and Blackshaw in an employee lounge in the radio station's offices where the two campaign officials had been watching the debate on closed-circuit television. Reporters also followed the debate from the lounge, as did Jay Novak from the Boschwitz camp. When Wellstone came into the lounge after the debate, he was ecstatic.

"I feel like David has climbed right up on top of Goliath's $6 million and is staring him right in the face," Wellstone told the reporters, borrowing Forciea's line and shaving off $1 million.

As Wellstone fielded questions from the press, Novak was on the telephone with Tom Mason, discussing what he should say to them. After he hung up, Novak said the debate was another win for Boschwitz. The debate "showed that he's in command of the facts, that he has a good deal of depth and knows what he's talking about," Novak said.

But Wellstone continued to put the Boschwitz campaign on the defensive, this time turning his attention to Novak. As reporters watched, Wellstone confronted Novak about his comments in response to "Looking for Rudy," in particular Novak's statement that Wellstone was "a self-promoting little fake."

"You know what really hurt? It was the part about being little," Wellstone said, pretending to have been truly offended, even though he had repeatedly made fun of his height himself. Caught off guard by this encounter, Novak swallowed and looked tense. Forciea and Blackshaw stood to the side trying to conceal their smirks. They knew that after eighteen months of effort, Wellstone finally was gaining momentum and was starting to control the contest with Boschwitz.

Their money problems also were about to be resolved. When word about the poll leaked out on the day of the debate, lobbyists and party leaders who had ignored Wellstone for so long rushed for the bandwagon. D. J. Leary, a Democratic public affairs consultant whose political newsletter had dismissed Wellstone, was the first through the campaign headquarters' door. He gave Blackshaw a hearty handshake, a $250 check, and a promise to tout Wellstone in the next newsletter.

Blackshaw and other staff members were thrilled to see the money and the interest, but they also were annoyed. "I now know what it's like to be patronized," Sam Kaplan said at an October 24 fund-raiser. "Before, I felt like I was being patted on the head by people saying, 'How nice it is for you to take care of the little guy.' Yesterday, I started getting calls from the party regulars saying, 'You know, we've been with you from the beginning.' "

Still, their righteous annoyance with the latecomers did not prevent them from accepting the money. In the three days immediately following publication of the poll, Wellstone's mailbox overflowed with checks. Rock star Don Henley sent a $1,000 check by Federal Express from California. Sarah Brady's handgun-control PAC sent $4,500 the same way. Even the National Abortion Rights Action League (NARAL), which had repeatedly ignored or rejected Wellstone's requests for help, opened its checkbook and sent $1,000 the day after the poll was published. NARAL sent an additional $1,000 within the week.

"It's literally raining money," Forciea said at a Minneapolis rally for the statewide Democratic ticket the day the poll was published. Outside Wellstone's headquarters, the street was clogged with double-parked cars as donors ran in with checks and new volunteers asked if they could help. Staff members were not able to call out because the seven phone lines were overloaded with incoming calls from people wanting to donate money, time, or both. In and out of the office, staff members were besieged by people asking how they could contribute funds.

"I took $1,300 from people handing me money," said deputy field director Dan Cramer. "It was really exciting. It was a real high. I walked out of the office after fifteen hours and I felt like I was flying. Normally, I walk out and you have to scrape me off the ground."

"I wish we took VISA and MasterCard," David Graham joked.

Liz Borg reacted with one of her trademark comments: "I feel some sort of weird karma about this."

In three days, Wellstone collected $96,000—more than 10 percent of the campaign's total take during the previous eighteen months. In addition, the DSCC, sensing that Wellstone might be a winner, immediately spent $100,000 on television time for him.

Nothing in Wellstone's style or message had changed. In essence, it was the same campaign, the same candidate who had announced that he was running eighteen months earlier. Only the poll numbers had changed. While Wellstone was delighted by the revitalization of his campaign, he knew that it was happening for all the wrong reasons. "It's something about polls and how they fit in that just doesn't make sense," he said as his staff worked overtime to record and deposit the campaign donations. "Everything happens because of polls, not the other way around."

"Ruddy: Zillion"

Indeed, the DSCC money meant that Wellstone could stay on the air with another imaginative ad from Bill Hillsman's team. In this one, called "Kids," Hillsman lowered the boom on Boschwitz with a bunch of tow-headed, curly-haired, freckle-faced, unfairly adorable preschoolers. "It's one of the meanest ads I've ever seen," Forciea said admiringly. "The idea of using four-year-olds to deliver the message—holy man!"

In the ad kids sit at a desk and use colored markers to write oversized checks to Boschwitz, then show them off with devastating grins. One boy proudly holds up his check, which he has filled in with childish letters: "Rudy. 13$. (Signed:) HARRY."

The sound of a cash register is heard: KA-CHING!

Another boy fills in his check with a red marker, giving "100000000" to "Rudy." He signs it "Sam."

KA-CHING! KA-CHING!

A girl shows her check made out to "Ruddy" for "zillion" and signed "Jessicca."

As these and other button-cute kids do their damage in rapid-fire sequence, Wellstone's voice-over says:

> If kids had money, maybe Senator Boschwitz would listen to them. If kids had money, maybe Senator Boschwitz would vote in their interest. If kids had money, maybe he wouldn't have one of the worst records in the Senate on children's issues. But kids don't have money. Boschwitz votes against their issues again and again. I'm Paul Wellstone. And I think it's time he paid.

The ad focused on a charge that had consumed Wellstone—that Boschwitz had failed to promote and vote for legislation that would help children, especially poor children. Boschwitz's zero rating by the Children's Defense Fund in 1989 was a stock element of Wellstone's stump speeches, along with attacks on Boschwitz's votes on child care subsidies and other issues important to parents. Wellstone did not try to accuse Boschwitz of being unfair only to lower-income children, and his broadening of the charge created a potent issue in suburban, two-income, middle-class families worried about day care and education. Indeed, while they were by no means scientific, nightly phone calls made by Wellstone volunteers during the week that the "Kids" ad ran detected big gains among suburban residents in their thirties and forties—parents, no doubt.

The beauty of this ad was that there was no way to respond. "How do you counterattack kids?" asked Wellstone adviser Pat Milan, who whistled in awe when he first saw the storyboard for the ad. "You can't do it and win. You can do it and be an Arab terrorist. . . . You take on kids and you're dead meat. What's your response? There is no response."

The ad ran for a week, October 22-29, without drawing any effective response from Boschwitz. It was then that Forciea grew more confident that the Boschwitz juggernaut was not all that it was cracked up to be.

From the Boschwitz camp, Tom Mason disputed the accuracy of the Minnesota Poll, but then he added that Wellstone had "not been defined very well by the media." He implied that Boschwitz's negative ads were warmed up and on the runway, that until then, the Boschwitz campaign was reluctant to launch an assault on Wellstone.

In hindsight, every armchair quarterback in the state claimed to have known that Boschwitz failed by not attacking earlier, but Mason had felt that an early assault on Wellstone was just too risky. With Wellstone and the media constantly drawing attention to Boschwitz's enormous financial advantage and safe lead in the polls, he had feared that criticism of the challenger would be perceived as bullying and mean-spirited. Mason also had figured that to acknowledge Wellstone in a Boschwitz commercial would increase the challenger's abysmal name recognition.

The latest poll results convinced Boschwitz and his aides that they could no longer merely counterpunch. They had to take the offensive. On Wednesday, October 24, the day the poll appeared in the *Star Tribune,* Boschwitz telephoned a number of reporters and told them he felt like "a caged tiger" and would be abandoning Washington that night, even if he had to miss votes, to get back home.

That afternoon, however, he found himself in yet another predicament that lowered his standing with voters. As the Senate considered an override of President Bush's veto of civil rights legislation, Boschwitz clumsily switched sides. Initially siding with the president and opposing the bill, Boschwitz now favored the override because he agreed with Wellstone's comment in their second debate that the veto would encourage racist "skinheads" and hatemongers like David Duke, then running for the U.S. Senate. Boschwitz said he voted for the override because he looked up and saw Duke sitting in the gallery watching the proceedings.

The reversal, widely reported in the media, could not have helped him with those on either side of the issue, or with un-decideds. Those in favor of affirmative action saw the flip-flop as insincere and an attempt to win votes away from Wellstone. Those opposed to the legislation saw Boschwitz as a traitor, giving in on what they considered the critical issue of racial quotas.

Confronted with evidence that this challenger that he had dismissed as a left-wing flake was now threatening to take his job away, Boschwitz returned to Minnesota to engage the enemy. On Thursday morning, October 25, he launched his own negative campaign by accusing his opponent of running one all along. "He says I'm mean-spirited, and I think Minnesotans know me better than that," Boschwitz said in the southern town of Mankato. "While [Wellstone] was out there huffing about, protesting and getting himself jailed, we fixed up the Farm Credit System."

Wellstone's staff quickly admitted to the arrests and provided more details. And after blistering Boschwitz for weeks for being isolated and alienated in Washington, Wellstone adeptly changed positions, attacking the incumbent for coming back to Minnesota. Noting that Boschwitz missed a key debate on the farm bill so he could rush home to help his party, which was disintegrating in the turmoil caused by the Jon Grunseth sex scandal, Wellstone jabbed, "He should be lining up votes there, not playing politics back here. He wasn't just elected to represent Republicans."

Undoubtedly Boschwitz would have preferred to gear up a full-fledged attack on Wellstone, but the Grunseth fiasco entangled him in an intraparty melodrama that would take up three days of precious campaign time.

On the afternoon of Thursday, October 25, Grunseth signaled that he would drop out of the governor's race, but then he met with wealthy contributors who persuaded him to stay in the race. That night, in a Bloomington hotel ballroom packed with reporters and supporters, Grunseth treated Minnesota voters to a bizarre spectacle. On live television, he tore up his withdrawal speech and vowed to stay in the contest. Bob Weinholzer, then the candid chair of the Minnesota Republican Party, acknowledged that the evening's events reflected poorly on the party. "If it looks like we don't have our act together, it's because we don't," he conceded.

For scores of tearful Grunseth fans in the hotel that evening, the biggest villain was Rudy Boschwitz, who had pressured Grunseth to quit. Boschwitz spent the evening in western Minnesota, keeping in touch with the events in Bloomington by phone. Despite his absence, Boschwitz was the target of angry Grunseth forces who believed that Boschwitz was trying to force Grunseth off the ticket to save himself.

Kathy Worre, a leading figure in the party's conservative Christian wing, actually said at one point that she and many other conservatives were likely to vote and work for Wellstone, just to punish Boschwitz. "He came out and threatened Jon," Worre told reporters. "Rudy Boschwitz is the one that killed him. . . . Rudy Boschwitz will lose, no matter what happens, whether Jon stays or leaves."

Before the night was out, Dick Senese had heard an unfounded rumor from his contacts in Duluth that Grunseth supporters wanted to contribute money to Wellstone in retaliation against Boschwitz. Senese doubted the rumor's authenticity, but he knew that it signaled that Boschwitz indeed was in trouble within his own party.

A detailed insiders' account in the book *There Is No November* by Grunseth's top campaign managers, David Hoium and Leon Oistad, portrays a desperate and manipulative Boschwitz, concerned primarily for his own skin. Days before Grunseth's aborted withdrawal from the race, according to Grunseth aide Elam Baer, Boschwitz agreed verbally to cover as much as $75,000 of Grunseth's campaign debts if Grunseth would drop out, a charge Boschwitz denied. (Grunseth subsequently lost a lawsuit against Boschwitz that alleged that Boschwitz broke a verbal agreement on this matter.)

Boschwitz was constantly on the verge of going public with a call for Grunseth to drop out, according to Grunseth's aides. Despite these backroom tactics, Boschwitz remained coy in public. When reporters pressed him, he replied diplomatically, trying to conceal his intimate role in this intrigue.

The Ticket Leader Goes Down

Grunseth doggedly remained in the race for three more days, but as he tried to douse the swimming pool controversy, two *Star Tribune* reporters confronted him on Saturday, October 27, with a new set of allegations. At the Minneapolis law office of a Grunseth supporter, reporters Paul McEnroe and Allen Short handed Grunseth a photo of Tamara Taylor, a striking thirty-two-year-old blond, who claimed to have had an intermittent nine-year affair with Grunseth that overlapped both of his marriages. Their latest tryst, she said, had been just one year before, long after his supposed "wild years" had ended.

Presented with her allegations, Grunseth acknowledged that he had had an affair with her, but he said it ended before his second marriage. As Sunday morning dawned, Minnesotans woke up to one of the wildest election stories they had ever read. On the front page of the state's largest newspaper, the headline read: "When did Grunseth 'wild years' end? Woman claims affair into '89; he says it was over 'long ago.'"

That same day, Taylor held a news conference to repeat her

story. She said she stepped forward because she believed the young women's accounts of the nude pool party. Grunseth himself had told her that there was nude swimming, she said.

With his campaign hopelessly mired in sordid allegations about his personal life, Grunseth decided on Sunday to surrender. Grunseth aides initiated a series of telephone negotiations with Boschwitz and his aides, and after securing what they believed was a gentleman's agreement from Boschwitz to help Grunseth pay his campaign debt, Grunseth announced his departure from the race. "It's wear and tear," he told the Associated Press. "It's just simply pure wear and tear. The whole thing becomes sickening. It's exhaustion, is what it is. Mental, physical, emotional exhaustion."

By the time Grunseth finally quit that Sunday afternoon, Boschwitz had become a pariah among many conservatives in the party. At first, the senator's campaign office was flooded with calls from Grunseth backers castigating him for his failure to support a fellow conservative. Within days, the first pieces of hate mail arrived.

11

HAND TO HAND COMBAT

With Jon Grunseth out of the gubernatorial race and Republican state auditor Arne Carlson serving as Grunseth's last-minute replacement, Rudy Boschwitz and his advisers knew exactly what was required to maintain his seat in the U.S. Senate. In the nine days left, they would pour all their money and energy into the long-awaited "defining" of their adversary.

Given his financial advantage and the proven effectiveness of negative campaigning, it was not surprising that Boschwitz chose television advertising as his preferred weapon. The ads began within the bounds of fairness. The first ad, which debuted October 25, 1990, superimposed an old photo of a frizzy-haired Wellstone onto a dollar bill in place of George Washington. The voice-over labeled Wellstone as a big-spending liberal: "Paul Wellstone isn't asking for our trust. He's asking for our money. And he wants us to send him to Washington to spend it. Get the picture?"

Another ad, called "Manure," hit on the same tax-and-spend issue, but with more humor. In this spot, which was based on ads in earlier campaigns in other Midwestern states, a farmer stood next to his cows, pitchfork in hand, and said: "He wants

to go to Washington and spend all that money on new programs; and he wants me to believe he won't raise my taxes! You
know, maybe Professor Wellstone ought to have my job, because
in my job we deal with that kind of thing all the time." Then the
farmer puts his pitchfork to work, throwing a clump of manure
into a truck.

Wellstone learned at this time that Boschwitz was preparing
an ad that claimed Wellstone had described himself to his students as a socialist. In an airport lounge after a full day of campaigning, Wellstone was met by a staff member who told him
that the ad, and several other negative ads, had been previewed
before a focus group by the Boschwitz campaign to judge the reaction. A woman who supported Wellstone over Boschwitz had
been inadvertently selected for the focus group, and she told the
Wellstone camp about the ads.

"Good, let the bastards run them," Wellstone said at the airport as he breathed deep, puffed out his chest, and hitched up his
pants. "It means we're close. This is the moment of truth. It will
either work or it will not work."

But Boschwitz did not air the socialist ad, which Novak said
was never even produced. "We were just testing out ideas. We
never expected to use it," Novak said. "We didn't know if we
could substantiate it, and we doubted we could use it even if we
substantiated it."

In addition to the television advertising, Boschwitz used his
personal appearances to "define" Wellstone as fiscally irresponsible. Boschwitz appeared at a press conference at the state capitol with New Mexico senator Pete Domenici, the top Republican on the Budget Committee, who was brought in for a fund-
raiser and to reinforce the message that Wellstone could not be
trusted with the federal budget. The two senators produced a
document that purported to show the effects on taxes and
spending of all Wellstone's proposals, including his universal

health care plan. They claimed that the bottom line was a staggering $700 billion, or half again as much as the annual federal
budget. Domenici charged that Wellstone's agenda was a "cruel
hoax." Referring to Wellstone's legislative proposals, he said he
had "never seen a more radical proposal."

This allegation—that Wellstone would make the federal deficit soar while also raising taxes—became the dominant theme of
Boschwitz's counterattack. Because Wellstone did, in fact, have
an ambitious agenda, he and his issues director, Ellen Anderson,
were forced into admitting that they did not expect all his programs to be put into effect at once, which amounted to an implied confession that his programs were indeed costly.

Wellstone fought back by protesting that Boschwitz's statistics unfairly lumped long-term goals, such as lower class sizes in
public schools, which the federal government does not pay for,
to produce the bottom line. Boschwitz's biggest distortion, Wellstone said, was that he neglected to tell the whole truth when he
included Wellstone's proposal for a Canada-style health care
program in the package. Boschwitz's calculation counted only
the taxpayers' total new costs and neglected to subtract the potential savings to many middle- and low-income Americans and
their employers, who currently pay for health insurance and
medical care in the private sector. Both Twin Cities newspapers
made these points strongly in their critiques of Boschwitz's ads.

To strengthen the attack on Wellstone as a free spender and
to rally mainstream Republicans, Boschwitz arranged for Senator Bob Dole of Kansas to join him at a campaign stop in Minnesota. But Dole, like Domenici, was a consummate Republican
insider, a blue-suited symbol of the Washington establishment
joining Boschwitz at the very time when the popularity of President Bush and all incumbents had reached a low point that year.
Pat Forciea made the most of this opportunity by emphasizing
Boschwitz's membership in the Washington club: "I'll be more

than happy to pay for the tickets of any more incumbent Washington senators who want to come back here," he said. "Tell [Boschwitz campaign manager Tom] Mason I'll let him use my American Express card to fly Bush out here, too." But Forciea knew that the Boschwitz attacks were taking their toll. Nightly telephone calls about two weeks before election day showed Wellstone's support starting to slip, particularly in the Twin Cities suburbs.

Two years earlier, Forciea watched the same thing happen to Michael Dukakis. He was tending to Dukakis's campaign in Minnesota, and it pained him to watch the candidate's inner circle in Boston remain passive for too long under Bush's attacks. By failing to respond to the Republican attacks, Forciea reasoned, Dukakis and the Democratic hierarchy failed to recapture the White House. Now, in control of this campaign, Forciea said he was determined not to repeat the Dukakis campaign's mistake:

> Boschwitz is trying to do to Paul what Bush did to Dukakis. I shouldn't let that happen. I'll feel very responsible for the loss because we can win right now. I watched the Dukakis campaign make all sorts of mistakes the last two months [of the 1988 election]. Now we'll see how much I learned.

One of his decisions was to air "Mud," another Bill Hillsman ad that took Boschwitz to task for his negative campaigning. Unlike the other ads, which focused on the incumbent's record on various issues, this one attacked Boschwitz for making misleading statements about Wellstone. As Wellstone, in a voice-over, describes Boschwitz's "inaccurate and recently downright nasty" campaign, globs of mud splatter on a photo of Wellstone. He concludes with a message for his opponent: "Six million dollars may buy a lot of mud, but it can't buy an election."

This was the only ad Hillsman had in the can. Because the

campaign had been so low on money, he had not been able to film ads to respond to the anticipated Boschwitz attacks, so he threw together a couple of quick spots. One was an attack on Boschwitz for coming back home to play politics while important votes were pending in Washington. The other was a "talking head" ad in which Wellstone looks into the camera and talks about his belief in the importance of politics as a vehicle for change—an ad demanded by Wellstone and some of his advisers who felt, over Hillsman's objections, that they needed at least one conventional ad in the television lineup.

Although television remained the dominant medium in the Senate campaign, Wellstone also had to fight a rearguard action on radio. By late October, Boschwitz had distributed seventy-five different radio ads to a hundred stations; each thirty-second spot was tailored to the local audience in every region of the state. The ads connected Boschwitz's Senate campaign to an issue of local importance or reminded listeners of his success in winning federal aid for them when they were stricken by drought. This was an audio version of Boschwitz's targeted direct-mail machine.

In sheer numbers, Wellstone could not match Boschwitz on radio any more than he could on television. But he could not cede the fight in that medium, and it became more of a battleground than Hillsman had anticipated. Radio presented Hillsman with the opportunity to have Wellstone discuss issues that were neglected in his television spots and to hit harder on the money issue. To maximize exposure, Hillsman booked time on the state's dominant radio station.

Class warfare was at the heart of Hillsman's TV commercials, but the issue was presented obliquely, with references to money and a portrayal of Boschwitz as unapproachable and beholden to special, wealthy interests. On radio, class warfare was waged explicitly with straightforward proclamations and charges against Boschwitz in an attempt to portray Wellstone as a working-class hero battling modern-day robber barons. In a spot on universal health care, Wellstone declared: "Affordable, dignified, and humane health care should be a birthright." About the savings and loan scandal: "Washington is ready to bill every taxpayer and yet the crooks are running free, driving fancy cars and living in expensive homes."

In October, during the budget stalemate in Washington, Wellstone recorded an ad entitled "Budget Crisis," in which he insisted that Boschwitz and other Washington leaders

> are finding out that their days of political trickery and deception are over. . . . Boschwitz [and others] . . . want to lighten the tax burden on the wealthy, unfairly raise taxes on the rest of us, cut Medicare benefits for our seniors, cut target prices for farmers, cut loans for students, cut benefits for veterans, and give the rich a free ride.

In this sixty-second spot, Wellstone managed to wrap a populist cloak around an appeal to the economic self-interests of just about every important demographic group.

In another radio ad, Hillsman found a way to remind voters of Boschwitz's infamous access stamps for campaign contributors. In a sixty-second spot called "Stamps," the announcer noted that the price of stamps would be increasing to thirty cents the following year.

"Think that's bad?" he asks. "Then just imagine if Rudy Boschwitz were postmaster."

The announcer explains that Boschwitz spent $3 million of taxpayer funds to send self-promoting mail to constituents and

> invented special stamps of his own so he'd know which letters to give special preference to. If you contributed $1,000, you got ten blue-colored stamps—a mere one hundred dollars per stamp.

So if you want your voice to be heard in Washington, you have two choices. Send Rudy Boschwitz a thousand bucks. Or vote for Paul Wellstone on November 6th.

Although Wellstone fought gamely on both television and radio, attracting media attention with his unconventional approach, his advisers felt that they needed to draw even more media coverage. To that end, Forciea announced to the press that Wellstone would be delivering a major speech in the state capitol rotunda on October 30.

Unlike most of Wellstone's stump speeches, this one was carefully scripted and staged. David Lillehaug wrote a draft that focused on the economic issues at the heart of Boschwitz's televised attacks and confronted Boschwitz for his style of politics. Against a backdrop of a huge American flag, and with dozens of his former students cheering wildly in the foreground, Wellstone, drawing heavily from Lillehaug's draft, came through with one of his most stirring addresses:

> Who are we? We show by our campaigns who we are. Political campaigns should be the best opportunities in politics. . . . But increasingly campaigns have become the dark side of politics for all too many incumbents, including Rudy Boschwitz. It all amounts to raising the big dollars, and too often it's in the boardrooms of the Exxons. . . .
>
> And then what's even more troubling is what's done with the money. Again, Rudy Boschwitz is a classic example. In September, we got the positive ads. Crisp, cool fall evenings, warm passion, coming into the living room, asking people to put on rose-colored glasses. A fantasy world where the incumbent was a perfect combination of Mr. Rogers, Captain Kirk, and Dr. Feelgood. . . . [Says he] cares about the environment, [that he's a] leader on child care, but not a very accurate representation of the voting record.
>
> But then come mid-October and late October, expensive

polling tracks tell of his lead evaporating. Rudy loses his cool. Desperation has struck. He decides to go negative and use the last million dollars in his kitty to hurl distortions and half-truths.

Apparently Rudy Boschwitz's paid handlers have told him he should talk about me as a spender, paint me as a spender, big spender.

Now remember, Rudy Boschwitz has been the man who's been in the United States Senate during this decade of the eighties, where we've gone from $970 billion to over $3 trillion of debt. Rudy Boschwitz was the senator who voted for Reaganomics. Rudy Boschwitz was the senator who traipsed to President Bush and said, "Please don't raise taxes on millionaires."

And yet somehow there's Rudy Boschwitz contending that I, this little guy from Minnesota, am going to send this country into bankruptcy. Well, well, I've got it. That charge is a bunch of Boschwitz.

Unlike Rudy, I'm not a millionaire. Sheila and I have to balance our checkbook every month. We have to scrimp and save to buy a bathroom fixture at [Boschwitz's store] Plywood Minnesota. And Rudy Boschwitz lecturing me on fiscal responsibility is like Leona Helmsley lecturing Mother Teresa on charity.

Bill Hillsman was in the hall with a camera crew, directing the taping of the speech for use in a commercial, but the single camera jammed and the commercial never was produced.

Gang Warfare

On the same day that Wellstone accused Boschwitz of unfair campaign tactics, Boschwitz stood before a crowd of business leaders in St. Cloud, adding new and false charges to his attacks on the challenger. In a brazen and reckless distortion, Boschwitz claimed that Wellstone had incited a group of farmers to vandalize power lines strung across central Minnesota. And he said that Wellstone "stole [government] records . . . or at least made light of it" during his work with poor people around the Carleton College campus. There was no evidence to back either accusation, but Boschwitz's accusations never were challenged.

Instead of trying to turn these unsubstantiated charges to his advantage, Wellstone found himself caught in one of the few blunders his campaign would make, a snafu that would briefly traumatize the candidate and his inner circle. Earlier in the week, the Minneapolis Urban League issued a press release announcing that a number of black organizations in the Twin Cities would conduct a mass literature drop for Wellstone and Governor Rudy Perpich. The last sentence stated that "members of the Vice Lords," a predominantly black street gang, would participate.

The release caught the attention of Mark Brunswick, a police reporter for the Minneapolis *Star Tribune,* who was intrigued by the notion of gang members as political volunteers. When Brunswick called Perpich headquarters, campaign manager John Stanoch cautiously distanced the governor from the event, saying the governor was not involved in planning it. Brunswick then called Wellstone campaign manager John Blackshaw, who likewise said that he was unaware of the planned gang involvement. Blackshaw promised to try to find out what was going on. He did, but he was unable to get through to Brunswick later that night.

In the meantime, Brunswick, facing a deadline, had talked to Wellstone's press secretary, Mark Anderson. Despite his title, Anderson was not authorized to speak for the campaign on sensitive matters. Nevertheless, he told Brunswick that the campaign would not discourage the gang's participation. "One of the key problems here is voter turnout," Anderson told Brunswick. "We are not going to discourage anybody from getting people to the polls."

The naiveté of the Wellstone staff, which had conferred on the campaign a sort of political virginity, nearly lost the election.

The article was published the next morning, Wednesday, October 31, and as Blackshaw read it over breakfast at Forciea's house, he sensed trouble. "This is going to be brutal," he said to Forciea's wife, Cathy.

At the state capitol, Pat Milan, who advised the campaign on advertising strategy, was so incensed by the misstep that he sat at his computer in the attorney general's office and banged out an angry essay he entitled "Paul Wellstone's Fatal Moment." After touring the capitol press corps offices to assess reporters' reaction to the story and to try to figure out how hard they planned to pursue it, he faxed a memo to Forciea's house in which he noted that the reporters thought Wellstone would not be able to wiggle out of this jam.

That same morning Boschwitz pounced on Anderson's comments at a news conference. Although he had scheduled the press briefing to focus on Wellstone's health care proposal, he began by bashing Wellstone for accepting the aid of a street gang. Boschwitz said it was proof that Wellstone was "on the left wing of his own party." The senator continued to denounce Wellstone as a candidate who "would accept the help from people who have made the lives of thousands miserable. It is just the kind of campaign that he has been allowed to get away with for so long." Boschwitz challenged Wellstone to reject the gang.

Blackshaw attended the Boschwitz press conference and tried to control the damage, telling reporters that Wellstone would neither welcome nor accept the help of the Vice Lords or any other gang. Then he lambasted Boschwitz for playing racial politics, but he recognized that Boschwitz had not initiated the story and that the issue would not be that easy to squelch. By the time he returned to the campaign office, a ten-minute drive from the capitol, more reporters had called. Blackshaw told other staffers that "we've got problems because people are not going to let this story die. . . . We've got to respond some way."

Blackshaw and Forciea huddled with Wellstone at Forciea's house and decided to hold a press conference that afternoon. For Blackshaw and Forciea, the strategy was clear: denounce the gang and attack Boschwitz. For Wellstone it was not so simple. "It was a real tough thing for Paul, because he really was very sensitive to selling out," said Blackshaw. "He kept asking me, 'Did you check with the black community? What are the black leaders saying?' "

Blackshaw made the calls, including a lengthy one with Richard Jefferson, the state's only black legislator. Jefferson, who had been active in trying to steer gang members into positive activities, offered to ask the Vice Lords to hold a press conference or join Wellstone at his afternoon meeting with the press. The last thing Blackshaw wanted was to have Wellstone appear side by side with the Vice Lords.

"I said, 'Richard, what we're going to have to do is we're going to have to distance ourselves from this thing like you wouldn't believe. We have no other alternative,' " Blackshaw recalled.

Jefferson told Blackshaw that he understood. "I told him not be concerned about that," said Jefferson, who later repeated the message directly to Wellstone when he saw him just before the press conference. "We all understood the politics."

Blackshaw reported back that there would be no repercussions if Wellstone distanced himself from the gang. With that assurance, Wellstone agreed to go forward with the press conference. Pat Milan arrived at Forciea's house to help prepare Wellstone for the press session and told him to be "laid back," to appear anything but frazzled. "I told him he had to smile," Milan said.

Instead, a visibly angry Wellstone stormed into the packed press conference at the State Office Building in St. Paul, where Boschwitz had held his own press conference that morning. Wellstone unequivocally disassociated himself and his campaign from the Vice Lords. "The Vice Lords are not a part of the Wellstone campaign," he said. "I condemn all gangs and all gang activities. My whole life has been devoted to nonviolence."

He then pressed the attack on Boschwitz, accusing him of trying to exploit racial fears and prejudices. By linking Wellstone with the Vice Lords, Boschwitz was employing President Bush's strategy of racial politics, Wellstone said. "In 150 years, Minnesotans have never seen a tactic like this used. . . . I consider it to be a tactic of fear, of dividing people by race," he said.

After the press conference, Wellstone began to have doubts about his denunciation of gangs. As he walked outside, he talked with issues director Ellen Anderson, Minneapolis field director Yvonne Malloy, and field organizer Scott Adams. Anderson, a former Carleton student who had taken a leave of absence as a public defender to work on the campaign, asked Wellstone why he had not said something about black kids and the need to get disenfranchised youth into positive activities.

"What do you people want me to do? I should never have been put in this situation," Wellstone retorted.

But Anderson's question stung. As Wellstone got into Blackshaw's Jeep along with Blackshaw and Mike Casper he wondered whether he had compromised himself in his desperation to win the election. In a loud and shaking voice, he said that the looks in the eyes of Anderson, Malloy, and Adams made him feel like a traitor.

"They made me feel like a sellout," Wellstone recalled saying. "Goddamn it, did I sell out?"

"Paul was just livid," Blackshaw said. Wellstone was furious that his staff had put him in this position, and he began to scream at Blackshaw, asking him how he knew the gang was involved in criminal activity, whether he had ever talked to the Vice Lords. "I don't want to say he was irrational, but that's what it was. He became irrational. He felt so sensitive to selling out," Blackshaw said.

As Blackshaw drove out of the parking lot, the three staff members were walking across the street and they looked back at the Jeep. "Look at that. They're looking at me like I sold out," Wellstone yelled. "Goddamn it, what am I going to do?" He told Blackshaw to stop the car so he could return to the press conference and retract what he had just said. He wanted to talk about the good things the Urban League was doing for black youths.

"He was screaming at me: 'You're the campaign manager. Why do you people do this to me?' " Blackshaw said. "There was so much screaming going on in my car."

Blackshaw kept driving, refusing to allow Wellstone to return to the press conference. When they arrived back at Forciea's house, Wellstone headed for the bathroom and Blackshaw told Forciea that Wellstone wanted to retract his statement. "You've got to be kidding me," a dumbfounded Forciea replied.

Forciea had a calming influence on Wellstone and was able to convince him that he had done the right thing. He insisted to Wellstone that "this was an instance where electoral politics needed to win out over cause politics," Forciea said. In fact, this was a real-life version of the academic discussions that Forciea and Wellstone often had in Wellstone's classroom. For years, Wellstone had brought Forciea to Carleton to speak to his classes about the tension between winning elections and clinging to a perfectly pure ideology. Forciea believed that a candidate could not abandon his or her philosophy, but, like Hillsman, he was not in politics merely to raise issues. He was in it to win, and that meant an occasional sacrifice on minor issues.

Now, as he spoke to Wellstone in his living room, Forciea knew that Wellstone was not inflexible. Based on their class-room discussions, Forciea knew that when there was a conflict between winning and ideological purity, Wellstone "understood both sides of it."

Indeed, after Blackshaw talked to black leaders on the phone, after black leaders also held a press conference that day to criticize Boschwitz over the gang issue, and after the Vice Lords announced that they would not participate in the litera-ture drop because they did not want to become a political pawn, Wellstone began to feel, however reluctantly, that he had done the right thing by distancing himself from the gang. But he la-mented the false choices politicians must make, especially on such a hot topic and at a time when both candidates are careen-ing madly toward the finish line:

> In a campaign like this, there's no time to educate the public. I wish it were otherwise. If I said I don't like the Vice Lords, but I understand what the Urban League was trying to do, the mes-sage would be that I did not denounce gang activity. I would have rather used it as an opportunity to educate people, to say to them that there is a mess in our society and we have to do something. That's what I didn't feel right about. It's like there is no room to spell out the complexity of an issue.

Boschwitz Bites Back

After battling over the Vice Lords issue all day, Wellstone and Boschwitz met that night in their next-to-last joint appearance, a live debate held in the studio of WCCO-AM radio. They sat side by side in the main studio, and the bad blood between them and their campaign staffs was unmistakable, the tension palpable. Wellstone's staff added to the antagonism by showing up with a film crew, violating an agreement that Boschwitz had secured from a WCCO producer.

Although the film crew distracted and angered Boschwitz's staff, it did not rattle the senator. He took the initiative in the debate and ripped into Wellstone with some of his most effective rhetoric, keyed to Wellstone's October 30 speech in the state capitol:

> Yesterday Paul Wellstone said we should judge a person by how he campaigns. So let's do that tonight. Paul, you finally pushed the little guy image too far. Yesterday, in a moment of humility, you compared yourself to Mother Teresa. Now isn't that a bit much?
>
> Paul, to listen to you, you would have every person who has been successful in life bow their heads in shame. . . . You want me to apologize for what I've accomplished in life, and I won't. . . . I started a business from scratch. I took a lot of risk, and I succeeded. And I'm proud of that fact. . . .
>
> You want the government to play an even bigger role in our lives. And worst of all, you would have Minnesotans believe that you can reduce the government debt, add billions, hundreds of billions of dollars in new programs and not raise their taxes. Come on! You know, Paul, you need to spend less time over there in the political science department, maybe a little more in the math department. It just doesn't add up.

This well-prepared attack took Wellstone by surprise. He tried to recover by describing Boschwitz's comments about the Vice Lords incident as a "Willie Horton type of tactic" and then issued the first of several challenges to drop all "negative" ads for the remainder of the campaign. "Give the people a holiday from this stuff," Wellstone said.

"Well, if they're sick of it in Minnesota, Paul, it's because you've been doing it about ten weeks, and I have not," Boschwitz shot back. "I have now decided that we have to define who Paul Wellstone is, what his views are, and that is part of the campaign."

Boschwitz also was more effective in deflecting Wellstone's attacks concerning the economic inequities of the 1980s. Instead of stubbornly insisting that all was well, as he did in the second debate, Boschwitz acknowledged the growth in the federal debt. But he also claimed to have been one of only thirteen senators running for reelection who voted for a deficit reduction program. He admitted too that farmers had been hurt by federal programs, but said the cuts in subsidies could have been worse.

When the debate shifted to health care, Boschwitz this time was ready with his own proposal, suggesting state initiatives such as "risk pools," and Medicare or Medicaid for uninsured and underinsured families and individuals. He also reiterated an unsubstantiated charge that Wellstone's proposal would close the world-renowned Mayo Clinic in Rochester, Minnesota. Mayo Clinic officials themselves refused comment on the issue.

Wellstone fought gamely on this subject, trying to make it clear that he favored a national health insurance program and not a nationalized system of doctors, hospitals, clinics, and product manufacturers, all employed by the federal government. Arguing that his type of plan was inevitable, Wellstone asserted that, "by the end of . . . the 1990s we will have some form of universal health care coverage and join all the other advanced economies in the world with something like that."

Finally, in response to Boschwitz's prediction that a Canada-style program would result in old people going blind while they wait for surgery, Wellstone countered that it was already happening: "We have terrible rationing in this country right now," he declared. "And you know what the sad thing is? It's rationing according to income. There are all sorts of our citizens in Minnesota and across this country who are rationed out. They don't have the money."

Before the debate ended, Wellstone issued two more calls for a cease-fire, and Boschwitz rejected both with aplomb:

> Well, I'd be very happy to agree, but after ten or twelve weeks of battering me on TV . . . now he suddenly says we should positively campaign. Apparently he likes to dish it out, but he doesn't like to take it. Well, politics is not for the fainthearted. . . . We will describe my opponent in these ads. We will not do so in a negative way, but in a factual way and, where we can, in a humorous way.

During a commercial break Wellstone renewed his offer of a truce on attack ads and he thrust his hand out to clinch the deal. "You can take your hand and go elsewhere," Boschwitz bit back. "You have run a very negative campaign." There was a palpable feeling that these candidates did not just disagree with each other; there was an immense personal dislike.

In the days after the third debate, Boschwitz delivered on his promise to "define" Wellstone. On the road, press secretary Jay Novak began carrying and showing to reporters a copy of Wellstone's Ph.D. dissertation, entitled "Black Militants in the Ghetto: Why They Believe in Violence." Novak also quoted Wellstone as saying that he used Saul Alinsky's *Rules for Radicals* in teaching a class about poverty politics.

But Boschwitz knew he could push the image of Wellstone as a socialist conspirator only so far. Boschwitz field director Chris Georgacas said that exhaustive research into Wellstone's background did not produce the kind of evidence that the Boschwitz camp had hoped to find—participation in a flag burning, membership in a socialist organization, or advocacy of nationalizing a major industry.

"[Wellstone] always walked up to the cliff [of radicalism] but never went over it," said Georgacas. "Our research showed that despite his perceived vulnerability on this score, there was nothing convincing or compelling enough to go with."

Wellstone's sure sense of the pragmatic limits of radical politics carried the day. Ironically, it was Boschwitz who may have had more to fear by raising the specter of socialism. As a college student in the 1940s, Boschwitz had briefly been a member of the Socialists League for Industrial Democracy, an episode he described to a newspaper writer in the 1970s as a normal idealistic searching. The result was that the Boschwitz camp had to tread carefully in this area, and it could venture no further than trying to portray Wellstone as an irresponsible, tax-and-spend liberal.

Again turning to television, the senator used increasingly hard-edged and distorted ads in which he accused Wellstone of being a threat to middle-income taxpayers and an enemy of senior citizens, an interesting counterpoint to Wellstone's portrayal of Boschwitz as an enemy of children. In one ad, entitled "Spending," a photograph of Wellstone's face is covered with a hand. The narrator says:

> Who is this guy? A proponent of uncontrolled government spending that would double the national debt. And double the taxes of everyone making over $20,000. Whose spending would cost the average Minnesota taxpayer an additional $2,300 a year. Who is he? Paul Wellstone. And while he says the rich should foot the bill, trouble is, he thinks you're rich.

This commercial kept running even though both metropolitan newspapers pointed out the distortions and false claims. "Nearly every major claim in this ad is inaccurate, misleading or distorted," wrote *St. Paul Pioneer Press* reporter Bruce Orwall.

Boschwitz used a similar technique for a spot called "Seniors." Again there is a picture of Wellstone's face, which eventually is covered up by an elderly woman's hand. The narrator says:

> Who is this guy who wants the federal bureaucracy to take over the American medical system? Who would take Medicare money from the seniors who need it so much and use it to fund his socialized health care plan? Who would eliminate Medicare coverage while doubling our personal income taxes? Who is he? He's Paul Wellstone. Not too smart for a college professor.

"This may be the most misleading political ad to air in the state this year," Orwall wrote. Both the *Pioneer Press* and the Minneapolis *Star Tribune* ran stories showing how Boschwitz's claims were based on far-fetched interpretations of Wellstone's health care proposal.

With less than a week left before election day, Boschwitz was emptying his bank account to ensure that no one missed these attacks. The ads ran day and night—during afternoon soap operas, during prime time, and on barely watched cable channels. He hunted down voters in their living rooms, cars, bathrooms—anywhere that television or radio signals could reach. He bought so much air time that some stations had to run his ads back to back to fit them all in.

The strategy worked, pulling down Wellstone's poll ratings and rattling the challenger. On Sunday night, October 28, after a late dinner, Wellstone sat on the edge of a chair in a Moorhead motel and angrily confessed that he constantly worried about the next attack:

> I wish I could say I'm at peace, but I can't. I don't want to lose on this basis. . . . I don't want them to get away with it. He doesn't deserve to win. It's become very personal. I'm going to do everything in my power . . . to make sure this bastard doesn't win.

Every day Wellstone fought back. On Thursday, November 1, he held a press conference to complain about almost $200,000 worth of anti-Wellstone TV ads paid for by an association of foreign auto dealers. Though some of his advisers suggested that he stress the Japanese interests behind the ads, the candidate rejected that approach as an appeal to xenophobia. "If winning requires that kind of [approach], I won't do it," he said. Instead, he attacked the ads as an "intrusion" by out-of-state interests.

The next day, November 2, Wellstone tried to counter Boschwitz's attacks concerning Medicare by surrounding himself at a press conference with doctors dressed in white coats. The physicians denied that Wellstone's health care plan was socialized medicine and claimed that tens of thousands of their colleagues supported the proposal. The event got little coverage.

Instead, Friday's news belonged to Boschwitz, who traveled to Rochester with his party's new gubernatorial candidate, Arne Carlson, for a meeting and rally with President George Bush. With an enthusiastic crowd of about three thousand at John Marshall High School, the rally offered the senator a perfect opportunity to be photographed with the president. Wayne Newton sang the national anthem to an audience waving placards that read "Tootie Fruity, Oh Rudy," and Bush and Boschwitz soaked up the cheers.

"We urge you, we cry out, send Rudy Boschwitz, our friend, your admired senator back to Washington, D.C., for six more years," Bush exhorted.

Wellstone rolled into Rochester in his campaign bus that same day, hoping to draw a contrast between the privilege of *Air Force One* and his battered vehicle. "These are the people who brought us the mess," Wellstone said, earning a share of the news reports that night. "Rudy Boschwitz has run out of gas."

That same day, the Wellstone campaign learned about a potentially damaging radio ad Boschwitz was running on the Iron Range. Wellstone would take people's sporting rifles away, the ad alleged, and Wellstone's environmental policies would close all the eastern steel mills and miners on the Range would be out of a job again. The ad was aimed squarely at Wellstone's strongest base of support, and it focused on issues that had worked against liberal candidates on the Iron Range in the past.

The Steelworkers union, one of the first major PACs to endorse and contribute to Wellstone, reacted quickly. David Foster, director of Steelworkers District 33, was in Pittsburgh that day, but when he learned about the ad, he telephoned the union's political operative, Bob Rootes, who was back in Minnesota, and they put together a tough response. The union had concluded months ago that there was no evidence that the Clean Air Act would close blast furnaces and throw miners and mill workers onto unemployment lines. Foster's statement said:

> By raising the specter of job loss on the Iron Range, Rudy Boschwitz has once again shown his true colors as a fear-mongering apologist for the interests of big business polluters. Boschwitz's views on the environment are identical to those of the USX corporation and other steel and mining companies whose mismanagement of the industry led to a decade of misery for tens of thousands of steelworkers.

Although Wellstone and his team were fighting back each day, they clearly were on the defensive now after months of being the political aggressors. And with the success of the Rochester rally, enthusiasm and momentum appeared to be taking hold in the Boschwitz operation. Hoping for a continued upward swing, Tom Mason told reporters that the rally would be followed by a massive television buy and get-out-the-vote effort.

But while Boschwitz had all the money he needed to saturate

the airwaves with his commercials, he had fallen behind in his field operations. Moreover, the intraparty squabbling resulting from the sex scandal in the gubernatorial race severely handicapped the Republican Party's grassroots operations, which were key to getting its voters to the polls. The party had scheduled what it called "the world's largest literature drop" for October 20. Volunteers would attach hundreds of thousands of plastic bags—bearing Boschwitz's photo on the outside and filled with Republican campaign flyers—to doorknobs all over the state.

But the Grunseth scandal, breaking just five days before the scheduled drop, forced Boschwitz field director Chris Georgacas to rework the whole operation at the last minute. He excluded Grunseth literature from the bags and edited Grunseth out of a thirty-minute videotaped pep talk and instructional aid for volunteer workers. When only about half of the expected volunteers showed up because of the divisions within the party, the event was scaled back drastically.

Georgacas said the damage was crucial because it ruined Boschwitz's main effort to show that his campaign had grassroots elements, that it was not just money and ads. But Georgacas also confessed that the grassroots organization had already been seriously weakened by constant raids on his budget for more TV advertising and telemarketing efforts.

The substitution of Arne Carlson on the Republican gubernatorial ticket complicated the get-out-the-vote telephone effort that had been planned for the weekend before the election. Boschwitz's staff knew that voter-turnout calls to supporters of the defunct Grunseth campaign could produce an anti-Boschwitz vote, and calls to pro-choice Carlson supporters might produce a Wellstone vote. Nevertheless, Mason said he expected more than 500,000 calls to be made over the weekend, compared to 700,000 DFL calls.

Because of the smaller literature drop and the decision to spend virtually all of the campaign's money on television ads, Georgacas knew that Boschwitz risked being perceived as a television candidate who had little showing of popular support. Throughout the campaign, there were no Boschwitz bumper stickers, no lawn signs, no hint of the candidate's presence other than on television.

By contrast, Wellstone's field operation was kicked into high gear. The airwaves belonged to Boschwitz, but Wellstone's forces had uncontested control of the streets. At seven o'clock each morning, before dawn, Wellstone supporters fanned out to key commuting locations around the Twin Cities, armed with steaming cups of coffee and large green Wellstone banners. The campaign was too poor to buy billboards, so staff members and volunteers stood on freeway overpasses, beside highway entrance and exit ramps, and along major bus routes holding Wellstone signs. In the parlance of the campaign, they were "doing a visibility."

"We're doing it at fifteen spots this morning," Liz Borg said one morning as she, Dave Graham, and two volunteers, Margaret Anderson and David Kelliher, stood on a footbridge above Interstate Highway 94, the major artery between Minneapolis and St. Paul. "We want people to think there are campaigners all over the place."

With the help of union members, the campaign had made and distributed some 11,000 poster-sized lawn signs and placed 500 four-by-eight-foot signs on private property along freeways in the Twin Cities and in northern Minnesota.

"The thing about these close races is the GOTV [get out the vote] is everything," Forciea said as he drove through a St. Paul neighborhood and pointed to Wellstone lawn signs everywhere. "It's the bumper stickers and lawn signs that must be driving the

Boschwitz people nuts. All the money in the world can't force people to go out and put those things up."

To complement the low-tech, grassroots efforts, Wellstone and his advisers kept up their attack on Boschwitz, this time turning to radio to deliver the message. In "Rimshot," an announcer speaks in the style of a stand-up comic:

> OK, so I'm watching TV the other night, and who comes on but Rudy Boschwitz saying he's a—quote—world spokesman on the global environment. [The sound of a rim shot (BA-DA-BOOM!) and a burst of laughter from a nightclub crowd] You wanna hear a really good one? Rudy Boschwitz said, "I'm concerned about our children's health . . ." [BA-DA-BOOM! More laughter] ". . . and then actually voted against a bill funding—are you listening here?—CHILDREN'S IMMUNIZATIONS. Excuse me? Rudy? Can we talk about this?

The nightclub sounds fade, and Wellstone's voice cuts in: "Fortunately, there is a way for you to have the last laugh. Vote for Paul Wellstone on November 6th."

In another spot, called "Addicted to Cash," the announcer says that besides addictions to alcohol, drugs, and even sex, "a new addiction has been discovered in Minnesota." Then a man with a maniacal voice begins to read from Boschwitz's frank memo about how he enjoys raising campaign money.

"Clearly, here is a man obsessed with cash—a man addicted to money," the announcer says. "Sadly, these are comments made by Senator Rudy Boschwitz on how to win reelection. Help Rudy Boschwitz get the help he needs for this terrible addiction. Vote for Paul Wellstone on November 6th."

When Forciea played "Addicted to Cash" in his car's cassette deck—ironically, after he had just slipped out of a Wellstone fund-raiser—he said he was not going to put it on the air. "This one is too mean even for me," he said.

On November 1, when Forciea awoke in the middle of the night to find a pile of Wellstone lawn signs set afire on his front lawn, he changed his mind. Later that morning the ad began to run.

Good Luck on Tuesday

Wellstone and Boschwitz met for the last time in public on Friday evening, November 2. Hostility filled the KTCA-TV public television studio in downtown St. Paul, where the two candidates gathered for a final, last-minute addition to their series of debates. Within minutes, the debate became another bitter, awkward, finger-pointing confrontation. The candidates practically climbed across the show's host, Eric Eskola, to get at each other.

"I need to respond to rank hypocrisy," Wellstone said, pointing at Boschwitz. Wellstone accused Boschwitz of trying to strike fear in senior citizens with the distorted Medicare ad. "When you run that ad and it has no foundation in truth and you scare the hell out of senior citizens, making a claim that's not true, then I think what you've done is shown this is a desperate campaign. No one runs ads like that."

Boschwitz bristled: "He's lecturing me as though he was a professor at school. You know, you're in the real world right now, Paul. Lighten up a little bit. Have a good time here. Lighten up."

Wellstone fired back:

To be a professor may be something humorous to you. It may be humorous to a millionaire. But I have been a teacher. I'm very proud of having devoted my life to education. . . . What I'm trying to point out here tonight is that in the final days of this campaign, to run these kinds of ads, you may think it's flippant, but people in Minnesota won't go for it. This is absolutely poisonous.

In this meeting, there was no clear winner. The debate remained mired in charges and countercharges, and neither candidate looked terribly statesmanlike or sharp. Off-camera, the bitter exchanges continued. As they walked out of the studio, Boschwitz needled Wellstone: "Good luck on Tuesday. You'll need it." Wellstone adviser David Lillehaug, who was between Wellstone and Boschwitz, spun around and confronted Boschwitz. "That was out of line," he snapped.

Later that night, however, it looked as if Wellstone would indeed need some luck. On Friday and again on Saturday night, November 3, just days before Tuesday's election, the state's two major media polls reported trends ominous for Wellstone. The WCCO/*St. Paul Pioneer Press* poll showed Boschwitz was favored by 49 percent of the voters, while 40 percent said they would vote for Wellstone. The *Star Tribune*/KSTP-TV Minnesota Poll reported an identical point spread—51 percent for Boschwitz and 42 percent for Wellstone.

The analyses accompanying the polls, however, were filled with disclaimers about an unpredictable electorate. The WCCO/ *Pioneer Press* poll, for example, found that almost two-thirds of those surveyed felt that it was "time for a change." And despite the lead, Tom Mason sounded genuinely concerned. "It's the most volatile electorate I've ever seen. We see spurts and faults everywhere," he told the *Star Tribune*.

Although the polls were demoralizing for Wellstone's forces, they kept up a brave, confident public face, and they kept focusing attention on Boschwitz's negative ads. "Rudy Boschwitz is engaged in a campaign of deceit, untruth, and distortion," Blackshaw said. "He doesn't deserve to hold elected office."

Nonetheless, the prevailing opinion by Saturday afternoon was that the natural laws of politics had reasserted themselves and that Boschwitz, by virtue of his carpet-bombing television campaign, was back on top and climbing away.

As he left the television studio after the final debate, Lillehaug counted himself among those who felt that Wellstone would be defeated. "It was a sense of helplessness because of Boschwitz's ad onslaught," he said. "I watched the TV ads every night that week and a Boschwitz ad was on every fifteen minutes and a Wellstone ad would poke up every now and again."

Lillehaug also was aware that a *Star Tribune* tracking poll did not bode well for Wellstone. And when he saw Boschwitz brimming with confidence at the Friday-night debate, Lillehaug assumed that Boschwitz's polls also were telling him he would win.

"I think Boschwitz felt he was in the catbird seat," Lillehaug said.

12

OVER THE TOP

The Wellstone campaign coming into the final weekend was shrouded in that moment of blackest darkness before the dawn, and it showed on Wellstone who, one day after the Vice Lords meltdown, blew up again.

Filming an ad at about 11:30 P.M. Thursday, a camera operator was not able to find the one cut out of more than a dozen that was suitable and that fit in thirty seconds. The operator asked Wellstone to do another take, and he suddenly turned on the hapless operator, shouting, "Why are you doing this to me?" He stormed out of the studio. The operator finally found the cut he wanted, and Wellstone came back and apologized.

"I don't think a lot of people saw that side of Paul," John Blackshaw said, noting that Wellstone's emotionalism may have helped him handle the late-campaign stress. "The beauty about Paul is that he vented his anger. He vented all the time, which was fine." But that habit of loudly releasing pressure and verbally abusing subordinates, which his handlers disregarded during the tense finale to the campaign, would prove to be a problem in his first year in office.

With Boschwitz reasserting control of the situation and Wellstone growing visibly distraught, yet another reversal was in store, one of the most memorable pratfalls ever witnessed in Minnesota politics. On Friday and Saturday, more than two thousand people received letters addressed to Boschwitz's "Friends in the Minnesota Jewish Community." The two-page letter, printed on Boschwitz campaign stationery, began:

> The United States Senate race is an extraordinary event for our community this year. Both candidates were born as Jews and historically this may be a first. But from there on the difference between them is profound.
>
> One, Paul Wellstone, has no connection whatsoever with the Jewish community or our communal way of life. His children were brought up as non-Jews.

The letter tarred Wellstone for his association with Jesse Jackson and, by extension, with Palestinian Liberation Organization leader Yasir Arafat and "the notoriously anti-Semitic [Black Muslim] Louis Farrakhan." Wellstone "represents a disturbing element in American politics" because he "has never disassociated himself from any of Jesse Jackson's policies."

Boschwitz, by contrast, came from a family with a rich Jewish history, the letter continued: "His grandfather was a Rabbi as were six preceding generations of Boschwitzs," it said.

"People with problems find their way to Rudy, including Minnesotans and Jews from all over the U.S. They know he is a 'mensch,' "—Yiddish for a decent and respectable person.

The letter recounted Boschwitz's work in the Senate on behalf of Israel, and added that

> much has been written of Rudy's activities as a "shadchan" [matchmaker]. He holds four parties for Jewish singles each year in Washington and helped to get a Jewish singles group organized in the Twin Cities. Over 1,000 people sometimes attend his functions and dozens of marriages have resulted. Why does

Rudy do it? He believes that it is essential to the survival of our people. . . .

Everyone who knows Rudy knows that he is very family oriented and justly proud of his family. Rudy, Ellen and their four sons are a credit to our community and to the State of Minnesota.

The intent of the letter was clear. It did not simply contrast the candidates' stands on foreign and domestic issues that might be of concern to Jews. Rather, by citing Boschwitz's role as a "shadchan" and his strong belief in Jews marrying Jews, in contrast with Wellstone's interfaith marriage, it implied that Boschwitz was the better Jew.

The letter was signed by fifty-one individuals or couples, including some of the state's most prominent businessmen. The reaction was sudden and overwhelmingly negative, the first wave coming mostly from those Jews who got the letter. Ironically, Wellstone backers Sylvia and Sam Kaplan were among them. After they read it Saturday morning, they rushed to the campaign headquarters. As they drove there, Sylvia, dialing from her car phone, called the signers she knew. One responded with a win-at-all-costs coldness. "Whatever it takes," the woman said. Others said they had not seen a copy of the letter before they agreed to let their name be used, and they were horrified to learn that it was a personal attack. One of the signers called Wellstone, weeping in apology; others sent him contrite letters.

Two leading Twin Cities rabbis, Bernard Raskas and Stephen Pinsky, publicly denounced the letter for its tone and content. One recipient told newspaper columnist Doug Grow that "for one Jew to question the Jewishness of another Jew is something that is totally inappropriate. It is something the worst anti-Semite wouldn't do." Other Jews strongly objected to Boschwitz's implication that Jews were monolithic in their support for the conservative Israeli government and its resistance to trading land for peace. Still others faulted him for impugning guilt by association with Jesse Jackson.

"Boschwitz did for us what we could not do for ourselves," said Sam Kaplan, who had despaired of ever making Wellstone acceptable, let alone popular, among Jewish leaders. But here was an issue that many Christians and secular humanists could understand, too, and it helped Boschwitz with almost nobody.

Those who knew of Boschwitz's profound pride and hard work for his people, his faith, and Israel could understand why he wanted to compare himself with Wellstone. His cultural identity had deepened as he aged, and nothing grated on him like the false Jewishness he perceived in Wellstone. To be constantly compared to Goliath, the ancient Palestinian, while Wellstone was portrayed as the great Jew, David, did not help.

Moreover, the feelings expressed in the letter were shared by some Jewish leaders. Wellstone had been shunned by an overwhelming majority of prominent Jewish contributors to the DFL. In early October, when he met with about forty prominent members of the Twin Cities Jewish community, Wellstone was questioned about his religious faith in a way that Sam and Sylvia Kaplan, who arranged the meeting, found offensive. One participant asked Wellstone how he could run for the Senate and be a Jew, yet never have traveled to Israel. Others accused Wellstone of denying his faith, of being a "self-hating Jew," and of "coming out of the closet" about his Jewishness only because he thought it would be politically beneficial.

"Apparently the word spread that Paul was trying to pass himself off as a legitimate member of the Minneapolis Jewish community, heaven forbid," Sam Kaplan recalled with sarcasm.

But Wellstone also had ardent defenders. At the meeting with Jewish leaders, for example, Terry Gips of the International Alliance for Sustainable Agriculture made an impassioned statement about how Wellstone, in the face of anti-Semitism and death threats, had courageously identified himself as a Jew during his work with the farm protest group Groundswell. "It was just unspeakable and absolutely unwarranted that any Jew would question his Jewishness," Gips said.

The Boschwitz letter was a response to what he felt was unfair criticism within the Jewish community. One rabbi delivered a blistering critique during a service, asserting that Boschwitz's voting record on social issues was "antithetical" to Judaism. "I could tell that just tore at Rudy," said Tom Mason. "It just hurt him, because his personality, his whole being is Jewish." Boschwitz, known as the "rabbi of the Senate" because of his interest in Jewish issues, decided to write his own letter to the Jewish community.

Media coverage at first indicated that the letter had been written by a supporter. But Boschwitz himself took responsibility for it, and for good reason. The letter was almost entirely his work. Press secretary Jay Novak recalled that the letter was developed and finalized earlier in the week. Boschwitz did much of the writing on a bus trip that started in the northern Twin Cities suburb of Fridley and ended in the southwestern Minnesota town of Marshall.

The first version, faxed to supporter Ruth Aaron when the campaign bus made a stop just outside the Twin Cities, said that Wellstone's "children were raised in their mother's faith [Baptist]." Aaron objected to that phrase, Novak said, because it looked as if Boschwitz was criticizing someone's religion. Novak said he told Boschwitz that "you're going to piss off the Baptists."

"Rudy was incredulous, and said, 'I wouldn't do that,' but he finally agreed and said, 'Go ahead and use whatever version you want,' " Novak recalled. "Mason and I got together later that day and changed it to 'non-Jews.' I still don't think Rudy understood our objection. To him it was akin to a farmer telling people in a farm district that his opponent was making a false claim to being a farmer."

Wellstone, touring the state by airplane for a series of press conferences, learned about the letter by phone on Saturday afternoon. While he was speaking in Marshall, Sheila, who was with him, called the campaign office to tell Blackshaw about Boschwitz radio ads in which Minnesota congressman Vin Weber accused Wellstone of favoring abortion through the ninth month of pregnancy and for such purposes as sex selection. Then Blackshaw read her the beginning of the Jewish letter.

"Oh my God," Sheila replied. "I don't know if I'm even going to tell Paul about this." Blackshaw insisted that she had to because reporters were calling, asking for a response. After Wellstone finished speaking, he called Blackshaw, who read him the entire letter.

"God, when is this going to stop?" Wellstone said.

That evening, when Wellstone returned to St. Paul, he was met at the airport by television reporters, who were featuring the story prominently on the night's news. Asked to comment on the letter, Wellstone crystallized the issue for the state's overwhelmingly Christian population.

"I guess the senator is criticizing me for marrying a Christian," he said.

This response angered some Jews, who saw it as a subtle attack on observant Jews. And there was much speculation after the election that the letter and Wellstone's response may have capitalized on anti-Semitic sentiments. Given a choice between a total Jew and one who had fallen away and even allowed his children to be brought up as Christians, went this theory, any anti-Semites in Minnesota's overwhelmingly Christian and Gentile electorate would take the latter. But Wellstone's response also drove home the point that Boschwitz had gone beyond the pale. This was an attack on an opponent's marriage vows.

"Romance conquers all," said Sylvia Kaplan. "And anyone who tries to get between true love is bad."

That night's news coverage focused on two items in the Senate race—the letter and fresh poll results that showed Boschwitz up by 9 points. Tim Droogsma, Boschwitz's press secretary in the Senate office, was sitting at home in Red Wing, Minnesota, watching television that night and remembered the double coverage of the latest poll and then a reference to the Jewish letter. "I gave a massive sigh of relief [at the poll news] and then thirty seconds later there was this feeling that we were in trouble again."

On Sunday morning, with stories about the letter on the front page of the *Pioneer Press* in St. Paul and the cover of the metro news section of the *Star Tribune* in Minneapolis, the Jewish letter quickly began to crowd out all other issues. Novak recalled: "We got about fifty calls from people who said they would switch their votes. They weren't crackpots either. They left their names. All of a sudden we could just feel it slipping away."

Over in the Wellstone camp, Sunday was a day of exhilarating and dizzying ascent, like an aircraft pulling out of a steep nosedive. Wellstone too was getting calls, but calls of support, some from people in mixed marriages, "from Lutherans married to Catholics to Norwegians married to Swedes," Sam Kaplan said.

A Turd in the Pool

Clearly, the letter and Wellstone's response to it bolstered the growing feeling among many television viewers, reporters, and editorial page editors that Boschwitz had gone too far and had become too personal in his attacks. There already was a sense that Boschwitz was playing too loose with the facts and was too negative in the last week before the election. The *Star Tribune,* for example, felt compelled to break with tradition and publish an editorial on election day entitled "The lowest political blow of them all" that said voters should be outraged by "the shameless letter" and tactics that "grossly stretch the bounds of truth and propriety."

That was the point the Wellstone camp was determined to emphasize in the closing days of the campaign, and his top advisers immediately realized that the letter was a grand opportunity. On Sunday morning, just before the start of a Wellstone press conference, Pat Forciea explained the game plan for the final three days: "The senator has dropped a turd in the pool and I intend [to make] him eat it," Forciea declared.

At the press conference, held in a Minneapolis senior citizen high-rise, the most respected figure in Minnesota politics, Walter F. Mondale, finally emerged. Using language considerably less earthy than Forciea's, the venerable DFLer gave Boschwitz a hard spanking. Mondale opened by saying that he had watched the race from afar (he actually had been an influential fund-raiser at a critical period) and found it "amusing" at times. But things had gotten out of hand, he implied, and now he had no choice but to intervene. Reminding Minnesotans that the race was for a seat he once occupied, Mondale raked Boschwitz for a "relentless, brutal, heavily financed, and, in my judgment, untruthful television assault." He noted that exaggeration in politics is unavoidable, but that Boschwitz's ads went "beyond any kind of conceivable standard for honesty and permissible exaggeration."

Novak responded that if Mondale were a statesman he would have prevented Wellstone from attacking Boschwitz in the first place. But Mondale's blast was devastating. It was carried on all the news shows Sunday night, the most-watched time slot of the week, along with the escalating furor over the Jewish letter, and the two events had a synergistic effect.

Immediately after the Mondale press conference, Wellstone drove to the St. Paul airport to catch a flight to Duluth for some last-minute campaigning. At the airport, Forciea showed him a copy of a newspaper ad scheduled to run in the following day's papers:

> FOR GOD'S SAKE, SENATOR, ENOUGH IS ENOUGH
> Last Saturday, Rudy Boschwitz's campaign made an issue of Paul Wellstone's wife for being a Christian and criticized Wellstone for raising his children as "non-Jews."
>
> He's lied about Paul Wellstone's record on issues ranging from Medicare to gun control. But now what he has done simply goes over the line.
>
> In the last week, Boschwitz has shown Minnesotans he is a mean-spirited man who will do anything to keep Minnesota's seat in the U.S. Senate.
>
> It's too late, Rudy!

Incredibly, as Wellstone reviewed the ad in the airport lounge, he objected to the use of "mean-spirited."

"What do you call what he's doing to you?" Forciea asked, dumbfounded. Wellstone walked away without answering. The newspaper ad and a similar radio ad ran frequently on the last few days of the campaign, the "mean-spirited" phrase intact.

Also on Sunday, Bill Hillsman worked furiously to create an ad that highlighted the negative press reviews that Boschwitz was earning for his tactics. The commercial showed headline after headline criticizing Boschwitz. "And now Boschwitz has made an issue out of the fact that Paul Wellstone's wife is a Christian and that his children were brought up as non-Jews," the commercial said. "Obviously, Rudy Boschwitz will say or do anything to save his seat. But it's making a lot of Minnesotans sick." Then a shot of Boschwitz's smiley-face signature faded into "Mr. Yuk," a sticker symbol that warns children away from poisons.

Boschwitz's ads angered Wellstone; the Jewish letter infuriated him. Now, on the Sunday-afternoon flight to Duluth, Wellstone succumbed to his emotions as he described the blow to his family. Tears welled up in his tired eyes, and when they streaked down his cheeks, he stopped talking, turned away, and bowed his head. His shoulders rose and fell with the deep breaths he took to compose himself. A minute later, he spun back around, his eyes moist and mean.

"I want to grab him. It's this last letter about Sheila and the kids that I want to kill him with. I want there to be this revulsion by Tuesday. I want people to have this feeling that what he has done now is despicable."

Wellstone was torn between a survivor's will to fight on against overwhelming odds and a deep sense that the battle had been lost. "I don't have $6 million. I can't hit back," he said. "He couldn't win on the issues. He might not yet. But I'm a little pessimistic. I have to stay strong, to stay up. But I'm pessimistic."

When the plane landed back in St. Paul that evening, Wellstone was met by aides who showed him a transcript of the Boschwitz radio ad on abortion he had heard rumors about a couple of days earlier. The ad said Wellstone supported abortion in the ninth month of pregnancy and under all circumstances.

"These guys are slimeballs!" he shouted in the charter terminal lobby. Two men working behind a counter looked up.

"Sorry, you guys," Wellstone said. "I'm usually more even-tempered than this, but this guy is a slimeball."

"That's OK," one of the men replied. "Have a nice day."

Wellstone was joined that Sunday evening by his wife and their daughter Marcia and son Mark. They drove to the Chatfield Inn, a bed-and-breakfast in St. Paul owned by Wellstone supporters who had given him a key so he could sleep there whenever he needed to stay overnight in the Twin Cities. Wellstone sat in the living room, waiting to meet Forciea and fretting over what to do about the attack ads.

"We should sue him tomorrow," Wellstone said, furiously tapping his heels on the carpet. "Doesn't matter. Can't win."

"Don't say that, Dad," Marcia said.

Wellstone left the room, and Sheila asked Mark if he had offered his father encouragement and support. He had not.

"You should say something to him," Sheila said.

"What the hell am I supposed to say?" Mark shot back.

Sheila reached into her purse for a tissue and dabbed her eyes with it.

After a short stay at the inn, Wellstone and his family prepared to go to a DFL rally in downtown St. Paul. As they stood to leave, Mark grabbed his father's hand, slapped him on the back, and clasped his shoulder, holding on for several moments. Neither uttered a word. Wellstone was touched by the gesture of support and gripped Mark's hand tightly in return.

By the time he got to the rally, Wellstone was back in riproaring form. Happy hour was well under way at the Landmark Center, a cavernous restored federal building jammed full of hundreds of boisterous, sign-waving DFL supporters, many of them tired but inspired after a long weekend of telephoning and knocking on doors. One sign said "G.O.P. Stands for Get Outa the Pool." And they sang this song to the tune of "Bye, Bye Blackbird":

> Pack up all your shirts of plaid, nasty ads, IR cads,
> BYE, BYE BOSCHWITZ
> Scrap your special interest PACs, campaign hacks, money sacks,
> BYE, BYE BOSCHWITZ
> Clean those privileged fat cats out of D.C.

Deficits and bombs are all you gave me
End our legislative blight
Wellstone's right
For the fight
BOSCHWITZ, BYE BYE.

Although all the candidates on the DFL ticket spoke, Wellstone had clearly become the star of the show. His rhetoric was
never hotter, nor more emotional, nor briefer: "You give me so
much courage and strength. This is, I believe, the moment of
truth in Minnesota politics. . . . I understand the wholesomeness
and goodness of Minnesotans. I've never been more certain that
they will reject the attack ads and we will win this election." A
cacophony of screams and a surging crowd enveloped him as he
stepped off the platform.

On the final day of the campaign, at a rally on the University
of Minnesota's Duluth campus, Wellstone returned to the same
theme: "I believe in the faith and goodness of the people. I'm
tired, but my soul is rested. I'm at peace."

Boschwitz spent the last day in his southern base, with a
swing through Winona, Rochester, Mankato, and Sioux Falls,
South Dakota, the major media center serving southwestern
Minnesota. Jay Novak remembered that Boschwitz ended his
day with a dinner at the upscale Twin Cities suburban Cocolez-
zone restaurant with best friends U.S. Senator Slade Gorton of
Washington state and U.S. District Judge James Rosenbaum. "I
remember thinking we should be doing something other than
having dinner," Novak said.

Wellstone's forces, meanwhile, were lathered up and ready to
work all day and night. The candidate and his brain trust—
Forciea, Blackshaw, Lillehaug, Casper—now placed their fate in
the hands of the twenty-six-year-old Liz Borg and her fuzzy-

cheeked field staff. They had spent months rehearsing for this one-act, one-performance play and now they were eager to perform.

On Monday night, as Boschwitz dined in style, Wellstone drove to three locations—the American Federation of State, County and Municipal Employees union offices in St. Paul, the Central Labor Union building in Minneapolis, and the Sabathani Community Center, where he had announced his candidacy eighteen months earlier. These were the hubs for an all-night literature drop. Wellstone and Governor Rudy Perpich were scheduled to address the volunteers, but the energy of the crowd was so high that organizers had trouble keeping the volunteers from grabbing stacks of literature and going to work before the candidates arrived.

"Our people [about 150 of them] were chafing at the bit," said Kris Blake, who supervised one of the locations. "Perpich and Wellstone showed up at ten after eleven and gave their speeches, but you couldn't hear anything but the screaming. Within five minutes after they were finished, the building had emptied." Dan Cramer, who supervised another 150 volunteers at a different location, recalled that "it was like a riot." People were climbing over tables to get maps for their routes so they could go. Elsewhere, volunteers were overrunning phone banks, where callers were reminding Wellstone supporters to get out and vote.

From the three hubs, volunteers fanned out to blanket every car in Minneapolis and St. Paul with Wellstone/Perpich literature reminding people to vote. The routes spreading out from Blake's hub were supposed to take five hours, but so many volunteers showed up with so much enthusiasm that they were done in half the time. Stuart Wagenius, vice president of the Carleton College student Democrats, told the Carleton newspaper that he was placing literature on cars in Minneapolis around

3:00 A.M. when he was confronted by a factory worker who demanded to know what he was doing. Wagenius explained that he was working for Wellstone.

"Bless you," the factory worker said.

Finished with the literature drop, Blake spent the next three hours driving through Wellstone's strongest neighborhoods, confiscating lawn signs for use in the morning "visibility" campaign. At 5:00 A.M., dozens of volunteers streamed into Wellstone headquarters, picked up their signs, and planted themselves at more than two dozen prime commuting locations.

The Verdict

Election day turned out to be mild and pleasant over most of the state, except for some light snow in the Republican south, yet another small godsend for Wellstone.

After having breakfast in a local café, Paul and Sheila Wellstone waited at their Northfield home for the campaign bus to take them to vote. On an end table in their living room was a book that Wellstone had started reading: *Little Victories,* about a schoolteacher's work with disadvantaged students.

The campaign bus driver, Paul Scott, who had retired from the Greyhound bus company rather than cross picket lines when drivers went on strike in March 1990, arrived with the bus and an admonition for Wellstone. "Promise me one thing," he said to the anxious candidate. "If you ever buy another bus, talk to me first."

Boschwitz voted at about noon at his precinct in the Minneapolis suburb of Plymouth. He tried to relax and meet with friends, and he even went to a dentist that day.

And then it was over.

Leaked information from early exit polls, including one by the Cable News Network, indicated that Wellstone was ahead and would win by a few percentage points. Voter Research and Surveys of New York, the exit poll subscribed to by the major media in Minnesota, did not project Wellstone a winner until after midnight. But everybody seemed to know what would happen.

For Boschwitz's inner circle, the end came early and was almost anticlimactic. Novak recalled that Mason got a call from a reporter earlier in the day reporting heavy turnout, an ominous sign for a Republican incumbent in a volatile race. Mason disappeared in his office to call other sources and to confer with pollsters. "At about 12:30, Tom came into my office, looked stricken, and said, 'We're going down,' " Novak said.

The two left the downtown Minneapolis campaign office, walked a few blocks to a restaurant, and broke their self-imposed rule against drinking during the day. Mason ordered a beer and Novak had a rum and Coke. Mason, who had lost an upset victory four years earlier to populist Tom Daschle in South Dakota, said, "Oh well, it's only a career." Novak said, "Let's just keep running the ads." Later they joined their workers at the Thunderbird Hotel for the planned victory party. Novak said he tried to sound upbeat to reporters. Instructions to Boschwitz campaign staffers the previous Saturday proved to be good preparation; they had been warned not to whoop it up or rub it in.

Wellstone broke one last convention of politics before the game was over. Rather than staying confined at home and maintaining a false calm, he dashed to Minneapolis for a few more hours of campaigning during the evening rush hour. He ran through downtown, hugging strangers, shaking hands, working the bus stops. The reaction was phenomenal. He was recognized by hundreds, horns honked, people waved and called out to him as if they sensed that he was their senator. It was perhaps the most electric moment in a high-energy campaign.

Neither candidate declared victory or conceded defeat before bedtime, although the outcome was soon obvious at both victory parties. Boschwitz signed off rather glumly, saying that he was in a "cliffhanger" for the first time in his life and that he was fortunate to have his wife and sons and twelve years in the Senate. Republicans were holding out hope for absentee ballots; some 400,000 had been mailed out to likely GOP voters. He said he intended to sip some more on a Portuguese brandy that a relative from Illinois had brought. "I had a little nip of that and that settled me down," Boschwitz said on television.

"You're history," Lillehaug said to Boschwitz's televised image in Wellstone's twelfth-floor suite at the Holiday Inn Minneapolis.

Dozens of staff members and well-wishers, including a line of party officials and DFL politicians, streamed through the door to congratulate Wellstone. "This campaign is totally unprepared for this," Lillehaug said with bemusement. "In a way, it's cute. I'm not used to this. I come from Mondale Inc."

As the results trickled in, Wellstone wanted to run downstairs and mingle with supporters, but his staff knew that emotions were running so high that he would be mobbed and crushed. Finally, a few minutes before midnight, Wellstone was permitted to go down and address the crowd. Forciea urged him to restrain himself, to forgo his habit of waving his arm over his head to fire up the crowd. This crowd did not need any more incitement to celebrate.

"I would just let it roll over you tonight," he advised.

Wellstone and his advisers took a freight elevator to the first floor, where Lillehaug, Forciea, Blackshaw, and others formed a flying wedge around Wellstone and made their way to the stage. Wellstone's statement to the giddy throng of mostly young people was a badly concealed victory speech:

We never had all the money, but I had you. We've traveled thousands of miles on that old green bus [and now that bus is] within inches of its destination. If present trends continue, that bus is going to take a U.S. senator to Washington.

I said at the beginning that the most troubling thing is the way people are disengaged by politics. This is one of those campaigns that's much more important than the candidate. Politics is about the improvement of people's lives. This has been a different campaign.

On stage with Wellstone, but standing at the rear, hidden behind an enormous banner, Forciea bowed his head. He had been wound tightly all night, looking at the results with his goalie's mentality, too nervous, too fearful of making a mistake to enjoy the game. At last he was unwinding. He embraced his wife in a long, tight hug; she wiped her eyes. Bill Hillsman, who carried a flask of scotch in his back pocket and wore a bewildered look on his face, asked Forciea if it was really over.

"It's a victory," Forciea nodded.

"Ya-HOOOOOO," the ad man shouted.

Forciea walked off the stage and into a hallway by the hotel's kitchen. There he stood, his arms folded across his chest, a tad short of breath and emotionally overwhelmed. He credited the twenty-one- and twenty-two-year-old staff members with giving him emotional boosts and reason to hope over the last week. His voice quavering, he said:

It's so much bigger than helping Paul win. It's very humbling to be part of this. Ninety-nine times out of a hundred—shit, a hundred times out of a hundred—when a well-heeled incumbent lowers the boom on a challenger, it's over. It makes me proud we were able to get back off the mat. . . .

The only good thing about Jesse Helms winning is now he's going to have to deal with Paul Wellstone in the United States Senate.

"He's going to be in his face," Sam Kaplan added.

"Every day," Forciea agreed.

Outside the hotel, delirious and drunken Wellstone supporters whooped it up. The *Carletonian* newspaper captured the
scene of college-age kids hanging off the back of Wellstone's
green bus, which was parked outside:

> "You see this baby?" they call out happily to passersby. "This
> here's Harry Truman's GRAND-NIECE!" One of them almost
> topples off the bus as he thumbs his nose at the line of Jaguars
> and Mercedes parked across the street in front of the Hyatt-
> Regency where Arne Carlson's campaign is celebrating.

Inside, shortly after midnight, Liz Borg celebrated Wellstone's win and her twenty-seventh birthday. She told a friend
what she wanted: a push-up bra and a motorcycle jacket. She
also needed a new car. Her Dodge Colt, which carried her
through 50,000 miles of campaigning, died that afternoon as she
delivered lists to a phone bank, but the breakdown did not upset
her. "I knew everything was going to be all right," she said.
"They have subways in D.C."

Other staffers crowed, too. "He [Boschwitz] spent $1 million in
the last week and his numbers went down," laughed Scott Adams.

With Wellstone safely back upstairs, Blackshaw said he felt
like crying. Forciea teased him: "How we doing in Margo-
Forehead?" It was a reminder of Blackshaw's mispronunciation
of Fargo-Moorhead soon after he arrived from California. At
12:22 A.M., Lillehaug popped the cork on a bottle of champagne. He filled two glasses, gave one to Paul and the other to
Sheila, and said: "Paul David Wellstone, I hereby christen you
United States Senator."

When it was all over, Wellstone had beaten but not thrashed
Boschwitz, 911,999 votes to 864,375 votes, or a margin of 50.5
percent to 47.9 percent. (A third candidate, Russell Bentley of

the Grassroots Party, got 1.6 percent.) The average margin per precinct was twelve votes.

Despite Governor Rudy Perpich's even better showing in his home base of northeastern Minnesota and the Iron Range, he too was thrown out of office, losing to Arne Carlson by a slightly larger margin than Boschwitz lost to Wellstone. A third incumbent, U.S. Representative Arlan Stangeland, an undistinguished Republican who had gotten into trouble making phone calls at taxpayer expense to a woman friend, also was bounced.

Minnesota, alone among the states, had followed through on the anti-incumbent sentiment detected throughout the nation during the campaign. It had a new moderate Republican governor, a new populist progressive U.S. senator, and a new six-to-two Democratic margin in the Minnesota delegation to the U.S. House, the most lopsided margin in decades. Conservatism, it could be argued, had taken a thrashing.

For days the Twin Cities media and opinion leaders were steeped in analysis, marveling at the outcome. The results attracted national postmortems too, although the extraordinary and well-publicized events of the Grunseth scandal and Boschwitz's Jewish letter quashed any weighty pronouncements about the Wellstone victory's being a harbinger.

Boschwitz, who awoke on his sixtieth birthday to the first defeat of his political career, took calls at his headquarters the next day from, among others, former president Ronald Reagan, President George Bush, and Vice President Dan Quayle. At his concession press conference, Boschwitz put on a brave face, saying he was "very much at peace." He praised Wellstone with the highest compliment this hustler could give: "I congratulate my opponent. He was an aggressive and resourceful campaigner. He simply outhustled us." He added that Wellstone "brought a much greater sense of philosophy and purpose" to his campaign than had his previous opponents.

Wellstone, as if he could not stop running an unconventional campaign, was not content to bask graciously in the victory. He seemed drained and curiously withdrawn, but he made news with a startling commitment to serve no more than two terms. He had not made the promise during the campaign, he said, because it would have looked like a trite and calculated maneuver to win votes.

Despite an earlier threat not to say anything decent about Boschwitz, Wellstone promised on the day after the election to continue the "wonderful constituent service" that Boschwitz had been known for. Two days later, when Boschwitz issued an eloquent apology for the Jewish letter, Wellstone called the statement "powerful" and said it showed "a tremendous amount of sincerity and conviction."

On the day after the election, in a speech in the state capitol rotunda, Wellstone's ebullience resurfaced briefly. He grinned widely, waved his hand over his head, and told off a newspaper that had described him as being only five feet, four inches tall. "I'm five-five-and-a-half, not five-four, *Pioneer Press*," he said, laughing. "I have some power now. I can insist on these things!"

But then he was serious again. He thanked his workers for their "shoe-leather power." He thanked Minnesotans for giving him "this incredibly sacred trust." And he predicted that he would not be the last of his kind to win. "A day of reckoning is approaching," Wellstone said.

EPILOGUE

As Boschwitz's handlers began to test possible attacks against Wellstone during the campaign, they asked the people in one small focus group what they would think if they learned that Wellstone actually was "a socialist."

Campaign manager Tom Mason recalled that one elderly woman piped up: "Well, Rudy's a socialist too. Have you ever seen him at the state fair? He's open, he's there for everybody." Mason said that other people in the group, most of them highly educated professionals aged forty-five and over, nodded in agreement. Nobody pointed out the difference between "sociability" and "socialism." The lesson Mason drew from this incident is that the public's ignorance is frightening, or that Minnesotans may deserve their reputation for excessive politeness.

Wellstone would see another meaning in the woman's response. He was convinced that Americans are no longer terribly fearful of labels such as socialism or liberalism and are ready once again to accept government programs and progressive solutions. And he was convinced that people are ready to accept a revitalized federal government that attempts to provide more economic security for all citizens and goes to work once again on chronic social problems. His stunning victory, Wellstone hoped and believed, made the point.

The political establishment—both in Minnesota and nationally—mostly rejected the notion that there were any lessons in Wellstone's victory for other states or for presidential politics. Even some DFLers still believe that Wellstone did not win the election, that Boschwitz lost it. This school of thought tended to be promoted by the same people who dismissed his chances from the beginning. "For so long, people said he couldn't win," said his first campaign manager, Kris Blake. "So when he won, they had to come up with an explanation for why they were wrong. People still don't want to accept [that] he won because he ran a better campaign."

Some Boschwitz supporters went so far as to suggest that the outcome was utterly meaningless, that it was all a result of the dynamics surrounding the Grunseth scandal, the budget deadlock, and the Jewish letter, and that if the election had been held a day earlier or a day later, any time other than November 6, the outcome would have been different. Elsewhere in the nation, Wellstone's victory was chalked up in part to Minnesota's being a liberal enclave.

It was argued further that Minnesotans never really knew what they were getting, that Wellstone's real political nature was unknown to many voters or glossed over by the media. Scott Cottington, a Washington consultant from Minnesota who managed Boschwitz's 1984 campaign, noted that responses to late-campaign polling suggested that many people voted against Boschwitz to punish him for something. But those voters did not really expect him to lose, nor did they intend him to, Cottington said. Toward the end of the campaign, Wellstone and his aides sometimes fed this notion of meaninglessness, attaching fatalistic interpretation to the strange twist of events. His adviser

David Lillehaug, for example, talked about how the "planets lined up" for Wellstone.

But persuasive evidence abounds that issues and philosophy and attitude were important factors in Wellstone's success. His victory may have had something to do with the power of a growing disenchantment with both Wall Street and Capitol Hill and the beginning of a new and aggressive strain of progressive populist politics.

It is simply not true that Wellstone hid his identity or that voters did not know what they were getting. The media typically described him—and usually dismissed him—as unusually far to the left for a DFLer, a true believer in liberalism, a prairie populist, a protester, even a radical. Wellstone's lifelong role as an advocate for the poor, for labor, for women and children, and for the environment was widely publicized. There was little doubt that he was a liberal of the bleeding-heart variety. Boschwitz himself, with his blizzard of ads toward the end of the campaign, made it abundantly clear that Wellstone was a champion of big spending by the federal government.

The Jewish letter is presumed to have done enormous damage to Boschwitz, and surely it took a toll, maybe even made the difference. But it may have been more of a final straw than a knockout punch from nowhere. Lots of anecdotes suggested massive voter reaction to the letter, but it is also likely that many people used it to seal a choice they already were about to make. Even if the letter had not been written, Mondale and Wellstone in the last few days before the election still would have been denouncing Boschwitz's negative ads, which were perceived by many to be far too harsh and distorted. Without the distraction of the Jewish letter, Wellstone might even have been able to concentrate more on refuting Boschwitz's attacks on his Medicare and health care proposals, and he might have recaptured some of the elderly voters who voted disproportionately for Boschwitz.

Going into the last weekend, and before the story of the Jewish letter broke, Boschwitz's lead was only slightly larger than the lead that Jim Nichols held in the polls over Wellstone just before the DFL primary election. It is difficult to measure precisely the impact of Wellstone's grassroots effort, but it surely was a bonus that pollsters could not account for in either the primary or the general election. Moreover, Minneapolis *Star Tribune* tracking polls showed Wellstone surging back again on the Saturday before the election—before the Jewish letter detonated in the news media on Sunday and Monday. Boschwitz was in serious trouble, with or without the letter. He himself has discounted it as a singular cause of his defeat.

As for the Grunseth matter, a number of polls indicated that Wellstone had caught up with Boschwitz before the Grunseth debacle really unfolded. A veteran Republican strategist, Twin Cities consultant Bill Morris, said his own surveys showed Wellstone ahead of Boschwitz by a two-to-one margin in affluent south Minneapolis neighborhoods in early October. "[Boschwitz] collapsed first among independent ticket splitters, and the DFL base for Wellstone was pretty much intact by the end of September," Morris said.

Wellstone's internal poll, taken October 16-17, just two and three days after the first Grunseth allegations surfaced, found that Boschwitz's margin had shrunk to 7 percentage points, 46-39. The crucial *Star Tribune*/KSTP-TV Minnesota Poll that showed Wellstone within 3 percentage points was begun just four days after the Grunseth story broke, and before it became clear to rank-and-file Grunseth supporters that Boschwitz was angling to have their candidate removed. Undoubtedly Grunseth's problems contributed, perhaps significantly, to Boschwitz's slide, but Mason and the experts have never been able to explain exactly what was happening in the minds of a great mass of voters to directly connect Grunseth's bizarre problems with family-man Boschwitz, and to explain a 15-point advance by Wellstone over a two-week period. During this weekend, some of Wellstone's most effective ads were portraying him as a likable antagonist of the system, and other ads were challenging Boschwitz's benign image.

During this critical period, the national news was dominated by the budget deadlock in Washington and Bush's and Boschwitz's opposition to new taxes on the wealthy, a development that sent other highly favored Republican Senate incumbents tumbling in the polls. In mid-October, Jesse Helms trailed Harvey Gantt by a margin of 41-49, and Republican senator Mark Hatfield of Oregon was behind Democratic challenger Harry Lonsdale 44-50. But the budget deadlock had to be considered more than just a lucky break or a peripheral influence that miraculously helped challengers. It was a bread-and-butter issue that helped define conservatives and liberals, and it was at the heart of the difference between Wellstone's and Boschwitz's philosophies.

Some Republican insiders in Minnesota agree that there was unique appeal in Wellstone's outsider pitch and championing of class issues, and that Boschwitz's weaknesses were rooted in the very issues and criticisms Wellstone focused on. Mason himself, by the summer of 1992, acknowledged that Wellstone "was on to something. I didn't think so then, but I do now."

Elam Baer, a prominent Independent-Republican strategist and a director of the Grunseth campaign, said that it was common knowledge among party insiders that Boschwitz's support was broad but shallow and that a combination of his conservatism and lack of accomplishment had become a recognized problem. "Our pollster [Washington-based Neil Newhouse] was telling us as early as September that Boschwitz had a real race on his hands, and he was telling me in mid-October that he thought the race was a toss-up," primarily because of the souring of the national mood, Baer said. Baer believes Boschwitz erred grievously by not attacking Wellstone earlier, but also by presenting himself as a powerful Washington insider "at precisely the wrong time." Although Baer believes running against money and the rich will not work for most other Democrats, he described Boschwitz as "uniquely vulnerable in that area and Wellstone as uniquely able to push it."

"I will give him this," Baer said of Wellstone. "He stuck to the theme of the big guy-little guy and was so persistent over such a long period of time that it came through to people."

There is some hard evidence that Wellstone got through to the groups to which his message was aimed. A poll of 1,817 Minnesotans as they left the polling booths, conducted by television networks ABC, CBS, NBC, and CNN, showed a pattern that fit the Wellstone message, not a helter-skelter jumble that one might expect from a chaotic, last-minute desertion from Boschwitz because of Grunseth and the Jewish letter. This exit poll by Voter Research and Surveys, and a comparison of actual returns in selected precincts in previous years, indicate that Wellstone won with a combination of stronger appeals to his political base and by reaching moderate, independent suburban voters who were worried about their own financial condition and that of the nation.

The exit poll showed that Wellstone did best among an assortment of middle-class folks—young voters and baby boomers, liberals and independents—but also among those who had a pessimistic view of the economy and those who thought their own financial condition had deteriorated.

For instance, he prevailed (53 percent to 47 percent) among those aged 18 to 29, and among the baby boomers, aged 30 to 44 (51 percent to 49 percent). This powerful demographic bulge is finally beginning to vote in greater numbers and it comprised more than half of the voters in Minnesota in 1990, according to the poll. Wellstone was beaten (54-46) among those in the most prosperous bracket, 45- to 59-year-olds, and among those over 60 (losing 53-47). The latter group undoubtedly was influenced by Boschwitz's eleventh-hour attempt to convince the elderly that Wellstone would abolish Medicare.

Wellstone's support was almost directly correlated to income. He won (53-47) among those with an income less than $15,000 and he won (55-45) among those making between $15,000 and $30,000. He tied (50-50) in the $30,000 to $50,000 bracket and lost (58-42) among those making more than $50,000.

The exit poll also revealed an interesting division based on perceptions of the state's economy and the nation's. DFLers are proud of Minnesota's relatively robust economy, which they flaunt in the face of free enterprisers who claim that its high taxes and public spending are bad for business. Those who thought the state's economy was doing well (58 percent of the sample) voted for Wellstone (53-47) while those who thought it was not good (38 percent) favored Boschwitz (52-48). Conversely, those who thought the national economy was doing well (only 30 percent of the sample) voted for Boschwitz (63-37), while the overwhelming 69 percent who thought the national economy was declining favored Wellstone (54-46). Wellstone lost among those who thought their own financial condition was better than two years earlier (58-42) and among those who felt their condition had not changed (53-47). But he clobbered Boschwitz (64-36) among those who thought their situation was worse.

The most pronounced indicator in the exit poll was a question about whether the country was headed in the "right direction" or was "off on the wrong track." Among those who thought the former, Boschwitz won (66-34). Among those who thought the latter, Wellstone won, by exactly the same margin. There were slightly more of the pessimists.

Wellstone performed better than Senate candidate Hubert H. Humphrey III in a similar 1988 exit poll among DFLers (by 2 percentage points), Republicans (by 4 percentage points), and independents (by 14 percentage points). At the same time, Wellstone was 13 points higher than Humphrey among self-described liberals, and 12 points higher among union members, suggesting that he revitalized the liberal-labor wing of the party.

A perusal of actual returns, broken down by region, also lends credence to the argument that his message got through to the middle class.

Wellstone carried only twenty-six of the state's eighty-seven counties, but he took all the most populous regions. He won by the big margins necessary in the DFL strongholds in Minneapolis, St. Paul, and the Iron Range. Although he lost most of southern and western Minnesota, he did much better than projected in these rural, conservative districts. He even snatched a couple of these counties away from Boschwitz, who had won them solidly in his previous two elections. Wellstone's stronger than expected showing in rural areas may have been a result of his high visibility in the farm protest movement in the mid-1980s. And he carried Mower County, where the Hormel strike occurred.

The most surprising result was his sweep of all five of the most heavily populated Twin Cities counties, including the prosperous suburbs of Washington and Dakota Counties. Wellstone's margin in Dakota County, to the south of the cities, was very thin, but it was unthinkable to experts back in September and October that he would have such strong appeal in this upscale suburban haven that has all the marks of a Republican bastion. This fastest-growing county in the state is being populated with young and middle-aged two-income, upper-middle-income families, baby boomers. Wellstone's message, particularly his pledge to invest in children through education, surely was a factor in his victory there. His emphasis on environmental issues and his advocacy of abortion rights also helped carry these precincts.

Nationally, Minnesota's reputation for liberalism undoubtedly contributed at first to skepticism about the meaningfulness of Wellstone's victory. But in fact, the state has been highly competitive in statewide elections; at least two of the top three officeholders (governor and U.S. senators) since 1978 have been Republicans. Its reputation is exaggerated by Democrats' successes in presidential elections and by their fairly consistent dominance of the state legislature over the past twenty-five years. But the presidential vote has been strongly affected by the fact that the Democratic nominee for president or vice president was a Minnesotan (Humphrey or Mondale) in five of the six elections between 1964 and 1984. Even so, Reagan came within 4,000 votes of beating Mondale in Minnesota in 1984.

Minnesota also deserves at least some credit as a bellwether state for national trends in politics. It was an early Republican stronghold and remained so for most of the post-Civil War period, but then produced one of the dominant populist leaders in the late nineteenth century, Ignatius Donnelly, and Minnesota became a hotbed for the movement. A few years later it sent forth a little-known but important progressive Democratic reformer in Governor John A. Johnson, who was a top competitor for the Democratic presidential nomination in 1912. In the Depression, Minnesota offered a progressive populist counterpart to the demagogic Huey Long in Governor Floyd B. Olson. It elected in the next decade one of the first of a new breed of Republican internationalists and moderates in Governor Harold Stassen. Then came Senator Hubert H. Humphrey, a pioneer of the civil rights and antipoverty movements. Swinging back again, Minnesota signaled the coming Reagan revolution in the

1978 election, in which Republicans, led by Boschwitz, swept DFLers out of both U.S. Senate seats, out of the governor's office, and out of the majority in the state House.

Minnesota's political junkies will be arguing for years about why Wellstone won and whether he would have succeeded without this or that occurrence, but these speculations miss the point that Wellstone did not need to win in order to prove his case. All he needed to do was show that his new brand of populist progressivism could be competitive, that it would not be laughed out of the voting booth, that he could come within a few percentage points of a Republican who had trounced previous moderate opponents. He made that case irrefutably, and he did it despite the handicap of a severe money shortage, despite being declared a goner by the news media, and, at least initially, despite getting little help from his own party.

Outside of Minnesota in 1990, congressional incumbents scraped through by much narrower margins than in previous years, but most made it back to Washington. Vermont actually elected a card-carrying socialist, Bernard Sanders, in a statewide election for its only seat in the U.S. House of Representatives, and Ann Richards, the tough-talking populist who taunted George Bush so unmercifully at the 1988 national convention ("Poor George . . . he was born with a silver foot in his mouth") was elected governor of Texas, one of the nation's conservative bastions. In spite of the Sanders and Richards victories, there was no nationwide trend toward the left.

A number of other analysts, however, were more than willing to identify Wellstone as a forerunner of a coming stampede toward progressive populist causes. Robert Kuttner, one of the most bullish proponents of a revitalized progressive populism, hailed Wellstone's campaign as precisely the kind of winning formula he called for in *Life of the Party,* a book he wrote before the 1988 elections. In the book, Kuttner explained why he thought economic populism would unlock the White House gates for the Democrats:

> Democrats do not do well when they offer bloodless technical solutions or when they try to compete with Republicans as advocates of Adam Smith's invisible hand. Harry Truman said it best: When the voters have a choice between a Republican and a Republican, they'll pick the Republican every time. Democrats do best when they develop broad, embracing, expansive visions, combining national purpose with economic advancement, and rally masses of non-rich voters. Democrats can regain their status as majority party only by rebuilding a majority coalition of ordinary wage- and salary-earning people, whose political and economic interests are not identical to those of the wealthy.

"Wellstone," Kuttner said in an interview, "is an example of a guy who's carrying out that scenario." He noted the successes in the late 1980s of a cluster of young, aggressive populists of the Upper Midwest, including presidential candidate and senator Tom Harkin of Iowa, Representative Byron Dorgan and Senator Kent Conrad in North Dakota, Senator Tom Daschle in South Dakota, and Representative David Obey in Wisconsin. Wellstone showed that "Democrats win when they persuade ordinary people that they are there to advance their interests . . . but only when you do it on pocketbook issues," Kuttner said. "If you emphasize those, they're willing to forgive you for avant-garde views on cultural issues, gay rights, civil liberties, even environmentalism."

Kevin Phillips was another who saw Wellstone's victory as a vindication of his prophecy of a Democratic revival. In a lecture in Minneapolis in early 1992, Phillips took note of a *Fortune* magazine poll showing that one-third of Americans think there should be no millionaires and other polls that show 80 percent support for new surtaxes on top incomes. Phillips ticked off a number of disadvantages that Democrats still faced, including the fact that they have been too "collusive" with the interests they should be opposing and far too responsive to special interest leverage.

Wellstone's experience also illuminates some stubborn disadvantages that progressives will face, chiefly in the area of foreign affairs and military posture. His lonely battle against the Gulf War in his first few months in office epitomized how out of step the movement is with the basic desire of most Americans to exert force and to remain the undisputed top-dog military force in the world. Public opinion may be shifting a bit, finally, on defense spending, but many citizens suspect that world has become only a little less dangerous.

The biggest problem of all for progressive populists may be the cost and redistributive nature of their economic agenda. Neither Wellstone nor any other leader these days is explicit or blunt in admitting that a heavier tax load—not just on the superrich but also on much of the upper middle class—will be necessary in order to balance the budget and to provide the universal rights to health and education that progressives admire in European countries. This is a huge pill to swallow.

The health care system proposed by Wellstone could, for instance, result in somewhat less satisfactory service and higher taxes for millions of upper-middle-class people who are relatively satisfied with their coverage. The underlying principle of economic progressivism is sharing and redistribution. Progressive populists may have a difficult time convincing a majority of voting Americans that in the long run they will fare better under the cumulative effect of many new progressive policies. The task is made tougher yet by the fact that voter turnout in the United States, for a variety of reasons, rises with income.

There is no denying that the odds are high against a sweeping success by economic populists. With the exception of the New

Deal era, which came after the equivalent of an economic holo-
caust, the American business establishment has pretty much had
its way throughout American history. Most progressive gains
have been incremental. Anxious as ordinary people are, most
Americans probably are afraid of moving too fast. The image of
the current system as a goose that lays golden eggs and that must
be protected at all costs is a powerful one, despite the competi-
tiveness of European nations with far more intrusive and confis-
catory governments.

Populist historian Lawrence Goodwyn in his book *The
Populist Moment* argued that "the hazards facing the organizers
of democratic movements such as Populism have been, and remain, awesome." Referring to "patterns of deference" instilled
in working Americans over generations, Goodwyn said that
Americans have no "culturally sanctioned way to express their
anxiety politically. A heartfelt but unfocused discontent about
'politics' has therefore become a centerpiece of the popular sub-
culture across the nation."

Others, taking a longer view, see a fairly steady advance in
modern history by the forces of democracy and equality, more
control by common people over all aspects of their lives, and an
invincibility to this cause. Among them is Paul Berman, a historian of the left who wrote a provocative piece in 1991 for the
New York Times Magazine, "Still Sailing the Lemonade Sea,"
about the future of progressive principles in the United States.
Like many others, Berman believes that without a militant communist menace on the horizon, with the failure of extreme and
totalitarian socialism, the left finally has some room to operate.
"For the first time since 1914, the idea of progress [as advanced
by the left] seems something other than a demagogue's dangerous slogan," Berman wrote. "Idealists do win. Freedom spreads.
Something about the unstoppable course of history, some small
piece of that idea, does seem to be true."

Four years and two elections after achieving what he hoped would be a tide-turning event, Paul Wellstone and the populist progressives were still waiting for their country to continue on this "unstoppable course." Wellstone admitted in the summer of 1994 that his election "wasn't quite the harbinger some of us thought," but he nevertheless claimed to have helped change the atmosphere in Washington to a "politics of possibilities."

Universal health care was on the table but the reality still appeared to be far in the distance. Polls showed that antitax, antigovernment sentiment was still strong. There was nothing approaching a consensus on how to address the frightening plight of the underclass and the working poor other than imprisoning a large percentage of the population, the standard response to the emergence of crime as the nation's top concern.

Before the decisive and humiliating sweep of November 8, 1994, a spate of victories by other populists, even progressives, replicated Wellstone's grassroots campaign methods, style, and attitude in both parties.

Exactly one year after his election, on election night 1991, Wellstone actually thought the revolution might be under way. That night he boarded an Amtrak train in Washington, D.C., and a few hours later he was in a downtown Philadelphia hotel suite with Democratic Senate candidate Harris Wofford and his supporters, who had gathered for an election-night party, win or lose.

Wofford had no business bringing champagne to this party, according to conventional wisdom a few weeks earlier. He had waged a campaign that was uncannily similar to Wellstone's, something that was widely reported after the fact. Wofford was a little-known liberal activist straight from the 1960s, a former college president, promoting an unabashedly progressive agenda, including a radical health care plan dismissed by his detractors as "socialized medicine." Wofford's message was crafted by consultants Paul Begala and James Carville, both of whom were celebrated in the national media for their bold and imaginative exploitation of class issues amidst a deepening recession. After the Wofford victory, Carville, nicknamed the Ragin' Cajun, went on to lead Bill Clinton's successful presidential campaign, flavoring it with a large dollop of Louisiana populism.

Wofford's opponent, like Wellstone's, was a popular politician—Richard Thornburgh, a former governor and a former U.S. attorney general, a cabinet member who was considered a personal friend of President Bush. At one point, Wofford was some 40 percentage points behind Thornburgh in the polls, and although he had narrowed the gap dramatically, few in Washington thought Wofford could go all the way. After all, Republicans had won nine consecutive U.S. Senate races in Pennsylvania.

Recalling a luncheon with Senate Democrats earlier that day, where the caucus line was being rehearsed, Wellstone said:

> People were talking, saying, "Even if Wofford doesn't win, it's a victory. We have to be prepared to talk about a victory." But I thought he would win big. It was in the air. He [Wofford] and I that summer had this conversation about how Thornburgh had just come out claiming that he "walked the corridors of power." I turned to Harris and said, "This is a gift from God."

Wellstone's hunch paid off. He was the only senator who made the trip to celebrate with Wofford an astounding special-election victory that was the talk of the political world for weeks.

The following year, 1992, produced campaigns that were among the most antiestablishment and populistic in recent American history. The Democrats, of course, recaptured the White House with a southern centrist whose policies and philosophy were unquestionably to the right of Wellstone's. But

Democrats of all stripes were preaching populism amid a darkening national mood brought on by recession, major failures in the nation's business sector, and a growing perception that government was paralyzed by special-interest money and incapable of addressing a general decline in the national welfare. As the year unfolded, huge blocs of voters seemed to fall under the spell of one populist leader after another.

On the left there was Jerry Brown's angry crusade to "take back America" from the rich, the polluters, and the professional politicians. On the right, David Duke and Patrick Buchanan stoked racist, nationalist, and ethnocentrist impulses, rallying ordinary people against non-Christians, nonwhites, foreigners, and job-exporting international capitalists. Even middle-of-the-roaders had their populist in Ross Perot, an entrepreneur who appealed to the "radical middle" and who denounced the domination of lobbyists and special interests over both parties. Each of these men claimed to be the hero who could take on villainous elites and special interests in Washington or on Wall Street and return control of the republic and long-term prosperity to ordinary people.

However ripe the masses appear to have been in 1992 for a progressive message, the left had to be disappointed by the fate of its presidential candidates. Wellstone's favorite, Iowa senator Tom Harkin, fell by the wayside early. Former California governor Jerry Brown, whose rhetoric matched Wellstone's almost perfectly at times, shone for a while but eventually lost as a result of the perception that he was just too strange and inconsistent.

Finally, the battle was won by Arkansas governor Bill Clinton, only a part-time populist and a sometime progressive. Clinton's tendency to promise all things to all people confused and encouraged progressives. During the campaign, Wellstone and even some Republican critics noted that his promises added up to the most leftist economic plan since George McGovern's candidacy in 1972. It included a historic expansion of federal benefits in higher education and health care, a redistribution of wealth through higher taxes on the wealthy and tax credits for the poor, a doubling of the rate of post-cold war Pentagon cuts, and a massive public works rebuilding program financed by the federal government. Others would characterize it as the most radical proposal since the great liberal economic reforms of the Depression era. However it might be labeled, the Clinton program directly challenged the laissez-faire capitalism prescribed by a ruling conservative Republican coalition, an administration that was presumed by many political experts to have an indefinite lock on the White House and national economic policy.

But the president turned out to be more like the kind of Democrat Wellstone fought against in Minnesota, accommodating to business interests, sidetracked by divisive issues such as gay rights, and unable to capitalize on his mandate to deliver universal health care or a new tuition-aid program.

Outside the presidential scene, however, antiestablishment challengers, mostly on the left, were taking back offices they lost in the 1970s and 1980s. After Wofford's victory, liberal and progressive women—double outsiders—were scoring knockouts in U.S. Senate elections in California, Washington, and Illinois. The biggest shock of all was when a triple outsider, a black woman considered hopelessly left-wing by many in her party, Carol Moseley-Braun, defeated incumbent Illinois senator Alan Dixon in a Democratic primary and went on to win in the general election.

Candidates all over the country, at the national and the local level, were using the themes and tactics pioneered by Wellstone. Dozens of candidates two years later were adopting their own fund-raising codes, swearing off big money and contributions from political action committees, inspired by Jerry Brown's refusal to take more than $100 from any one source. Governor Clinton's advisers consulted Wellstone's at length before launching their own bus tours immediately after the Democratic National Convention in New York.

Wellstone, who at first felt virtually alone in the Senate, saw new comrades such as Russ Feingold of Wisconsin, Patty Murray of Washington, and Ben Nighthorse Campbell of Colorado as "cut out of the same cloth."

After four years in office, he confessed to disappointment that more progress had not been achieved on "committing resources to the progressive agenda, on education and children and health care. . . . I find myself indignant with these cut-cut-cut Democrats. Their major allegiance is still to the bondholders and the private interests."

But the 1990s, through the first half at least, had become "more of a public-interest decade than a private-interest decade," Wellstone argued in the summer of 1994.

And most of all, Wellstone was greatly encouraged by the rise of a new breed of "rock-the-boat" politicians, not all as progressive as himself, a group that he believes had become "one of the central dynamics of American politics in the 1990s."

But these fairly isolated and modest success stories for progressives were soon overwhelmed by the 1994 election results, one of the most complete turnabouts in modern political history and a devastating and demoralizing blow to Democrats. In the aftermath of the election, few progressives even tried to make the case for a coming renaissance for their values and policies.

Republicans, pounding single-mindedly on the antitax, antigovernment theme and helped by the voters' disenchantment with Clinton, took complete control of the Congress for the first time in forty-two years. They gained ground almost everywhere in state and local governments. In the year before, Republicans, albeit moderates, accomplished the unthinkable in winning mayoral races in Los Angeles and New York City, the previously untouchable Democratic urban bases.

In Minnesota, two earnest and honest DFL candidates with essentially the same agenda as Wellstone were defeated. In both cases, the winning Republican campaigns relied heavily on conventional ads and large campaign contributions, more or less politics as usual.

One of the DFLers, gubernatorial candidate John Marty, promoted Wellstone-style reforms in campaign finance and ethics, along with a redistribution of the tax burden from the middle class to the rich. Marty was defeated by a larger margin than any DFL gubernatorial candidate since the 1940s.

Marty modeled his grassroots campaign organization on Wellstone's—taking no more than $100 from anyone and no PAC money—but many DFLers felt he lacked the senator's charisma, power, and anger. And Marty faced a fairly popular Governor Arne Carlson during the peak of an economic boom, which tends to take the edge off populist anger and tends to help incumbents. No incumbents for major office in either party were defeated in Minnesota in 1994.

The other DFLer, U.S. Senate candidate Ann Wynia, despite strong support from Wellstone's coalition, lost a contest for an open seat by a few percentage points to U.S. Representative Rod Grams, the most conservative, antigovernment politician Minnesota has sent to the Senate in at least fifty years.

Conservatives and Republicans were jubilant, and most establishment DFLers were saying "I told you so."

On one hand, Wellstone had to alter the previous summer's analysis of the politics of the 1990s: "This is not what I expected—[I expected] that this would be a public-interest decade," he said.

On the other hand, Wellstone speculated hopefully that it was "not a defining election. . . . We saw a change vote in '90, a change vote in '92, and a change vote in '94." Even Republican conservative Minnesota leader Vin Weber carefully warned Republicans that the election might have been another antiestablishment reflex and they should not assume that long-term success was guaranteed.

As most other DFLers were talking about having to change their thinking and reevaluate their basic positions on issues, Wellstone continued to cut a figure of progressive defiance, even as there were rumors of a primary challenge from some unknown centrist DFLer within his own party in 1996. There was no note of conciliation or retreat from Wellstone.

Two weeks after the election, he said: "This Contract [with America, a campaign manifesto engineered by House Speaker Newt Gingrich] is mean-spirited, it's not Minnesota, and I'm going to be fighting it. . . . These cuts in capital gains taxes are going to take food out of the mouths of babies and I'm going to provide clarity on that. The worst thing Democrats could do is to fold to the Gingrich agenda. . . . And I'll be right smack in the middle of this debate."

Dennis J. McGrath, 39, was born and grew up in New York City, where he graduated from the City University of New York with a bachelor's degree in English. After graduation, he served as a New York City Urban Fellow for the city's police department. McGrath joined the *Minneapolis Tribune* (now the *Star Tribune*) in 1978. He has covered agribusiness, police, city hall, and, since 1988, state and government politics. McGrath has won several awards for reporting, including a first-place Associated Press Award for his coverage of a 1993 controversy over telephone bills in the Minnesota House of Representatives. He lives in Minnetonka, Minnesota, with his wife and two children.

Dane Smith, 45, was born in Corpus Christi, Texas, grew up in Anchorage, Alaska, and served four years in the navy as an aviation structural mechanic. He came to Minnesota in 1973, enrolled at Inver Hills Community College, and transferred to and graduated from the University of St. Thomas with a bachelor's degree in journalism. Smith was hired in 1977 by the *Minneapolis Star* to cover the northern Twin Cities suburbs and he later covered state government and politics. In 1980, he joined the *St. Paul Pioneer Press*, where he covered city and county government for three years and served as Washington correspondent for three years. He has covered state politics and government for the *Star Tribune* since 1986. Smith has won several awards for reporting and in 1989-90 studied economics and history at Stanford University as a John S. Knight Fellow. He lives in St. Paul with his wife and three children.